LANDMARKS

OF THE

DECCAN

THE AUTHOR

LANDMARKS

OF THE

DECCAN

A COMPREHENSIVE GUIDE TO THE
ARCH AEOLOGICAL REMAINS OF THE
CITY AND SUBURBS OF HYDERABAD

SYED ALI ASGAR BILGRAMI, ASAFJAHI

ISBN : 978-93-5324-573-3 (HB)

First Published, 1927

Published, 2020

Published by

Facsimile Publisher
12 Pragati Market
Ashok Vihar, Ph-2
Delhi-110052
E-mail: books@facsimilepublisher.com

Printed at: G. Print Process, Delhi.

Landmarks of the Deccan

Author: Syed Ali Asgar Bilgrami, Asafjahi

Landmarks
of the
Deccan

A Comprehensive Guide to the Archæological Remains of the City and Suburbs of Hyderabad

BY

SYED ALI ASGAR BILGRAMI, ASAFJAHI

Ag. Director of Archæology

(1922-1924)

Asst. Secretary to H.E.H. the Nizam's Government, Judicial, Police & General Departments

HYDERABAD-DECCAN:

PRINTED AT THE GOVERNMENT CENTRAL PRESS

1927

CONTENTS

DEDICATION

TO

LIEUTENANT-GENERAL HIS EXALTED HIGHNESS, ASAF JAH, MUZAFFAR-UL
MULK-VAL-MUMALIK, NIZAMUD-DOWLAH, NIZAM-UL-MULK,
NAWAB MIR SIR OSMAN ALI KHAN BAHADUR
FATEH JUNG, FAITHFUL ALLY OF THE BRITISH
GOVERNMENT, SIPAH SALAR, SULTAN-UL
ULOOM, G.C.S.I., G.C.B.E.,
NIZAM OF HYDERABAD.

THIS BOOK
IS BY GRACIOUS PERMISSION
DEDICATED
BY
HIS EXALTED HIGHNESS'
MOST DEVOTED SERVANT AND FAITHFUL SUBJECT,
SYED ALI ASGAR BILGRAMI.

INTRODUCTION

This English edition of the "Maathir-e-Deccan." is the outcome of the favourable reception which was accorded to the Urdu edition of this book and the encouraging remarks made by the intelligentia in general.

I am greatly indebted to M. A. N. Hydari, Esquire, (Nawab Hydar Nawaz Jung Bahadur) the Finance Member of the Hyderabad Executive Council, whose interest in the Archæology of the State is well known, for his valuable suggestion to publish this English version, so that it may make a wider appeal both in the East and the West.

I am also grateful to Nawab Inayeth Jung Bahadur, an enlightened member of the Hyderabad aristocracy, and a great grandson of the late Prime Minister, Nawab Ruknud Dowlah Bahadur, for his ardently following me in most of my adventures when I used to hunt for fresh inscriptions in the ruined cemetries of forgotten ages.

It is hoped that the shortcomings of this little work may receive gentle treatment by its readers and that its co-ordinating data may be of some value to Archæological scholars.

I have inserted a Retrospect of the origin and progress of the Qutbshahi dynasty at the end of the text and revised this edition with many useful additions and reference and some minor inaccuracies have been removed.

HYDERABAD-DECCAN,
1st *March* 1927.

S. A. A.

PREFACE

(*To the Urdu edition.*)

THE antiquarian remains of His Exalted Highness the Nizam's Dominions are in no way less important in respect of their variety and interest than the chief monuments of the Indian Empire. Wherever you look, to whatever quarter you turn in His Exalted Highness' dominions, you will find them covered with the most varied remains of the past—remains that belong to every age from Palæolithic times down to the 20th century, remains which are representative of many peoples and of many creeds. Of prehistoric antiquities there is an abundance throughout the whole State particularly in the Southern and Eastern districts, where besides Palæolithic and Neolithic remains you have those very interesting monuments, the circular cairns and Monolithic tombs, which are generally classed as prehistoric.

Among the earliest records of the historic age, the rock inscriptions at Maski (Raichur) are unique in that they refer to the Emperor Asoka by his own name and thus once and for all place his identity beyond dispute. Then the cave temples and monasteries hewn from the living rock at Ajanta and at Ellora, afford especially valuable material for the study of Indian plastic and pictorial art, for these monuments, particularly the frescœs of Ajanta, have a far reaching significance in the historic art not only of this country, but of Asia in general. A large fresco painting in Cave No. I at Ajanta is still easily recognizable as a vivid representation of the reciprocated courtesy in the presentation of their credentials by the Persian envoys from Khusru II, king of Persia, who in 625 A.D. had received a complimentary embassy from Pulakesin—(608-642 A.D.) king of the Deccan (Vatapi), the modern Badami in the Bijapur district.

This picture, in addition to its interest as a contemporary record of unusual political relations between India and Persia, is of the highest value as a landmark in the history of the art. At Ellora, the paintings which once adorned the walls of the caves, have now all but perished and only the more durable sculptures remain.

The Thousand-Pillared Temple at Warangal (Hanamkonda), the temples of Amba Jogai (Mominabad) and Tuljapur, an almost unique structural Chaitya-hall at Ter in Osmanabad district and the remains of Alampur of the early Mediæval age, are likely to prove very enlightening as links between the earliest Buddhist stupas and later temple architecture. At Ittagi, Palampet and Anwa, there are some of the most perfect and most splendid examples of Chalukyan style. The ancient remains of old Paithan (Prathisthana) and the buried temples of Patancheru, Alwampalli (Mahbubnagar district) and Karimnagar, offer a remarkably wide scope for exploration and research.

The chain of Saracenic buildings begins with the early Muslim conquerors, Qutbuddin Mubarak Khilji and Muhammad Tughlaq; the imposing monuments of the Bahmani dynasty at Gulburga, the towering Chand Minar at Daulatabad, the tomb of Ahmad Shah Wali at Bidar, the palatial Madrasa of Mahmud Gawan and the Badshahi Ashur Khana in which the lapse of so many centuries have failed to rob the freshness and resplendence of their Persian enamelled tiles. The mausoleum of Ali Barid, the finely proportioned Mecca Masjid, the Char Minar and the tombs of the Qutb Shahi Kings of Golconda may be ranked among greatest Architectural creations of the East and they by themselves tell the tale of Muslim genius in Architecture and of the bygone glory of the rulers of the Deccan.

The peculiarities of these splendid groups of antiquities have drawn towards them Western explorers and Oriental scholars as far back as 1665 or even 760 A.D. when Monsieur Thevenot, the famous French traveller or the Chinese pilgrim Hieun Thsang first visited these lands.

These memorials of the past being a great national asset, the State as well as the people have every reason to guard and to cherish them with the most zealous care. The Government of His Exalted Highness the Nizam in consequence, is taking great pains to preserve them for posterity. Apart from the educational value of these ancient monuments the beauty which pervades their line and their colour, their delicate grace and their massive strength, the beauty which enshrines their stately walls and battlements, their pillared halls and soaring minarets, and the beauty of the graven or painted forms combine in themselves the best traditions and ideals of the Indian genius and tells the history of the bygone generations.

Ever since the inaguration of the State Archæological Department in 1914 (1323 Fasli) a good number of reports and journals, illustrated by photos and drawings, have been published which deal in detail with the account of the Archæological remains of the dominions.

Mr. Henry Cousens was the first to compile a list of Antiquarian Remains of the Nizam's Dominions in 1899. This list, apart from being incomplete, was prepared in a summary manner and consequently it is difficult to form any adequate idea of the monuments which have been described in it. To wit, the monuments of the entire city and suburbs of Hyderabad have been dealt with in a single leaf of this list.

In 1922, When Mr. Ghulam Yazdani, the permanent Director of Archæology of the State, proceeded on deputation to Europe and Islamic countries for a period of 2 years, I was put in charge of this Department by the Gracious Farman of His Exalted Highness, and as in the course of discharging my interesting duties I had the privilege of going through the valuable data collected by the Department and also by having the occasion of constantly visiting and examining these ancient monuments, I felt the necessity of preparing a comprehensive descriptive list of the ancient monuments of these Dominions and first of all the remains in the premier city and its suburbs engaged my attention. The present volume may be taken as the first instalment of this undertaking, and conditions being favourable, I propose to compile lists of the antiquarian remains of the four Subahs of the Deccan, in the same fashion.

The monuments mentioned in this volume are situated in the city and suburbs of Hyderabad and in listing these monuments I have followed the principles laid down by the Superintendent, Archæological Survey of India, Northern Circle.

The uninscribed monuments have been dated with reference to the reign of the contemporary emperor and in the general description of the monuments the following rules have been adhered to :—

No.—Number of monument.

a.=Name of monument

b.=Situation

c.=Owner

d.=Class

The following classification of monuments has been adopted.

I. Those monuments which from their present condition and historical or archæological value ought to be maintained in permanent good repair.

II. Those monuments which it is now only possible or desirable to save from further decay by such minor measures as the eradication of vegetation, the exclusion of water from the walls and the like.

III. Those monuments which from their advanced stage of decay or comparative unimportance, it is impossible or unnecessary to preserve.

The monuments in class I and II are further subdivided thus :—

I-*a* } Monuments owned and maintained by Govern-
II-*a* } ment.

I-*b* } Monuments owned and maintained by private
II-*b* } persons.

I-*c* } Monuments owned by private persons but main-
II-*c* } tained by the owners and by Government jointly or by the Government exclusively.

No comment is necessary as regards monuments coming under class I, but of those in class II it will often be found necessary to carry out sufficient initial repairs over and above those specified, to put a building in such a state that those minor measures will afterwards suffice to keep it in a tolerably fair condition.

Because a building is put in class III on account of its very dilapidated condition, it does not follow that there should be any unnecessary haste in converting it into road metal. It may still be a monument of interest as long as it keeps together.

(*e*)=Date.
(*f*)=Inscriptions.
(*g*)=General condition.
(*h*)=Should be protected or protection unnecessary.
(*j*)=Notes and general description.

A few of the inscriptions and their plates which have been incorporated in this book have already appeared in the *Epigraphia Indo-Moslemica* which is being edited by Mr. Ghulam Yazdani and published under the auspices of the Government of India. The photographs of the kings, etc., and the monuments are the property of the State Archæological Department—the former having been copied from the British Museum collection are quite authentic. In describing the monuments I have as far as practicable classified them according to the year of their erection, inasmuch as the list of contents has been prepared in chronological order. I have divided the book into two parts. In the first part are set forth the monuments of the city and environs of Hyderabad; in the second part, all the monuments of Golconda have been described in one group for the convenience of the tourists.

I am greatly indebted to Sir John Marshall, the Director-General of Archæology in India, for his kind and ready permission to reproduce the blocks of Golconda and Hyderabad inscriptions in my book.

S. A. ASGAR BILGRAMI,

HYDERABAD-DECCAN,
1*st January*, 1924.

LIST OF AUTHORITIES.

(1) Alamgir Nama, by Muhammad Kazim, Bibl. Ind. 1868.

(2) Baghe Char Chaman, by Maulana Abbas. (Lucknow Edition).

(3) Basatinus-Salatin, by Muhammad Ibrahim Zubairi. (Hyderabad Edition).

(4) Bernier's Voyage to the East Indies, by John Pinkerton. Vol. 8, (London Edition, 1811).

(5) Bustane Asafiyah, by Manik Rao, Vithal Rao. (Hyderabad Edition).

(6) Dabistane Mazaheb, by Zulfiqare Ardastani (Bombay Edition).

(7) Epigraphia Indo Moslemica, by Mr. Ghulam Yazdani.

(8) Gulzare Asafiyah, by Khanezaman Khwaja Ghulam Husain Khan. (Hyderabad Edition).

(9) Hadiqatul Alam, by Mir Alam. (Hyderabad Edition).

(10) Hadiqatus-Salatin Qutbshahi (MSS.) by Mirza Nizamuddin Ahmad.

(11) History of the Deccan Vol. 3. Silsilae Asafiyah (Agra Edition).

(12) Kanzul Lughat. (MSS.).

(13) Madras in the Olden Times, by Mr. Talboys Wheeler.

(14) Maathire Alamgiri, by Muhammad Saqi Mustaid Khan. Bibl. Ind. 1871.

(15) Maathirul Kiram, by Mir Ghulam Ali Azad Bilgrami, (Agra Edition).

(16) Muntakhabul Lubab, by Khafi Khan. Bibl. Ind. 1869-74.

(17) Nujoomus-Sama, by Moulvi Mirza Muhammad Ali. (Lucknow Edition).

(18) Roz Namae Vaqae Darul Jihad, by Nimat Khan Ali. (Bombay Edition).

(19) Salafatul Asr, by Syed Ali Khan Madani. (MSS.)
(20) Tarikhe Farishta, by Muhammad Qasim. (Bombay Edition).
(21) Tarikhe Muhammad Qutbshahi, (MSS.).
(22) Tawarikhe Farkhunda, by Ghulam Qadir Khan Bidri. (MSS.).
(23) Tarikhe Zufra, by Girdhari Lal. (MSS.).
(24) Tuzuke Qutbshahi. (MSS.).
(25) Vaqae Mamlakate Bijapur, Part 3. by Moulvi Bashiruddin Ahmad. (Agra Edition)

LIST OF MONUMENTS.

LIST OF ILLUSTRATIONS.

THE CHRONOLOGY OF THE QUTB SHAHI DYNASTY

924 A.H. / 1518 A.D. — 1098 A.H. / 1687 A.D.

(E.I.M.)

No.	King	Birth	Accession	Death
1	Sultan Quli, Qutbul Mulk Qutb Shah I. ..	849 A.H. 1445 A.D.	924 A.H. 1518 A.D.	950 A.H. 1543 A.D.
2	Jamshed Quli, Qutb Shah II., son of (1) ..	..	950 A.H. 1543 A.D.	957 A.H. 1550 A.D.
3	Subhan Quli, Qutb Shah III., son of (2) ..	950 A.H. 1543 A.D.	957 A.H. 1550 A.D.	..
4	Ibrahim Quli, Qutb Shah IV., son of (1) ..	936 A.H. 1530 A.D.	957 A.H. 1550 A.D.	988 A.H. 1580 A.D.
5	Muhammad Quli Qutb Shah V., son of (4) ..	973 A.H. 1566 A.D.	988 A.H. 1580 A.D.	1020 A.H. 1612 A.D.
6	Muhammad Qutb Shah VI son of Mirza Muhammad Amin son of (4)	1001 A.H. 1593 A.D.	1020 A.H. 1612 A.D.	1035 A.H. 1626 A.D.
7	Abdullah Qutb Shah VII., son of (6)	1023 A.H. 1614 A.D.	1035 A.H. 1626 A.D.	1083 A.H. 1672 A.D.
8	Abul Hasan, Tana Shah Qutb Shah VIII. ..		1083 A.H. 1674 A.D.	1111 A.H. 1699 A.D.
			Extinction of the Dynasty 1098 A.H. 1687 A.D.	

PART I.

No. 1.

(*a*)=Old Bridge. (New).

(*b*)=Near Karvane-Sahuwan.

(*c*)=Government.

(*d*)=Ia.

(*e*)=986 A.D.
1578 A.D.

(*f*)=The following inscription, written in Nasta'liq is set in the archway.

بعہد شاہ اسکندر شدہ تعمیر پل یکسر * ز سعی راجہ چندو لعل از سابق بود بہتر
بہ شادان رسید ندا جائے غریبے بہر تاریخش * ز سیل اینک بود محفوظ چون
اندر صدف گوہر - تحویل پورن سنگھہ داروغہ سنہ ۱۲۳۶ھ (۱۸۲۰ع)

Translation.

"During the reign of Shah Iskandar by the endeavours of Raja Chandu Lal, reconstruction of the bridge was done better than before;

Shadan received the invisible cry "Ja-ey Ghari-be" (unique place) for its chronogram; it will henceforward remain safe from floods, as the pearl in the oyster. 1236 1820 A.D.)

In the charge of Puran Singh Darogha."

(*g*)=Good.

(*h*)=Should be protected.

(*j*)=Fourteen years previous to the foundation of the new city of Hyderabad, this bridge was constructed during the reign of Sultan Ibrahim Qutb Shah IV, chiefly with a view to afford easy egress and to avoid the risk of life which attended the nocturnal visits of Prince Muhammad Quli to Bhagmathi, a courtesan, who resided in the village of Chichlam, near Shah Ali Banda.

On one occasion when the Prince set out from the fort of Golconda to pay a visit to this sweetheart, the overflow of the Musi river did not deter him from crossing the river on horseback, and when his father, Ibrahim Qutb Shah, was informed of this venture of the Prince's, he forthwith ordered the construction of this bridge which was completed at a cost of Rs. 1,00,000.

"Sira-tu-hul Mustaqim[1]" $\frac{\text{986 A.H.}}{\text{1578 A.D.}}$ gives the year when the erection of this bridge was commenced and the chronogram of its completion is .

زتحت او گذرد ماء ز بر او گذریم - ازین سبب شده تاریخ او گذرگه ما

سنه ۹۸۶ھ م ۱۵۷۸ع

"The water flows under the bridge and we pass above it; for this reason its chronogram is Guzargahema (our passage) $\frac{\text{986 A.H.}}{\text{1578 A.D.}}$ The word 'ma' bears a double interpretation, as it also signifies water and consequently the chronogram may also mean (passage of water), although the word 'ma' has no hamza at the end.

After the famous flood of 1236 A.H. (1820 A.D.) during the reign of Nawab Sikandar Jah, Maghfirat Manzil, Asaf Jah IV, this bridge was reconstructed and in commemoration of this incident inscription (*f*) was set by Maharaja Chandu Lal Bahadur Shadan, the then Prime Minister. After the last flood of 1326 A. H. (1908) the superstructure of this bridge was again repaired on an extensive scale during the reign of Nawab Sir Mir Mahboob Ali Khan Bahadur Asaf Jah VI, Ghufran-Makan, and the masonry walls were replaced by railings of pierced Ashlar.

The bridge has a row of 22 arches and its dimensions are (L 600 × W 36 × D 42) Ft. Though one of the

(1) According to "Tuzuke-Qutbshahi" (MSS), it was constructed in the course of 8 months only, at a cost of one lac; as it was ordered by the King to be completed before the next winter and the year of its erection was 986 A.H. vide Gulzare Asafiyah P. 15. This word means 'Its path is straight.'

oldest examples of Qutb Shahi architecture in the city of Hyderabad, it is still in the best state of preservation.

Purana Pul (Old Bridge) is the name given to it during the Asaf Jahi reign, but in the Qutb Shahi period it was called Pul-e-Narva(1) (Narva Bridge).

No. 2.

(*a*)=Kohe Sharief (Moula Ali Hill) (New*)

(*b*)=Near Malkajgiri village.

(*c*)=Government.

(*d*)=IIa.

(*e*)=Ibrahim Qutb Shah's reign, about $\frac{\text{986 A.H.}}{\text{1578 A.D.}}$

(*f*)=On and in the vicinity of Moula Ali Hill the following inscriptions are fixed.

(1) On the Ashur Khana of Khush-hal-Khan, the Musician.

خوشانصیب که خوشحال‌خان بکوه شریف * بحسن‌نیت پاک و ز روی صدق و صفا
کمان و مسجد و عا شورخانهٔ ذیشان * سرا و تکیه برا ه خدا چو کرد بنا
خرد بسال بنا ها بگفت مصرع خوش * بنا نهاد بقانون خوب و روح افزا
سنه ۱۲۹۳ھ (۱۸۲۳ع) راقم سید حسین علیخان عفي الله عنه

Translation.

"By good fortune Khush-hal Khan with true and sincere intention, to seek the pleasure of God, erected the Arch, the Mosque and the grand Ashur Khana, the inn and the fakir's stand on the venerable hill.

"For the chronogram of these erections the divine wisdom composed this nice hemistich. The foundation was laid judiciously and inspiringly 1293 A.H. (1823 A.D.). Written by Syed Husain Ali Khan, may God pardon him.

---

(1) Tawarikh-e-Farkhunda by G. Qadri Khan of Bidar (MSS).

In Telugu language Narva means a causeway.

* This word indicates that either these monuments have been discovered by the author or the relative inscriptions or their historic account is now being for the first time published with accuracy and precision.

(2) On the Arch of Khush-hal Khan.

دمان و مسجد و عاشور خانهٔ ذیشان * طرز مسجد عالی ز راه صدق و صفا
ز هے نصیب که خوشحال خان بکوه شریف * بنا نهاد بقانون خوب و روح افزا

Translation.

"By good fortune Khush-hal-Khan judiciously and inspiringly laid the foundation of the Arch, the Mosque and the grand Ashur Khana; the dignified Mosque was erected with sincere intention."

(3) On the black slab of Chihl-Cheragh, (lamp stand), near the steps of the hill.

(۱) و یسبحونه و له یسجدون - الا ذقان سجدو بکیاً - و ما الرحمن واسجد
لا تسجدوا و اسجدو ا

(۲) ولله یسجد من فی السموات و الارض - ان الله یسجد لهم اسجدوا
لا یسجدون سجدوا - فاسجدوا و اقترب سجدا

(۳) بنا کرد ی سجده بکوه علی - که بی بال سران(؟) بحیدر علی سنه ۱۲۲۴ھ (۱۸۰۹ع)

Translation.

(1 & 2) Verses from the Quran relating to Sijdah.

(3) "On the hill of Ali the act of falling down in adoration started, ... Hydar Ali. In the year 1224 A.H." (1809 A.D.).

(4) On carved teakwood over the door outside the mausoleum of Mah Laqa Bai.

سرو گلستان نازگلبن باغ ادا * عاشق حیدر بجان جاریهٔ پنجتن
چونکه زحق در رسید مژدهٔ جاء الاجل * کرد قبولش بجان گشت بهشتش وطن
هاتف غیبی ندا - اد بتاریخ او * راهئ جنت شد آه ماه لقائے دکن
سنه ۱۲۴۰ھ م ۱۸۲۴ع

Translation.

"Cypress of the garden of grace and rose-tree of the grove of coquetry, an ardent *inamoratu* of Hydar and suppliant of Panjtan. When the tidings of the advent of death arrived from God, she accepted it with her heart, and heaven become her home. The voice of the invisible speaker called for her chronogram, Alas! Mah Laqa of the Deccan departed for heaven 1240 A.H." (1824 A.D.).

(5) Carved on teakwood over the door inside the mausoleum of Mah Laqa Bai.

کنیز شاه مردان راج کنور * سخاوت پیشه و اخلاق آرا
چو محمل بست ازین دنیای فانی * عجب بگذاشت دختر سرو بالا
بخوبی بهتر از لیلی و شیرین * خطابش مه لقا و عرف چندا
برای انبساط روح مادر * بنا کرد این مکان فرحت افزا
بسال رحلت او گفت هاتف - بیا مرزد خدا آن عاجزه را ۱۲۰۷ھ (۱۷۹۲ع)

(*Translation*)

" Raj Kunwar, the suppliant of Shahe-Mardan (Ali) was magnificient and of good nature. When she passed away from this mortal world, she left a unique daughter of cypress stature, who is in quality, better than Liela and Sheerin, her title is Mah Laqa and commonly called ' Chanda .' For the blessedness of her mother's soul she built this pleasant abode. For the chronogram of her demise the invisible speaker said, may that supplicant be forgiven by God 1207 A.H." (1792-A.D.).

(6) On a well outside the mausoleum of Mah Laqa Bai.

سبیل نذر مولا علی ۱۲۹۴ھ (۱۸۳۳ع)

(*Translation*)

" Water dedicated to Moula Ali 1294 A.H." (1833 A.D.).

(7) On a loose stone slab near the grave of Chanda Bibi, which belongs to some other building.

نذر مولا چندا بی بی بنت راج کنور بائی که از حضور نواب غفران مآب آصفجاه
ثانی میر نظام علیخان بخطاب ماه لقا بائی سرافراز در سنه ۱۲۳۱ھ مرتب
ساخت - (سنه ۱۸۱۵ع)

(*Translation*)

" Chanda Bibi, daughter of Raj Kunwar Bai upon whom was conferred the title of Mah Laqa Bai by His Highness Nawab Ghufran Maab Asaf Jah II, Mir Nizam Ali Khan prepared this in 1231 A.H. (1815 A.D.) dedicating it to Maula (Ali)."

(*g*)=Good

(*h*)=The arch and the inscriptions should be protected.

(*j*)=According to the 'Tuzuke Qutb Shahi' during the reign of Ibrahim Qutb Shah IV, Yaqoot, a Eunuch, was staying at Lallaguda for a change. On the night of 17th Rajab he saw in a dream that a man came to him clad in green Arabic garb and asked him to accompany him to see Janabe Amir, (Hazrat Ali) who was waiting for him. Yaqoot followed him and saw Hazrat Ali seated on the summit of the hill on which his mausoleum now stands Yaqoot saluted him and remained standing for some time without any discourse from either side. The following morning he went up the hill and saw the hand and side mark of Hazrat Ali engraved on the same stone where he was seen seated during the night. Yaqoot caused the marks to be hewn out of the stone and had a masonry arch built there and made offerings on 17th Rajab in the name of Hazrat Ali. When this incident was related to the king, he also visited the hill to pay his respects. The mosque which is situated to the south was erected by Sultan Ibrahim Qutb Shah. This Urs (ceremony) is still observed annually on 17th Rajab. Later on, Phiki Bi, daughter of Syed Muzaffar, Minister of Tana Shah, who used saltless food became mujawir of this shrine, and is buried in the Northern enclosure. Then Nawab Ruknuddowlah Bahadur, Prime Minister of Ghufran Maab, Asaf Jah II, who succumbed to the wounds inflicted on him by one Faizoo Gardee in 1189 A. H., is buried in his garden close to the steps of the hill. Vikarud-Dowlah, Nazim of Hyderabad is also buried in his garden close by. Samsamud-Dowlah originally built a wooden canopy opposite the mosque of Ibrahim Qutb Shah and also a wooden hall near the shrine, but this wooden canopy and hall were afterwards replaced by masonry by Nawab Samsamud-Dowlah Bahadur and Mah Laqa Bai, respectively. Nawab Asaf Jah II, had the outer door and other out-houses built and conferred the Jagir of Charlapalli for the mujawirs and sweepers, crier-to-prayers, drum beaters and gong-strikers and for other expenses of the shrine. A Naqarkhana (the place where drums are beaten at stated intervals) was built by Maharaja Chandu Lal Bahadur, and a Baradari by Raja Rao Rambha Jiwant Bahadur. Near Kamargah a huge arch was built by Jamal Saheb, Azmat Jung manager of Zafarud-Dowlah Bahadur, Mubarizul Mulk. On the route through which the Sandal is carried up a big arch, a mausoleum, an Ashurkhana and a repository for drinking water were built by the musician Khush-hal Khan[1] who was the instructor of Mah Laqa Bai. On the outskirts of the hill Mah Laqa Bai had a mosque and Karwansarai built and in the centre of a beautiful garden is situated the last resting place of Mah Laqa and her mother. The new Shahabad stone steps leading to the hill were constructed by the order of His Exalted Highness the Nizam, soon after his accession to the throne. The decoration of the shrine with glass-work was done by the late Nawab Imdad Jung Bahadur, but it has been completed by Nawab Shah Yar Jung Bahadur.

There is another hillock opposite the Maula Ali hill, which is called ' Qadam Rasul,' on which sacred relics of the Prophet were deposited by Muhammad Shukrullah Khan, a servant of Nawab Ghufran Maab, Asaf Jah II. He also had a portion of the revenue of Trimulgherry village assigned for the expenses of this place; a mosque was also built here by the same gentleman. The steps leading to this hill were constructed by Kazim Ali Khan. On the southern extremity of this hill there is a baradari, (citadel), which is ascribed to Syed Muzaffar, Minister of Sultan Abdullah Qutbshah VII, and Tana Shah. The adjoining hill has several huge boulders piled one over the other; locally this is called Bhandoli[2] hill, and traditionally it is said to be a fort belonging to some old Railu Rajah[3]; remains of a stone

(1) He was the son of Karim Khan Ghugga, and was considered a master-Musician of his time. He is buried in his own garden there. " Gulzure Asafiyah."

(2) Bhandoli=a number of Jars borne one over the other.

(3) Tuzuke Qutbshahi. (MSS)

Char Minar.

gate and wall may still be seen here, it is also called the fort of Arjuna.

The Sandal of Moula Ali is annually carried on the back of a camel with great pomp from the grave yard of Rang Ali Shah; after this follows another Sandal for the safety of His Exalted Highness from the "Punja Shah," and is carried to the Maula Ali hill. This hill is 2017 feet above the level of the sea.

No. 3.

(*a*)=Char Minar.

(*b*)=Is situated in the heart of the city.

(*c*)=Government.

(*d*)=Ia.

(*e*)=999 A.H. (1590 A.D.)—1000 A.H. (1591 A.D.).

(*f*)=Nil.

(*g*)=Good.

(*h*)=Should be protected.

(*j*)=Bhagnagar or the present city of Hyderabad was founded by Sultan Muhammad Quli Qutb Shah V, in 999 A.H. (1590 A.D.). Sultan Muhammad Quli's sweetheart Bhagmati, resided in the Chichlam village which is now called Shah Ali Banda and the City of Bhagnagar was styled after her name, but after her demise it was denominated Hyderabad and seven years after the completion of the city, 'Farkhunda Bunyad[1] 1006 A.H. (1597 A.D.) became its chronogrammatic epithet. This name was changed to 'Darul-Jihad, Hyderabad' after the sack of the city by the Emperor Aurangzeb in 1098 A.H., and Farkhunda Bunyad was again adopted by the omission of the word 'Darul Jihad' by Shah Alam. When the foundation of the city was being laid, Sultan Muhammad Quli gave precedence to the building of Char Minar which is a prototype of Taziya[2]

(1) *Vide* Baghe-Char Chaman (p. 23) By Maulana Abbas.

(2) Owing to the outbreak of cholera the inhabitants fixed a huge Tazia in the heart of the city on Thursday, 1st Moharrum 999 A.H., so that it may serve as a charm to safegaurd them from the epidemic, and when it subsided, the huge building of Char Minar was constructed of stone and mortar at the same place. ("Tuzuke Qutbshahi.") (MSS).

or Taboot (representation of the tomb of Imam Husain). This square edifice is situated in the heart of the city and is built of plaster and stone ; its four corners lie exactly toward the four cardinal points, each side measuring 60 ft. in length and 42 ft. in width. Its main building consists of four splendid arches—one in each direction, measuring 24 by 30 ft. containing a small cistern in the centre. Facing each arch are four highways ; several stairs lead to the upper story and the top portion is double storyed, composed of finely proportioned arches ; the four corners of the upper portion have four minarets (80 ft. high), each of which is again subdivided into four storeys. The entire building is composed of lime and stone and is full of fine stucco decorations, the height of each minar from the ground level is 160 ft.

The opinion of Monsieur Thevenot, the French traveller, that " there is no edifice like the Char Minar in the whole city which appears so splendid to the eye " is quite true to the present day. In the Qutb Shahi period the first storey was used as a Madrasa[1] and cubicle for the students, on the second storey there was a mosque and water reservoir where water used to come from the Jalpalli tank and from this top reservoir water was distributed to the inhabitants of the city and the Royal palace. A fine birdseye view of the picturesque city may be had from the top, but owing to the proximity of the Royal palaces of Chau-Mahalla and Panch-Mahalla, the public are usually not allowed to go upstairs, but on emergent occasions it is possible to obtain a special permit from the Sarf-i-Khas. It has been estimated that this glorious edifice was completed at a cost of 200,000 Huns[2] or 9 Lacs of rupees. After the extinction of the Qutb Shahi dynasty, during the Subadarship of Bahadur Dil Khan the South western minaret of Char Minar fell to pieces by the effect of lightning, but it was forthwith repaired at a cost

(1) The origin of the word Madrasah is given in the Tarikhe Zufra that this name was given to Char Minar because all necessaries of life were also procurable here.

(2) Hun, a gold coin, was equivalent of 4½ Moghal rupees.

of Rs. 60,000. During the reign of His Highness Nawab Nasirud Dowlah Bahadur, Ghufran-Manzil, Asaf Jah III, plastering of the entire Char Minar was done in 1258 A.H. (1824 A.D.) at a cost of a lac of rupees. A guard of Afghan City Police was stationed here in 1302 A.H. (1884 A.D). In 1304 A.H., (1886 A.D.) on the occasion of the visit of Lord Dufferin, Viceroy of India, to Hyderabad, iron railings were fixed round Char Minar with a gate on the Northern side. In 1307 A.H. (1889 A.D.) four clocks were set on the second storey of this building. On special occasions this building is illuminated by electric bulbs from top to bottom including a resplendent star and a crescent. The accompanying photograph depicts the northern side of Char Minar.

No. 4.

(*a*)=Char Kaman.

(*b*)=Opposite Char Minar.

(*c*)=Government.

(*d*)=Ia.

(*e*)=1001 A.H. (1592 A.D.).

(*f*)=None.

(*g*)=Good.

(*h*)=Should be protected.

(*j*)=After the completion of Char Minar a piazza of four sublime arches was built by Sultan Muhammad Quli Qutb Shah V, being formerly called, that on the West, " Daulat Khanae Ali , (The gate of Royal residence), that on the East, the Naqqar Khana," (gate of palace where drums are beaten), and generally the central area of the four arches was termed the " Jilau Khana " (Royal Vestibule).

At present these lofty arches which are used as passages through which a huge elephant with a canopied litter can easily pass, are called, (Northern) " Machli Kaman "— the fish Arch (a big fish made of bamboo and paper resembling a miniature æroplane is suspended in the centre of the arch on every lunar new year), (Southern) the Char Minar arch, (Eastern) The Kali Kaman or Kaman of Shambhoo Pershad, (the Black arch). (Western), Kaman Sher Dil or Sihr Batil, (the arch of lion hearted or Magic breaker). The Hyderabad Improvement Trust Board is now building excellent arches on either side of the road from Char Minar to Afzulganj by His Exalted Highness' command.

Formerly the Qutb Shahi palaces were situated towards the western arch, but the relentless hand of time has totally obliterated them. This portion of the land remained the residence of Qutb Shahi Kings and the Royal family, ever since the capital was shifted here from Golconda by Sultan Muhammad Quli V, till the last siege of Golconda in 1098 A.H. On the eastern side was the entrance to the Royal palace which was approached after crossing a courtyard, 1,000 ft. square; the gate of the Royal residence was a huge structure of sandalwood in which golden spikes were set. The adjoining outhouses were used as a sitting place for the nobles and officials. These noblemen used to come every morning with their retinue and attendants and after reaching the Royal vestibule which was in the centre of the four arches, the suite and retinue were left behind and they used to proceed unattended for the audience of the King. On either side of the Royal gate a few elephants remained standing day and night and inside the gate 1,000 foot, 200 African slaves and 1,000 horse used to be drawn up in rank and file. The four cornered octangular reservoir was intended for quenching the thirst of the army. In the southern enclosure was the Privy Council Chamber, in the Northern enclosure was the Royal wardrobe house and other Royal offices; the Northern enclosure consisted of four apartments where soldiers, stewards, clerks on night duty and armour bearers used to sit. In Chandan Mahal ordinary armour bearers attended alternately; in Gagan Mahal, Turks, Arabs and Deccani armour bearers used to assemble and the main apartment was reserved for trustworthy servants. Sajan Mahal was set apart for learned and virtuous men and the eastern enclosure was the public dining hall where thousands of deserving men were supplied with delicious food from the Royal kitchen every morning and evening*.

Four highways lead to different parts of the City through every arch and exactly in the centre of the four arches there is a reservoir, a view of which may be had from every direction, hence its name Char-su-ka-Hauz, (the four cornered reservoir). It is now called Gulzar Hauz; the old terrace with which it was surrounded was pulled down in 1313 A.H., (1895 A.D.) for the sake of widening the path, and an iron fencing was fixed in its stead. The Qutb Shahi Kings used to sit on the balcony of the Royal residence facing this reservoir.

No. 5.

(*a*)=Badshahi Ashur Khana.

(*b*)=Near Path-hargatti.

(*c*)=Sarf-i-Khas.

(*d*)=IIa.

(*e*)=1001 A.H. (1593 A.D.) 1005 A.H. (1596 A.D.)

(*f*)=The following inscriptions in the best Tughra style are engraved on Persian enamelled tiles, and are now published for the first time :—

(1) Over the Central niche.

نصر من ا لله و فتح قریب وبشرا لمومنین غلا م علی محمد قطب شاه سنه احدی والف

(*Translation*)

"Help is from God and the success is in view and so give this glad tidings to the faithful. The slave of Ali Muhammad Qutb Shah in the year 1001." (A.H.)

* Tarikh-e-zufra (MSS.)

(2) On the Western wall.

آیۃ الکرسی تا هوا لعلی العظیم - ابو المظفر محمد قلی قطبشاه خلد الله ملکه وسلطانه ۱۰۰۵ هجری

(*Translation*)

" Throne verse (Quran, Ch. II verse 256) Abul Muzaffar Muhammad Quli Qutb Shah, may God keep his Kingdom and suzerainty 1005 Hijri," (1596 A.D.)

(3) On the Western wall, in Tughra style

ان المساجد لله فلا تدعوا مع الله احدا - سنه ۱۰۰۳ھ (۱۵۹۴ع)

(*Translation*)

"The places of worship are for God, hence invoke not any other with God. In the year 1003 A.H." (1594 A.D.).

(*a*) بسم الله الرحمن الرحیم

" In the name of God, the merciful and compassionate."

قل کل یعمل علی شاکلته

(*b*) " Say, (O Muhammad) every one acts according to his designs.

(*c*) ابو المظفر سلطان عبد الله قطبشاه

" Abul Muzaffar Sultan Abdullah Qutb Shah."

(*d*), یا الله یا محمد یا علي

" O God ! O Muhammad ! O Ali."

(*e*) یا مفتح الابواب

" O opener of the gates."

(4) On the Northern and Southern walls in Tughra style.

اللهم صل علی محمد المصطفی وعلی المرتضی والبتول فاطمه وصل علی سبطین الحسن والحسین وعلی زین العابدین

" The Shiite Durad."

(*a*) توکلت علي خالقي

" I have relied on (God) my creator."

Badshahi Ashur Khana.

(b) وما توفيقی الا باالله

"Verily, there is no guidance except from God."

(c) اللهم صل علی النبی والوصی والبتول والسبطين والسجاد والباقر والصادق والکاظم والرضا والتقی والنقي والعسکری والمهدي عليهم السلام

"The Shiite Durud."

(d) ان المتقين في جنات وعيون وادخلوها بسلام

"Verily, let enter men, of piety, in paradise and fountains (of immortality), with peace."

(5) On the hall of Western wall.

چون نظام الملک آصف منزلت * کرده از بهر حسين توقير او
هست اين قدسي مکان آن امام * که بفرقان آمده تطهير او
گفت هاتف سال تاريخش چنين * کرده آصف جاه ما تعمير او
۱۱۷۸ ھ (۱۷۶۴ ع)

(*Translation*)

"Whereas Nizamul Mulk of the same dignity as that of Asaf (son of Barkhiya, Vazier of Solomon the Prophet) treated this abode with reverence, for the sake of (Imam) Husain.

"This holy abode is attributed to that Imam, whose purification has been mentioned in the Quran."

"The invisible voice thus spoke for its chronogram 'Our Asaf Jah repaired it' 1178 A.H." (1764 A.D.)

(6) On wooden panels of Northern and Southern hall

بهر احيائي طراز اين مکان تدبيرکرد * در دل مشرف اسد خالق چو اين تاثيرکرد
عهد آصفجاه ثاني آن شه عالی دکن * لامکان جاي امام ماکه او تعميرکرد
سنه ۱۲۵۰ ھ (سنه ۱۸۳۴ ع)

Translation)

"Deliberated for the renovation of the decoration of this edifice, when God impressed this in the heart of Asad, the Superintendent (of buildings). During the reign of Asaf Jah II, the King of Deccan. He constructed a non-existent abode of our Imam 1250 A.H." (1834 A.D.).

(7) Over the main entrance gate.

باب فیض امام عالمیان ۱۱۷۹ھ (۱۷۶۵ع)

"The gate of favours of Imam of the upper and lower worlds 1179 A.H" (1765 A.D.)

(g)=Fair.

(h)=Should be protected.

(j)=The inner hall is the oldest portion of this building. It was built by Sultan Muhammad Quli Qutb Shah V, at a cost of Rs. 66,000. It will be apparent from the above inscriptions that the construction of this building remained current from 1001 A.H. (1592 A.D.) to 1005 A.H. (1596-A.D.). The name of the reigning sovereign is inscribed on the western wall and also on the central niche, but the word Quli has been omitted in the latter inscription. The Persian enamel work was executed in the last year of the reign of Sultan Muhammad Quli in 1020 A. H. (1611 A.D.). Besides this the name and royal titles of Sultan Abdullah Qutb Shah VII, the grandson of Muhammad Quli, have also been inscribed in fine ornamental style which indicates that he took a considerable part in the renovation of this building. He also introduced the use of standards in this Ashur-Khana during the month of Moharram.

The addition of outer halls, which stand on a range of huge wooden colonnades was made during the reign of His Highness Nawab Mir Nizam Ali Khan Bahadur, Asaf Jah II as will be apparent from inscription No. 5. Inscription No. (7) was fixed by Nawazish Ali Khan Shaida,[1] a Mutawalli of this Ashur Khana, when the main gate was built by him during the reign of Asaf Jah II. In 1250 A.H. (1834 A.D.) Asad, the Superintendent of buildings, restored the decorations of the halls. In respect of age this Ashurkhana is older than Imam Baras of Hugli or Lucknow and its enamel work compares favourably with the best buildings of Lahore.

(1) Author of 'Ijaze-Ahmadi and Rauzatul At-haar.' He was also Musharraf and Mir-Samaan of Ghufran Maab.

and Multan. Notwithstanding the lapse of 3 centuries the freshness and resplendence of enamel tiles have maintained their brilliant lustre, and the excellence and beauty of their colours as also the arrangement and fitting together of joints are highly commendable. The wooden wainscotting of the roof is the characteristic of the old Asafiya style of Architecture. His Highness Asaf Jah II, conferred a Jagir yielding an annual revenue of Rs. 12,000 for the expenses of this Ashur Khana, and His Highness Nawab Sikandar Jah Bahadur, Asaf Jah III., made an addition of Rs. 2,000 cash to the existing annuity. The accompanying photograph of the central niche indicates the enamel work and caligraphical skill of the artist. The extensive courtyard of this building is now used as a public auction house.

No. 6.

(*a*)=Darush-Shifa. (New).
(*b*)=On the back of Darush-Shifa Police Station.
(*c*)=Sarf-i-Khas.
(*d*)=II (b).
(*e*)=1004 A.H. (1595 A.D.)
(*f*)=None.
(*g*)=Ruinous.
(*h*)=Worth protecting.

(*j*)=This double storyed hospital which has a square courtyard was erected during the reign of Muhammad Quli, Qutb Shah V., for the sake of the sick and the diseased; this was also used as a residential college for imparting Unani Medical education. There was also a Karwan Serai and a bath attached to it; but at present these are in a neglected and ruinous condition and require much restoration.

The Northern enclosure of this building contains a large standard (Alam) of steel which is always kept standing in a small room. The Mutawalli showed the author copies of 2 Royal deeds, which bear out that during the Qutb Shahi period one Agha Mohsin of Persia had brought with requisite authenticity a piece of fetters of the 4th Imam Zainul Abideen from Damascus (Syria), which was fixed in this standard and several miracles became manifest from this during the Qutb Shahi and Alamgiri periods, with the result that during the Qutb Shahi period one Hun per diem and 2 Huns in the reign of Aurangzeb, were allotted to it for flower and incense expenses. Both of the deeds bear no date, but on the top of the deeds are inscribed the words ختم بالخیر و السعادہ (Ended with peace and prosperity) which serve to indicate that they pertain to the reign of Sultan Adullah Qutb Shah VII, as after the seige of Golconda in 1066 A.H. (1655 A.D.) a peace was concluded on the distinct stipulation that the daughter of Sultan Abdullah should be given in marriage to Prince Muhammad. son of Emperor Aurangzeb and owing to Sultan Abdullah having no male issue, Prince Muhammad was acknowledged as heir-apparent to the throne of Golconda. Ever since the question of succession was thus settled Sultan Abdullah had the words (ختم بالخیر و السعادہ) engraved on his coins and also the Royal seals of Sultan Abdullah and Tana Shah possessed the same expressions, as the extermination of their house was contemplated by this perforced agreement.

In one of the out-houses of Darushshifa, four banners of the time of His Highness the Asaf Jah II, are kept under a guard of irregular forces.

There is also a Darush-shifa Mosque close by, where prayers are observed to the present day, built by Muhammad Quli V, and its style bears affinity to other Qutb Shahi mosques.

No. 7.

(*a*)=Jamay Masjid (Assembly Mosque).
(*b*)=N. E. of Char Minar.
(*c*)=II (a).

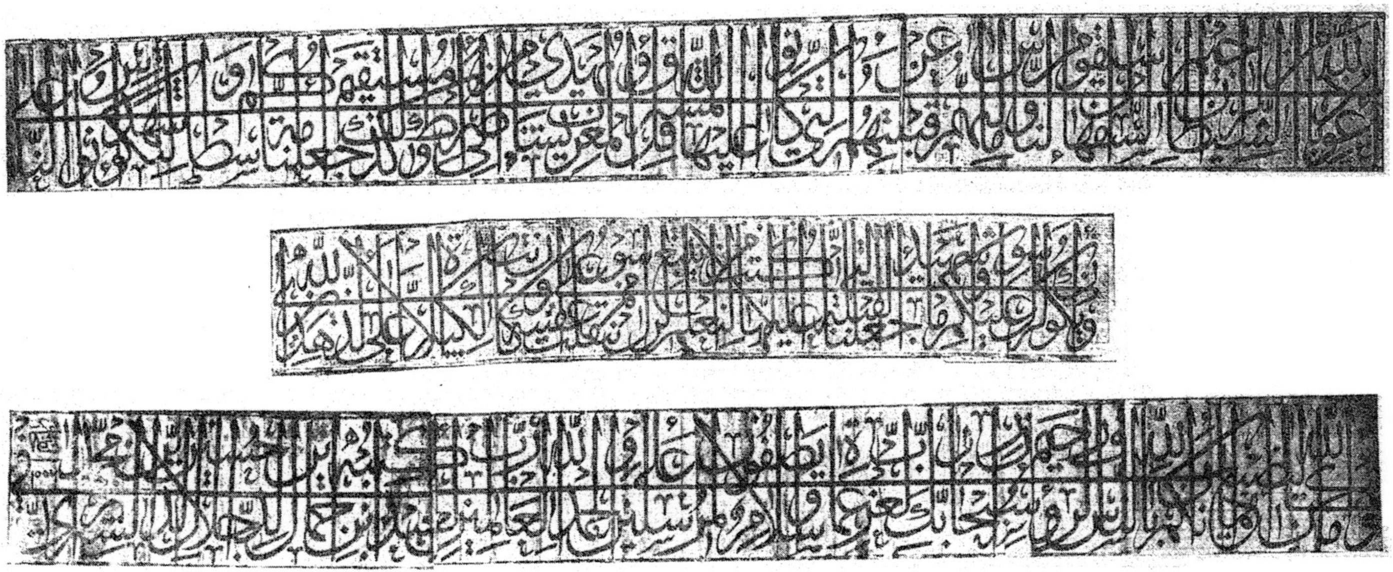

Jamay Musjid City (Naskh inscriptions.)

Jamay Masjid City (Nastaliq inscription.)

(*d*)=1006 A.H., (1597 A.D.)

(*e*)=The mosque has two inscriptions, one in Nastaliq script is fixed above the entrance gate, on black basalt (7×2 ft.)

The author's reading of this inscription, a photographic rubbing of which is herewith published is as follows :—

جهانداری بشاهان شهریاری * که نیکی دیده در عهدش نکوئی
دل آسایش کند جان تازه گردد * زلعلش سر زند چون گفتگوئی

زمین را رشک جنت کرده [1] خلقے * گلستان ارم گردیده روی
بامر عالی خود مسجدی ساخت * که در سقفش فلک گردیده گوی
مگر در پیش صحن او نماید * کند هر لحظه جنت رفت و روی

بنازم خوش در آنجا می نماید * تقاضائی مسلمانی غلوی [2]
کسے پرسد اگر تاریخ او را * زهے عالی بنائی خیر گوئی
تمام گشت بسعی ملک امین الملک حرره بابا خان

(*Translation*).

" The Lord of the world, the King of Kings, in whose reign the virtuous received generous treatment.

" The heart is consoled, the soul is refreshed, when his ruby (lips) make a speech.

" His courteous manners have made this earth the envy of Paradise and his (beautiful) face shows the rose garden of Iram.

" By his own exalted order he built a mosque, below the roof of which heaven revolves like a ball.

" In order that it (Paradise) may appear before its (mosque's) courtyard, the Paradise sweeps it every moment.

" I am proud of this that it is the manifestation of the exacting pre-eminence of Islam.

" Should anyone ask the date of its erection, say, " How excellent is this lofty benificient building," (1006 A.H.)

(1) The word (ہ) has been omitted by Mr. Yazdani in his reading (E. I. M. 1917-18, p. 44).

(2) Mr. Yazdani's reading is (علوی) (*Ibid*).

" Completed by the efforts of Malik Aminul Mulk. Written by Baba Khan."

The next inscription is carved in Tughra or Tauqia style and Thulth script, in the prayer niche. Its dimensions on both sides of the niche are (13×1 ft. 5 inches). It runs thus. (*vide* enclosed plate).

١- اعوذ بالله من الشيطان الرجيم -- يقول السفهاء من الناس ماوليهم عن قبلتهم
التی كانوا عليها قل لله المشرق و المغرب يهدي من يشاء الی صراط المستقيم و
كذلک جعلناكم امة وسطاً لتكونوا شهداء علی الناس -
٢- و يكون الرسول عليكم شهيدا و ما جعلنا القبلة التی كنت عليها الا لنعلم من يتبع
الرسول ممن ينقلب علی عقبيه و ان كانت لكبيرة الا علی الذين هدي الله-
٣- وما كان الله ليضيع ايمانكم ان الله بالناس لرؤف الرحيم- سبحان ربک رب
العزة عما يصفون وسلام علی المرسلين والحمد لله رب العالمين - كتبه العبد
جمال الدين حسين ابن[1] جلال الدين محمد الفخار الشيرازي فی
سنه ١٠٠٦ ھ (١٥٩٧ ع)

(*Translation*)

" Quran Chapter II, Verses 137, 138, written by the servant (of God) Jamaluddin Husain son of Jalaluddin Muhammad Al-Fakhkhar of Shiraz, in the year 1006 A.H. (1596 A.D.)

(*f*)=Fair.

(*g*)=Should be protected.

(*j*)=This assembly mosque which is one of the earliest of the Deccan mosques next to the famous Bahmani mosque of Gulburga, was built by Muhammad Quli V, in 1006 A.H. at a cost of Rs. 2 Lacs under the supervision of his Vazier and Mir Jumla, Malik Aminul Mulk[2], Alaf Khan Bahadur whose Amin Bagh is still famous. A school, a monastry and a bath was also attached to it but all of these have become dilapidated. The name of the reigning monarch is not mentioned but that of his Minister, Aminul Mulk is

(1) Mr. Yazdani has prefixed (ابن) before Jamaluddin in his reading, and his translation shows that the calligrapher was Jalaluddin and his father was Jamaluddin, while quite the reverse is the case (E. I. M. 1917-18, p. 44).

(2) He is buried at Patencheroo.

given in the inscription No. (1) and the name of the caligrapher is Baba Khan.

The character and style of the inscription carved in the prayer niche of the Great Mosque in Golconda Tombs, (No. 67) which will be dealt with in chapter II, is, to a great extent identical with those of inscription No. 2 of this mosque, although in the former the Quranic verse has been written up to (لرو ف رحیم) only, and the latter portion of inscription No. 2 *i.e.*, (و سلام علي المرسلين والحمدلله رب العالمين سبحان ربك رب العزة عما يصفون) has not been reproduced there. Evidently the caligrapher at Golconda has incessantly laboured to copy (71 years later in 1077 A. H.) this original specimen belonging to 1006 A.H. (1666 A.D.); although one of these caligraphers is an Arab and the other a Persian, and the characters of the Golconda mosque inscription are bolder and exhibit much force of form representing the finest example of Naskh script.

During the reign of His Highness Asaf Jah III, this mosque was extensively repaired and the wooden railings were fixed by Mir Abbas Ali Khan, Etisamul-Mulk Bahadur Mir Munshi, who died in 1230 A.H. (1814 A.D.).

Hafiz, Qari Mir Shujauddin, Khalifa of Shah Rafiuddin stayed in this mosque when he first came from Burhanpur, and engaged himself in imparting Arabic education to his numerous pupils of this place. The custom of committing to memory, the Quran and the recitation of Maulood of the Prophet became prevalent in the City through his exertions and influence.

Another mosque of the same age is situated near Karwan and is called Jali-Ki-Masjid, because close to the mosque stands the graveyard of Habibullah Shah in a trellised enclosure. It is a small mosque having 3 arched opening and on either margins of the prayer niche is engraved the following on black basalt. (New).

اعوذ بالله من الشيطان الرجيم سيقول السفهاء (تا) عما يعملون - كتبه العبد
محمد بن صالح شيخ حسين البحرانی سنه ١٠٠٦

" Quran ch. II. Verses 141-44.

" Written by the slave, Muhammad son of Saleh (son of) Shaikh Husain of Bahrain. The year 1006. (A.H.)."

In the prayer niche.

الٰهی تا ظهور صاحب الامر بود این سجده‌گه چون کعبه برجا

وان المساجد لله فلا تدعوا مع الله احدا

برای سال تاریخ بنایش بگفتا خانهٔ حق شد هویدا [1]

" O God, until the advent of Sahebul Amir (Mahdi, the 12th Imam), may this place of prostration survive like Kaaba.

" Verily the mosques are unto God, therefore invoke not any (other) with God.

" For the chronogram of its erection said, the abode of God became manifest."

By the side of the mosque an empty dome is situated, its inner roof stands on graceful props of *Averroha Carambola*.

No. 8.

(*a*)=Lingampalli Garden (New).

(*b*)=On the road to Moula Ali, near Lingampalli.

(*c*)=Paigah of Nawab Sir Khurshid Jah Bahadur.

(*d*)=III (*b*).

(*e*)=None.

(*f*)=Sultan Muhammad Quli V, 1018 A.H. (1609 A.D.)

(*g*)=Poor.

(*h*)=Unnecessary.

(*j*)=This garden which has an extensive area was laid during the reign of Sultan Muhammad Quli V[2] and was

(1) The hemistich fails to give the exact year.
(2) Hadiqatul-Alam. p. 305.

once famous for its fresh fruits. Later it was used as a delightful resort for recreation by Sultan Abdullah VII, who spent 3 lacs of rupees on its restoration and decorations[1]. Save the reservoir and walks, the other buildings are modern, which were erected by His Highness Asaf Jah III., in 1278 A.H. (1761 A.D.). This garden was presented by His Highness Asaf Jah V, Nawab Afzalud Dowlah Bahadur, to his brother-in-law the late Nawab Sir Khurshid Jah Bahadur. At present it belongs to the Khurshid Jahi Paigah.

No. 9.

(*a*)=Saidabad Mosque (New).

(*b*)=On the road to Sarurnagar, opposite the house of Nawab Dr. Sir Amin Jung Bahadur.

(*c*)=Sarf-i-Khas.

(*d*)=II c.

(*e*)=1014 A.H. (1605 A.D.) The reign of Md. Quli V.

(*f*)=The following inscription is carved on the well-proportioned prayer-niche of highly polished black basalt.

Over the central niche.

- قال الله سبحانه و تعالی

۲ - ومن اراد الآخرة و سعی لها سعیها وهو مومن فاولیک کان سعیهم مشکورا

۳ - عجلوا بالصلوة قبل الفوت

۴ - ربنا تقبل منا بالنبی و آله ۱۰۱۴ھ

۵ - و عجلوا بالتوبة قبل الموت

On either margins of the Niche.

۶ - اللهم صل علی المصطفی محمد و المرتضی علی و البتول فاطمه و السبطین الحسن و الحسین و صل علی زین العباد علي والباقر محمد والصادق جعفر والکاظم موسی والرضا علی والتقی محمد و النقی علی والزکي العسکري الحسن

۷ - و صل علی الحجة القایم الخلف الصالح الامام الهمام المنتظر المظفر المهدی محمد الهادی صاحب العصر والزمان و خلیفة الرحمن و سید الانس و الجان و المظهر الایمان صلوات الله وسلامه علیه وعلیهم اجمعین الی یوم الدین۔ نمقه عبده هم حسین شیرازی -

(1) Gulzare-Asafiyah.

(*Translation*)

1. " The glorifying God has said. "

2. " Whoever contemplates for the day of resurrection and makes befitting endeavours and he is faithful, verily, his endeavours will be rewarded."

3. " Hasten to say prayers, lest ye miss them."

4. " O God accept this from us for the sake of the Prophet and his descendants. 1014 A.H."

5. " and hasten to repent lest ye perish."

6. " Shiite Durud. Written by their slave (of the Prophet and the Imams above mentioned) Husain of Shiraz."

(*g*)=Fair.

(*h*)=Should be preserved.

(*j*)=This mosque, which was built 8 years after the erection of Jamay Masjid (No. 7.) during the reign of Sultan Muhammad Quli V, about 7 years previous to his death, is situated on the old Masulipatam Road in the village of Saidabad, 4 miles off the city. It is a very small building and must have been used by the Royal camp followers while the Qutbshahi Kings used to pass this village on their way to Hayatnagar[1]. The prayer-niche which is of highly polished black basalt bears the above inscription, in best Thulth of Tauqi' style, and resembles the inscription of Shukrullah guda mosque (No. 10), and it appears that the inscription mentioned in No. 10, was also written by the same caligrapher (Husain). The outer appearance of the mosque is so insignificant that no one could fancy that specimen of such a masterly piece of writing could be discovered here. The author is indebted to Nawab Dr. Sir Amin Jung Bahadur for this discovery.

---

(1) According to "Muhammad Qutbshahi," and " Hadiqatul Alam.' Sultan Abdullah Qutbshah encamped in Saidabad for a couple of days on two different occasions; once when he was taken by his mother Hayat Bakhsh Begum for the shaving ceremony to Hayatnagar on 24th Rajab 1041 A.H. and next time when he himself went on an excursion as far as Masulipatam.

No. 10.

(*a*)=Shukrullah Guda Mosque. (New).

(*b*)=Near Amir Pet, in the precincts of **Maula Ali Hill.**

(*c*)=Government.

(*d*)=III (a).

(*e*)=1019 A.H. (1610 A.D.)

(*f*)=The following inscription carved on a black basalt slab in best Thulth style, is now loosely placed on the top of the roof. The author's reading of the inscription is as follows :—

١ - قال الله سبحانه و تعالى. (٢) ومن اراد الآخرة و سعي لها سعيها
وهو مومن فاولئك كان سعيهم مشكورا (٣) عجلوا بالصلوة قبل الفوت
... ربنا تقبل منا (بالنبي و آله) وعجلوا بالتوبة قبل الموت
(٤) قال محمد نبي الكونين المومن حي في الدارين .... تاريخ
بناء مسجد ١٠١٩ هـ (٥) اللهم صل على النبي والوصي والبتول
والحسن والحسين و زين العباد والمحمد الباقر و جعفر الصادق والموسى
كاظم و على الرضا و المحمد التقى و على النقى والزكى العسكري الحسن
(٦) و صل على حجته القايم الخلف الصالح الامام الهمام المنتظر المهدى
خليفة الرحمن وسيد الانس والجان و مظهر الايمان صلواة الله . سلامه عليهم اجمعين

(*Translation*)

1. " The glorifying God has said "
2. " Whoever contemplates for the day of resurrection and makes befitting endeavour and he is faithful, verily his endeavour will be rewarded "
3. " hasten to say prayers lest ye miss them and hasten to repent lest ye perish."
4. " Mohammad The Prophet of both the worlds has said that the true believer is alive in both worlds, the date of the erection of mosque, 1019 A.H."

5. *and* 6. " Shiite Durud."

(*g*)=Dilapidated.

(*h*)=The inscription should be preserved.

(*j*)=In the precincts of Maula Ali hill, about a mile and a half beyond the back of Abban Saheb's garden near the village of Shukrullah Guda, a ruinous mosque stands on an elevated paved platform. According to the local tradition this loose inscription, which is not *in-situ*, was originally fixed over the outer archway of the mosque but owing to the dismantling of the arch, this inscription which is broken, with several parts missing, was reposited on the roof of the mosque, it measures. (9×6 ft.) and is in the form of an arch. It may be saved from further obliteration and decay by storing it below the roof of the mosque. The year of its erection (1019 A. H.) indicates that this mosque was built a year previous to the demise of Sultan Muhammad Quli V, and 13 years after the erection of Jame' Masjid (No. 7). Although at present this mosque has no special features, yet the excellence of the inscription serves to indicate that it must have been built under royal patronage. It is also probable that this spot may have been used as a Royal camp on the occasion of the visits of Golconda Kings to Maula Ali. Evidently no trace of any old habitation is visible here and as such, this mosque cannot be attributed, as an adjunct even of any tomb or graveyard as none exists close by. The mosque proper is in a poor state of preservation and contains fine mihrab recesses, and the steps which give access to it are fast disappearing.

No. 11.

(*a*)=Naubat Pahar and Fateh Maidan. (New).

(*b*)=Near Public Garden.

(*c*)=Government.

(*d*)=II (a).

(*e*)=The reign of Muhammad Quli V, 999 A.H. (1580 A.D.) 1020 A.H. (1611 A.D.)

(*f*)=None.

(*g*)=Fair.

(*h*)=Unnecessary.

(*j*)=This rock which is 300 ft. above the level of the ground, was used as a Royal health resort in the time of Sultan Muhammad Quli V. On the top of the hill there was a small garden and other buildings, out of which only a square room in the form of a huge stool, commonly called the stool of Satan exists now. It is believed that in the Qutb Shahi and later periods the announcement of Moghal Farmans from Delhi, was made from the top of this rock by beat of drums, hence the name of Naubut Pahar was given to it. During the last siege of Golconda the first camp of Emperor Aurangzeb was pitched in the extensive field below this rock and consequently after the conquest of Golconda this field was named Fateh Maidan (The Plain of Victory). Owing to its commanding view and historic associations the quarrying of stones from this rock has now been prohibited.

In 1270 A.H. (1853 A.D.) this maidan was first used for a military parade and in 1280 A.H. (1863 A.D.) and 1301 A.H. (1883 A.D.) respectively Major Rock and Col. Neville and

Gen. Nawab Sir Afsar-ul-mulk Bahadur commanders of His Exalted Highness the Nizam's regular forces had this field paved and turfed. It is now used as a race course and Polo ground and His Exalted Highness' birthday parade is held here annually.

No. 12.

(*a*)=Mecca Masjid. (New).

(*b*)=N. of Char Minar.

(*c*)=Government.

(*d*)=I (a).

(*e*)=1027 A.H. (1617 A.D.) 1104 A.H. (1669 A.D.)

(*f*)=At the Southern end of the courtyard there were six screens of pierced marble, which contained the following inscriptions, but when operations for the extension of the courtyard were taken in hand, these screens had been removed, and the inscriptions have not yet been refixed. The Southern courtyard of this mosque is used for the burial of Asafiyah Royal Family, ever since the burial place of Atapur No. (30) was abandoned owing to its very long distance from the city. The following members of the Asafiyah family are buried here :—

1. Umda Begam Saheba (mother of Asaf Jah II).

2. Tahniatun-Nisa Begum Saheba (mother of Nawab Sikandar Jah, Asaf Jah III).

3. Bakhshi Begum Saheba (Step mother of Nawab Asaf Jah II).

4. Chandni Begum Saheba (mother of Nawab Nasir-ud Dowlah Asaf Jah VI.

5. Dilawarun-Nisa Begum Saheba (mother of Nawab Afzalud-Dowlah Bahadur, Asaf Jah V.)

6. Imami Begum Saheba (daughter of Nizam Ali Khan, Asaf Jah II).

7. Khan Bahadur Begum Saheba (sister of Nawab Nizam Ali Khan, Asaf Jah II).

8. Burhanpuri Begum Saheba (Queen of Nawab Asaf Jah II, mother of Jahandar Jah Bahadur).

9. His Highness Nawab Mir Nizam Ali Khan Bahadur, Asaf Jah II, (Ghufran Maab).

10. His Highness Nawab Sikandar Jah Bahadur, Asaf Jah III, Maghfirat Manzil.

11. His Highness Nawab Nasirud-Dowlah Bahadur, Asaf Jah IV, Ghufran Manzil.

12. His Highness Nawab Afzalud-Dowla Bahadur, Asaf Jah V. Maghfirat Makan.

15. His Highness Nawab Sir Mir Mahboob Ali Khan Bahadur Asaf Jah VI, Ghufran Makan.

16. Mian Nek Roz (a Steward of Nawab Mir Nizam Ali Khan Bahadur, Asaf Jah II).

On the main gate of Mecca Masjid the inscription " the year 32 " indicates the regnal year of Aurangzeb which corresponds to 1100 Hijri (1688 A.D)

(1) بر روح پاک میر نظام علی مدام * خوانند با وضو همه اشخاص فاتحه
زین مصرع عجیب دو تاریخ را بخوان * مستوجب بهشت و با خلاص فاتحه
۱۲۱۸ ھ ۱۲۱۸ ھ

(*Translation*)

(On the grave of Gufran Maab)

" After performing ablution, all people should always read Fatiha, for the sacred soul of Mir Nizam Ali."

" From this strange hemistich read two chronograms."

"Deserving of Paradise (1218 A.H.) and Fatiha with sincerity[1]" 1218 A.H. (1803 A.D.).

(2) چون سکندر جاه از آفاق رفت * هر مکان شد از غمش بیت الحزن
برکشیدم آه گفتم سال او * راهئی فردوس شد شاه دکن
سنه ۱۲۴۴ ه

(*Translation*)

(On the grave of Maghfirat Manzil)

"When Sikandar Jah went from the world, every house became an abode of grief in bereavement. I drew out a sigh and said his chronogram, King of the Deccan travelled to Paradise 1244 A.H." (1828 A.D.).

(*a*) Ditto

کرد شاه دکن ز دهر کنار - در هزار و دو صد چهل و چهار

Translation)

"The King of Deccan retired from the world, in one thousand, two hundred and forty four."

(3) چو رفت نواب ناصر الدوله سوی جنت ز دار فانی
خداش بخشید و کرد بخشش بفضل و رحمت مقام والا
مه صیام از شهور بوده است و بود بست و یکم از آن مه
که داده اش ایزد بقصر جنت بصدر عزت مقام والا
سروش غیبی برای سالش بگوش جان خواند مصرع خوش
بناصر الدوله داد ایزد میان جنت مقام والا
سنه ۱۲۷۳ ه

(*Translation*)

(On the grave of Ghufran Manzil)

"When Nawab Nasirud-Dowlah went to Paradise from this mortal world, God, by his grace and mercy, forgave him and bestowed on him an exalted station."

"It was the month of fasting and was 21st of that month, that God gave him in a citadel of Paradise a high and exalted place."

---

(1) It also means that Chapters (1) and (CXII) of the Quran. should be recited as a blessing to the soul of the deceased.

" The invisible angel recited from his soul this nice hemistich for its chronogram, ' God gave to Nasirud-Dowlah an exalted place in Paradise ' 1273 A.H." (1856 A.D.)

(4) ربی العما لک ماح الجنه * ولمدو حدی فاح الجنه
قلت تاریخ وفات المرحوم * افضل الدوله راح الجنه
سنه ۱۲۸۵ ھ

(*Translation*)

(On the grave of Maghfirat Makan.)

" God of the universe adorned the Paradise and made it pleasant for my worthy of praise. I said chronogram of the death of the deceased, ' Afzalud-Dowlah retired to paradise' 1285." (1868 A.D.)

(5) (الف)روضه سلطان محبوب علی سنه ۱۳۲۹ ھ
(ب)وانه فی الآخرة لمن الصالحین سنه ۱۳۲۹ ھ
(ج)شد بفردوس برین غفرانمکان * میر محبوب علیخان بادشاه
مصرع تاریخ صدیقی بخوان * رحمت حق باد بر آن بادشاه
سنه ۱۳۲۹ ھ

(*Translation*)

(On the grave of Ghufran Makan)

(*a*) " Mausoleum of Sultan Mahboob Ali 1329 A.H."

(*b*) " Verily he is among the virtuous in the other world 1329 A.H."

(*c*) " Ghufran Makan, the King Mir Mahboob Ali Khan went to Paradise. "

" Siddiki, read the hemistich of chronogram, ' May the mercy of God be on that King.' 1329 A.H." (1911 A.D.)

(*g*)=Good

(*h*)=Should be protected.

(*j*)=The erection of this imposing mosque was started by Sultan Muhammad VI, in 1027 A.H. (1617 A.D.) under the supervision of Darogah Mir Faizullah Beg and Chaudhri Rangaiyah, alias Hunarmand Khan, with the help of nearly

8 thousand masons and labourers. The work of its construction continued during the reigns of Abdullah Qutb Shah VII and Tana Shah VIII, at a cost of 8 lacs of rupees, and it was completed after 77 years by the Emperor Aurangzeb in 1104 A.H.[1]. When the Emperor was requested for further decoration of the mosque he read this famous couplet.

کار دنیا کسے تمام نکرد هر چه گیرید مختصر گیرید

(Transactions of the world have never been completed by any one, (consequently) impose upon yourself as little as possible).

When the foundation of this mosque was being laid, it is related by all the contemporary historians that Sultan Muhammad VI, after inviting the learned and pious men of the City asked them to have the foundation stone laid by one who had never missed his prayers ; but none from the assemblage having come forward, he himself laid the foundation stone by saying that he had never missed even his 'Tahaj-Jud' (a prayer repeated after midnight) ever since his 12th year This is one of the most sublime and impressive mosques of the Deccan, and it is so extensive that nearly 10,000 men can easily say their prayers conjointly. The building is 225 ft. long, 180 ft. wide and 75 ft. high ; the outer enclosure is oblong whose terrace is 360 ft. each way. At a corner of the platform there is a cistern for ablution, with 2 long slabs measuring 8 ft. each, and it is said that these slabs belonged to a temple in Maisrum village, no traces of which are now left. The mosque is composed of triple vestibules measuring (195 × 126′ 8″) with fifteen arches in each row, and five masonic arches in front, the Northern and Southern extremities are surmounted by two large domes. The two lofty minarets in front, of the main

(1) Tuzuke Qutbshahi (MSS).

entrance gate and the Sundial of the courtyard, belong to the reign of Aurangzeb. The lofty colonnades and the prayer niche are fashioned out of one stone slab. According to Mons. Tavernier the stone for this niche was hewn out of the quarry by several hundred labourers in the course of five years and 700 pairs of bullocks carried it to the mosque. One of the rooms of the courtyard contains the hair of the Prophet and other sacred relics. Sultan Muhammad Qutbshah VI, named this mosque (بیت العتیق), a nickname given to the square temple of Mecca. The numerical value of 'Baitulatiq' is 1023, which gives the date of its erection according to the Hijri year, and corresponds to 1614 A.D. In the time of Aurangzeb it assumed the name of 'Mecca Masjid.' It is estimated that the total expenses of this mosque amounted to 3,000,000 lacs of Huns.

The following verse was composed by a poet and presented to the King in commemoration of its erection.

طواف کعبهٔ اشرف میسرت گر نیست * بیا به کعبهٔ ملک دکن عبادت کن

"If the pilgrimage (going round) of noble Kaaba is not attainable to thee, come and pray in the Kaaba of the Deccan." As regards the adoption of the name of 'Mecca Masjid' it is said that Muhammad VI, had some bricks made from the earth of Mecca which were fixed over the central arch. The compiler of 'Tawarikhe Farkhunda,' has given another version, that it being the peculiarity of Kaaba that it is at no time devoid of pilgrims, so is the case with Mecca Masjid that it has never been found without those, who come to say their prayers and for this reason the name of 'Mecca Masjid' was spontaneously adopted by the public and became renowned all the world over. During the Qutbshahi period 36 maunds of food was cooked and distributed to the poor every day, but during the reign of Khuld Makan (Aurangzeb) it was reduced to Rs. 12 per diem[1].

(1) Tuzuke Qutb Shahi (MSS).

No. 13.

(*a*)=Mausoleum of Mir Qutbuddin, Nimatullah Dashtaki Shirazi and Mirza Sharief Shahristani (New).

(*b*)=In Mughalpura, near the house of Ex-Kotwal.

(*c*)=Government.

(*d*)=II a.

(*e*)=1024 A.H. 1618 A.D.

(*f*)=The following inscriptions are carved on the graves.

(1) On the headstone of Nimatullah Shirazi's grave.

۱- الحکم لله - اللهم صل علی النبی و الوصی و البتول و السبطین و السجاد و الباقر
و الصادق و الکاظم و الرضا و التقی و النقی و العسکری و المهدی
علیهم السلام

۲- یا رب همه را بروز محشر بهره ز شفاعت علی باد
چون رفت ز دهر نعمت الله * از بار گنه بخلی باد
تاریخ وفات او چه جستم * حشرش بمحمد و علی باد　　سنه ۱۰۲۵ ه

(*Translation*)

" The Command is for God.

" O God, bless the Muhammad, the testator (Ali), the Virgin (Fatima), the two offsprings, the Sajjaad, the Baqar, the Sadik, the Kazim, the Riza, the Taqi, the Naqi, the Askari and the Mahdi, May peace be on them all.

(2) " O God, on the day of judgment, let all people profit from the intercession of Ali.

" As Nimatullah left the world, may he be void of sins.

" I deliberated for the chronogram of his death, ' May his rising (after death) be with Muhammad and Ali, ' 1025 (A.H.)."

(3) On the sarcophagus of the grave of Nimatullah.

۱- شهد الله انه لا اله الا هو و الملائکة و اولوا العلم قائما بالقسط لا اله الا هو ا
لعزیز الحکیم فی ۱۰۲۷ ه

(*Translation*)

"God hath borne witness that there is no God but He, and the angels and those who are endowed with wisdom profess the same and executeth the righteousness; there is no God but He, the Mighty, the Wise. In 1027 A.H."

كل من عليها فان ويبقى وجه ربك ذو الجلال والاكرام

"Every thing which is on it is mortal and the eternity is to God, the Glorious and Supreme."

اللهم صل على محمد المصطفى والمرتضى على والبتول فاطمة والسبطين
الحسن والحسين وصل على زين العباد على والباقر محمد والصادق
جعفر والكاظم موسى والرضا على والتقى محمد والنقى على والزكى العسكرى
الحسن وصل على الحجة القائم الخلف الصالح الامام المنتظر المظفر المهدى
محمد الهادى صاحب العصر والزمان خليفة الرحمن وسيد الانس والجان
ومظهر الايمان صلوات الله وسلامه عليه وعليهم اجمعين فى ۱۰۲۴ -

(*Translation*)

"*Shiite Durud*"

"O God, bless the chosen Muhammad; the agreeable (Ali); the chaste Fatima; the two offsprings Hasan and Husain; and bless on the ornament of pious persons, Ali; the learned Muhammad; the truthful Jafar; the forbearing Musa; the submissive Ali; the holy Muhammad; the Pure Ali; the virtuous Hasan Askeri; and bless the living proof, the worthy son, the expected the victorious and the dedicated, Muhammad the leader, the lord of the time, the viceregent of the merciful, the lord of mankind and genii, the manifestation of the faith; May God's blessing and peace be on him and upon them all. In the year 1024 (A H.)."

اعوذ بالله من الشيطان الرجيم آية الكرسى (تا) هم فيها خالدون - صدق الله
العلى العظيم والحمد لله رب العالمين - ۱۰۲۴ -

"I take refuge of God from the Satan who is execrated."

"Throne verse." (Quran)

"True is God, the high, the great and praise be to God, the Lord of all creatures 1024 (A.H.)"

حسبنا الله و نعم الوكيل نعم المولى و نعم النصير ناد عليا مظهر العجائب
تجده عونا لک فی النوائب کل هم و غم سینجلی بولایتک یاعلی یاعلی یا علی

"Sufficient is God to us and how most excellent is He (our) Counsellor and Lord and Helper."

"Nadi Ali."

1. On the headstone of Mirza Sharief Shahristani's grave.

اللهم صل علی النبی (تا)ا لمهدی علیهم السلام - وفات سیادت پناه نقابت
دستگاه جنت مکانی میرزا شریف در سیم ۱۰۲۹ شهر جماد (1) الثانی

"Shiite Durud ." The death of the asylum of Saiyids the strength of princes, of paradise abode, Mirza Sharief (occurred) on the 3rd of Jamadis-Sani 1029 (A.H.)."

2. On the sarcophagus of the grave of Mirza Sharief Shahrestani.

۱- شهد الله انه (تا)هو العزیز الحکیم فی سنه ۱۰۲۹
۲-کل من علیها فان (تا)و الاکرام
۳- اللهم صل علی محمد المصطفی(تا) علیهم اجمعین فی ۱۰۲۹
۴- اعوذ بالله من الشیطان الرجیم - آیته الکرسي - وفات سیادت پناه
مغفرت دستگاه مرحومي جنت مکانی میرزا شریف بتاریخ سیوم شهر
جمادی الثانی فی سنه ۱۰۲۹ -
۵-حسبنا الله و نعم الوکیل نعم المولي و نعم النصیر - ناد علی صغیر

(*Translation*)

1. "God hath borne witness that there is no God but He; and the angels and those who are endowed with wisdom profess the same; who executeth righteousness; there is no God but He the mighty, the wise. In the year 1029 (A.H.) ."

2. "Everything which is on it, is mortal and the eternity is to God, the Glorious and Supreme."

3. "Shiite Durud." "in the year 1029" (A.H.)

4. "I take refuge of God from Satan, who is execrated." "Throne verse." "The death of the asylum of

(1) The word (ي) has been omitted by the Caligrapher.

Saiyids, whose sins have been forgiven, the deceased, of Paradise abode, Mirza Sharief (occured) on the 3rd of Jamadis-Sani in the year 1029 (A.H.) ."

5. " Sufficient is God to us and how most excellent is He (our) Counsellor and Lord and Helper. Nadi Ali (short). "

(*g*)=Good.

(*h*)=Should be protected.

(*j*)=In Mughalpura lane, near the house of the Ex. Kotwal (the late Inayet Husain Khan Bahadur), in a vaulted narrow street two graves are situated side by side on two elevated terraces surmounted by two domes. The first one belongs to Kutbuddin *alias* Nimatullah and the second contains the remains of his son-in-law Mirza Sharief. The elevation of the terrace is about 5 ft. and sarcophagii of both are of polished black basalt and the script is carved in best *Thulth* character and Tauqia style.

These personages were members of the Qutbshahi family, inasmuch as that when Prince Abdullah Mirza was born of Muhammad Qutbshah VI and he was warned by the astrologers not to see the face of the Prince until he attained the age of 12 ; the King entrusted the fostering and the tutorship of the Prince to his paternal uncle Mir Qutbuddin, Nimatullah, who was also made Mir Jumla[1]. According to ' Gulzare Asafiyah ' Qutbuddin died five years after he was made a tutor to the Prince, and as Prince Abdullah was born in 1023 A.H. (1614 A.D.) it follows that the date of Qutbuddin's death ought to have been 1028 A.H.(1618 A.D.). Several inscriptions having 3 conflicting dates are to be found on the headstone and sarcophagus of his grave but in the author's opinion the date (1024 A.H.) mentioned in

(1) Hadiqatus-Salatin.

the inscription Nos. 3, (*b and c*) of the sarcophagus is the year of his death. If any other date is taken to be the year of his death it will be highly improbable to have the sarcophagus of one's grave inscribed prior to his death. Thus it shows that he did not survive long after the birth of the Prince.

No. 14.

(*a*)=The fort of Sultan Nagar (New).

(*b*)=Near Suroor Nagar (East).

(*c*)=Government.

(*d*)=III (a).

(*e*)=1030 A.H. (1620 A.D.)

(*f*)=None.

(*g*)=Dilapidated.

(*h*)=Unnecessary.

(*j*)=This fort was constructed by Sultan Muhammad Qutbshah VI, in 1030 A.H. (1620 A.D.) and is situated six miles to the East of the city. Prior to the erection of the defences and other buildings of the fort, a mosque was built by him in the centre of the fort, which is still extant, then the 'Idgah' the ramparts and other royal paaces were commenced. It had double defences and around the outer wall the work of digging a very deep trench (150 ft. wide) was started and after laying a base of mortar and stone (75 ft. wide) it was resolved to make a 24 ft. wide intrenchment when the foundation reached the surface of the earth. In the meantime when the work was in progress the King (Muhammad VI) died of typhoid fever and the fort which by then had cost 3 lacs Huns (14 lacs of rupees), remained incomplete. His son Sultan Abdulla VII, considering it to be inauspicious ordered the work to be abandoned. It would appear on referring to inscription (4) of No. 29 that this Sultan-Nagar was acknowledged to be the capital of the Qutbshahi kingdom in 1035 A.H. At present the outer wall and buildings are in a very dilapidated condition and are called Old Fort. According to Tarikhe Farkhunda' the stones of the defences of this fort were utilized by Nawab Mushirul Mulk Bahadur for the construction of Sarurnagar village in 1214 A.H. (1799 A.D.) It is unnecessary to demolish these ruined walls as long as they keep together.

No. 15.

(*a*)=The Necropolis of Mir Momin.
(*b*)=Near Mir Jumla Tank, (Sultanshahi).
(*c*)=Government.
(*d*)=II (a).
(*e*)=1031 A.H. (1621 A.D.)
(*f*)=There are a number of inscriptions carved on the graves in Thulth characters which represent caligraphy of no mean order and the old epigraphs are generally on polished black basalt. The following inscription of the reign of Muhammad VI, pertains to the tomb of Khadija Bibi, [1] daughter of Mir Ali

(1) The Mosque of Ghassalan (bathers of deadbodies) which is situated at the back of the Necropolis of Mir Momin, bears the following inscription in the prayer-niche, and establishes an interesting link to the tomb of Khadija Bibi. The inscription lays down that this mosque was constructed in 1034 A.H. as an adjunct to the grave of this lady. (New)

بنای این مسجد جهت ثواب عفیفه صالحه صالمه را کعه سا جد ه بیبی خدیجه
بنت میر سید علی استرآبادی شیخ آوند ۱۰۳۴

It is the local tradition that this lady was an aunt (paternal) of Sultan Abdullah. The mosque is so called because undertakers of the necropolis reside in the vicinity.

of Astrabad, which is crowned by a massive domed building. The polished black sarcophagus is engraved with verses from the Quran and other religious texts. The epigraphs which give the name as well as the date of the deceased's demise are as follows:—

(۱) درود شریف

(۲) کلمه شریف - قرآن سوره ۲ آیة ۲۵۶ - سوره ۳ - آیة ۱۶ - سنه ۱۰۳۲ ه

(۳) ناد علی صغیر - قرآن سوره ۳۳ - آیة ۵۶ فوت عفیفه صالحه صائمه
ساجده بی بی خدیجه بنت میر سید علی استرآبادی شیخ اوند
بتاریخ ۱۰ شهر جمادی الاول سنه ۱۰۳۱ ه

(۴)-قرآن سوره ۹۷-۱۰۹-۱۱۲-۱۱۴!

(۵)-قرآن سوره ۲- آیة ۲۸۵ - ۲۸۶

(*Translation*)

(1) " Shiite Durud. "

(2) " Shitte creed," Quran Ch. II. verse 256 and Ch. III. Verse 16, 1032 A.H. (1622 A.D.).

(3) " Nade Ali (*vide* Plate) Quran Ch. XXXIII, verse 56. The death of chaste, pious, fasting and devout Bibi (lady) Khadija, daughter of Saiyid Mir Ali of Astrabad, the Shaikh of Awand (Master of the Kitchen) (occurred) on the 10th of Jamadi I, 1031 AH." (1621 A.D.) (*vide* Plate).

(4) " Quran Chaps. (XCVII, CIX and XCII-XIV) "

(5) " Quran Ch. II. Verses 285-86 "

2.—On the grave of Ibrahim Beg the following is engraved. (1017 A.H.) (New).

چون بامر حق زدنیا رفت ابراهیم بیگ * رخت هستی را بسوی جنت المأوا کشید
دانه عیشی نچید و رفت از کشت حیات * مرغ روحش ز آشیان تن سوی عقبی پرید
شربت قندی نخورد از شکرستان وجود * ناگهان از دست ساقی اجل حنظل چشید
میوهٔ شاخ امید جد و اب خویش بود * زان سبب شد سال فوتش میوهٔ شاخ امید
(۱۰۱۷ ه)

Nade Ali over the grave of Khadija Bibi.

Epigraph over the grave of Khadija Bibi.

3.—On the grave of Mir Abu Turab Fitrat of Meshad is engraved the following quatrain which was composed by him at the time of his death in 1060 A.H. (New).

فطرت بتوروزگار دیرنگی کرد * ننواخت بمهر و خارج آهنگی کرد
آن سینه که عالمی درو می‌گنجید * اکنون زترد د نفس تنگی کرد

4.—The following quatrain which was composed by his son Mir Razi Danish is also engraved on the tomb of Mir Abu Turab. (New).

دانش مکن ای عنبار بر عمر دراز * کاید بزبان کم بسر عمر دراز
گیرم که چو عیسی بفلک بر شدهٔ * آید بچه کار بی‌پدر عمر دراز

(*g*)=The general condition is worthy of notice.

(*h*)=All the inscriptions and the tombs of Shah Charagh, Nurul-Huda, Mir Momin, Nimat Khane-Ali and Bibi Khadija, etc., should be protected.

(*j*)=Mir Momin of Astrabad a nephew of Amir Fukhruddin Samaki, came here from Persia during the reign of Muhammad Quli V, and was created a Peshwa and Minister of the State. He was held in great estimation on account of his learning, piety and poetry. After discharging his duties for sometime he disengaged himself from the affairs of the state and spent a retired life from the latter part of Muhammad Quli V's reign, till the time of Abdulla Qutb Shah VII. Years previous to the foundation of the City of Hyderabad, Shah Charagh, a holyman from Najaf (Mespot) had taken his abode at the place where he is buried now in the necropolis; formerly this place was a portion of Chichlam, (Shah Ali Banda), which was populated solely by Brahmans, Shah Charagh being the first Muslim to inhabit this place, and according to his last wishes his remains were also interred here. Later on, after the building of the City, Nurul-Huda, a pious man, took his abode near the tomb of the late Shah Charagh and ultimately died and was buried there. Several years afterwards Mir Momin of Astarabad purchased this land and bequeathed it for free burial of the dead, he also mixed the holy earth of Karbala in this land. A bath and a well was built by him and a place in the city called 'Mir Chauck' is attributed to this gentleman. The grave of Shah Charagh and Mir Momin are situated in roofless enclosures and are of polished black basalt. Mir Momin died in 1035 A.H. (1625 A.D.) and near the steps of his mausoleum is buried Mirza Ahmad (Muhammad) Nimat Khane Ali the famous satirist and poet and Superintendent of the kitchen of the Emperor Aurangzeb; an oblong polished slab of black basalt marks the grave of this great poet and is situated exactly below the first step of the mausoleum of Mir Momin. Besides this other distinguished personages such as, Mir Alam, Abul Qasim Khan, Sira Jul Mulk and Munirul Mulk, the late Sir Salar Jung I and II and other members of his family are buried in this necropolis. This grave-yard is still used as a burial place although it has become very overcrowded now.

No. 16.

(*a*)=The Bund of Ma-Saheba Tank.

(*b*)=On the road to Golconda *via* Saifabad.

(*c*)=Government.

(*d*)=II A.

(*e*)=1034 A.H. (1624 A.D.)

Over the facade of Rahim Khan Mosque. No. 17.

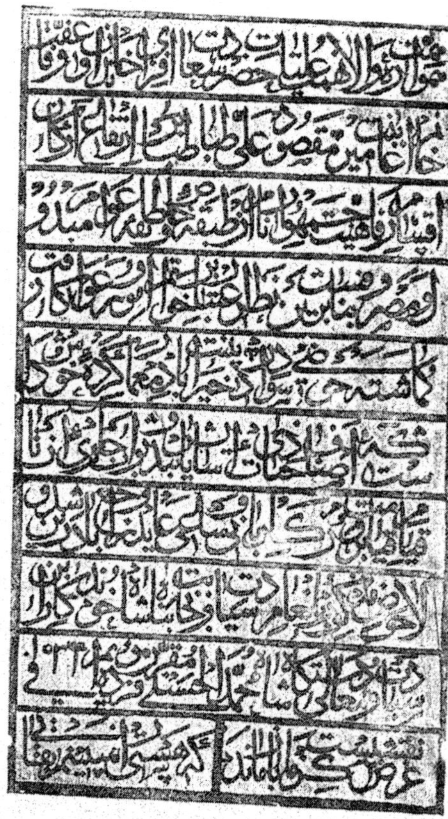

In the S. W. tower of
Ma-Saheba tank.

(*f*)=In the top storeys of the towers on either side of the bund there are two inscriptions carved on tablets of polished black stone in Naskh style. The text of these epigraphs is almost identical, the difference being that the inscription in the tower at the S. W. end of the bund does not contain lines 9 and 10 of the following inscription :—

۱- همواره همت والا نهمت علیا حضرت سعادت افزای خاندان عفت و وفا 1
۲- خانم آغا بنت میر مقصود علی طباطبا بر ارتفاع ارکان
۳- اقسام رفاهیت جمهور انام از طبقهٔ خاص و طائفهٔ عوام مبذو
۴- ل و مصروفست بنا برین نظر اعتبار بر خواتم امور و عواقب کار
۵- گماشته حوضی در سواد پنت 2 خیرآباد معمار کرده خوش دا 3
۶- شت که اصناف ذی حیات آسایش یابند و ثواب جاری آن تا
۷- قیام قیامت بر روزگار بانی و ساعی عاید و راجع باشد درین و
۸- لا حوض مذکور با نعام سیادت و نجابت پناه شاه خوندکار ابن
۹- سیادت و معالی دستگاه شاه محمد الحسینی مقرر فرموده ایم فی ۱۰۳۴
۱۰- غرض نقشیست کز ما باز ماند - که هستی را نمی بینم بقای

(*Translation*)

" The intentions full of high aspirations, of Her Highness, the source of felicity to the family of fidelity and chastity, the Khanum Agha, daughter of Mir Maqsud Ali Tabataba[4] is always bent and disposed to meet the requirements of the general public, consequently, having regard to the ultimate end of affairs and consequences of pursuits, a nice tank had been built which is situated in the vicinity of the

(1) Mr. Yazdani's reading is (و فا و عفت) which is not of the same Materes (خا نم آ غا) or (طبا طبا). (E. I. M. 1917-18 p. 47).

(2) Mr. Yazdani has given the translation of this word to be a Market, my translation (road) is based on the Hindustani and English dictionary of Duncan Forbes published in 1859 (London).

(3) Mr. Yazdani's reading is (خوش است). The three dots above the (ش) of the word (دا شت) conclusively decide the word to be (دا شت) instead of (ا ست). (E. I. M. 1917-18, p. 47).

(4) Mir Maqsud Ali Tabataba son of Syed Alauddin Tabataba was the Maternal grand-father of Muhammad Qutbshah VI. (Muhammad Qutbshahi) (MSS).

road of Khairabad, for the convenience of living beings of various classes; and that a continual blessing may rest till the Resurrection, upon the founder as well as on those who have assisted (in the building of the tank) now, in 1034 A.H. the above tank has been awarded (as Inam) by us (Sultan Muhammad VI), to the Asylum of Saiyids and person of noble birth, Shah Khundkar, son of the noble and Exalted Shah Muhammadul Husaini. In 1034 (A.H.) (verse). So that an impression from us may remain, as in existence we see no permanence (*vide* Plate).

(*g*)=Fair.

(*h*)=The towers containing the inscriptions should be protected.

(*j*)=The inscription depicts that this tank which was built by lady Khanum Agha, daughter of Mir Maqsud Ali Tabataba, was awarded by the reigning sovereign (Muhammad Qutbshah VI) to Shah Khundkar. Khanum Agha was the wife of Prince Mirza Muhammad Amin (son of Ibrahim Qutbshah IV) and mother of Muhammad Qutbshah VI. This tank is now-a-days called the 'tank of Ma Saheba' and 'Ma Saheba' was the by-name of Hayat Baksh Begam (wife of Muhammad Qutbshah VI) mother of Sultan Abdullah VII, who had built the village of Hayatnagar (No. 18). It appears to have been the practice to give this name to all the Queen-mothers of the Qutbshahi Kings, *vide* No. (19). Shah Kundkar to whom this tank was awarded as 'Inam,' was the son of Shah Muhammad (son of Shah Ali), who was the Peshwa (Minister) of Sultan Abdullah Qutbshah VII, and maternal grandson of lady Khanum Agha and a cousin of Sultan Abdullah VII.* The graves of Shah

* *Vide* Hadiqatus-Salatin (MSS).

Khundkar (No. 61) as well as that of Khanum Agha (No. 55) are situated in the mausoleum of Sultan Muhammad VI, and his inscription begins with the same address of ' His Exalted ' as that of Sultan Muhammad VI. The caligrapher has wrongly split the words in more than one line. These inscriptions are fixed in the top storey of these double storeyed rectangular towers of solid masonary, which stand on either side of the bund ; the upper storey consists of a hall with three arched openings and a terrace facing the water of the tank.

No. 17.

(*a*)=Mosque of Rahim Khan.
(*b*)=Near old bridge.
(*c*) · Government.
(*d*)=II A.
(*e*)=1053 A.H. (1643) A.D.
(*f*)=In the prayer-niche is inscribed in Thulth script, the Throne Verse, on polished black basalt and at the end of the verse the name of the calligrapher is given as Mir Ali[1]. who was a contemporary of Ali-ul-Katib and Mir Ali of Tabriz. The arches of the Mosque bear medallions of black basalt in which the words (یا اللہ یا محمد یا علی) are inscribed. The next inscription which is the longest of its kind begins in the form of a straight line, from the centre of the Northern minaret to its Southern end, covering the entire facade of the mosque. On a nice band of black basalt besides Shiite Durud and the Quranic phrase و بشرا لمو منین نصر من اللہ و فتح قریب the following verses are inscribed in poor Naskh.

(1) The compiler remembers an earlier inscription written by the same (P.T.O.)

ابعالی نشان رحیم خان * که از بندگان قطبشهست
صفائی مسجد او جانفزا (2) * چو تمام شد چو صبحگهست
بسال هزار و پنجاه و سه گفت سپهر (3) * که این سجده گاه مهر و مهست

(*Translation*)

"The August Rahim Khan, who is a servant of Qutb Shah.

"The serenity of his mosque is soul-inspiring; when completed, it is like the early morn.

"In the year 1053 A.H. (the poet) Sipahr said, verily it is the place of adoration of the sun and the moon." (*vide* Plate).

(g)=Poor. Measures for conservation may be taken to preserve the building from further decay.

---

caligrapher (Mir Ali), on the prayer niche of Husaini Mosque, which is situated near Mach-hli Kaman (city) in the Koocha-e-Nasim (the lane of Nasim). This is a small mosque of the same type as that of Saidabad (No. 9.) Its prayer niche of black basalt bears the Shiite Durud in best Thulth script and the following:— (New).

فی ع ۱۰۴۶ - کتبه العبد میر علی و حاجی مبارک - المسجد حسینی -

(In the year 1046 A.H. written by the Servant Mir Ali and Haji Mubarak. The Husaini Mosque).

The Medallions contain (یا الله یا محمد یا علی) and the word (یا علی) is inscribed in Tughra on either side of the prayer niche in four different styles.

The author cannot fail to notice another mosque of the same ilk which is situated near the Gandi-Bauli lane close by. It has no architectural beauty, but the excellence of its caligraphy justifies its placing on record. The facade of its Dalan contains the Muslim creed and the prayer niche of highly polished black basalt contains the Shiite Durud in best Thulth after which the following is inscribed. (New)

بانی مسجد صالحه زوجه بریصاحب بنت درگاه قلی در زمان سلطان
عبد الله قطبشاه تمام شد سنه ۱۰۶۹

(The builder of the Mosque (is) Saleha, wife of Baresaheb (and) daughter of Dargah Quli; was completed during the reign of Sultan Abdullah Qutbshah. The year 1069 A.H.)

(2) Mr. Yazdani has read this (صفائی مسجد جانفزائی او) although in the inscription there is no (ئی) in (جانفزا) (E. I. M. 1917-18 p. 48).

(3) Mr. Yazdani has given a translation of this word considering it to be a common noun, while it represents the *nom-de-guerre* of a poet (سپہر) (*Ibid*).

(*h*)=Should be protected.

(*j*)=This mosque which contains three arched openings is situated, close to the Toli Masjid, on a small terrace containing a prayer hall (27×18) ft. and two minarets stand on each flank. The peculiarity of this mosque is that the use of polished black basalt has been profusely made in the arches, minarets, mihrabs and the entrance gate. Opposite the paved court yard there is a well, and the platform contains nine un-known graves, none of which bears any inscription. At present it is generally known as "Nirkhi Mosque," because the Nirkhi Nawabs used to say their prayers here.

No. 18.

(*a*)=Hayatnagar (Sarai of Hayat Ma Saheba). (New).

(*b*)=Beyond Sururnagar.

(*c*)=Government.

(*d*)=III a.

(*e*)=Sultan Abdullah Qutb Shah's reign 1035 A.H. (1626 A.D.)

(*f*)=None.

(*g*)=Fair.

(*h*)=The mosque and the Karwansarai should be protected.

(*j*)=Hayat Bakhsh Begum, (Hayat Ma) mother of Sultan Abdullah Qutb Shah VII, built this village, in 1035 A.H, by the name of Hayatabad, which is situated about 9 miles East of the City of Hyderabad; between the 6th and 7th mile, a milestone masonry pillar of Qutbshahi reign may be noticed. In the royal palaces of this village, the ceremony of the first shave of Sultan Abdullah Qutb Shah was celebrated by his mother on a very grand scale, successively for twelve days in 1041 A.H. (1631 A.D.) and the expenses of these celebrations are said to have amounted to 2 lacs of Huns[1]. Outside these royal buildings a grand mosque, on a terrace measuring about 150 feet each way, is situated inside a very extensive Karwansarai. The mosque proper is composed of 5 double arches of massive masonry and is flanked by two lofty minarets. The prayer-niche is made of plaster and bears no inscription. During the reign of His Highness Asaf Jah VI, this mosque was thoroughly repaired, but at present its roof appears to be badly in need of repairs; it should be made watertight and the rank vegetation which is to be seen on the outer surface of the mosque should also be eradicated. The mosque is floored by the local ashler stones and the facade is decorated in stucco. The centre of the terrace contains a small cistern for ablution. The extensive court yard is about (450 × 400) of an oblong shape and it is surrounded on all sides by several hundred double rooms of massive masonry which were intended for the use of travellers: hence it is called the "Sarai of Man Saheba." The Sarai and the mosque are entirely uninhabited now-a-days and are situated at a little distance from the existing village. There are 3 lofty entrance gates of the Sarai, on the Northern, Eastern and Southern directions, but only the Eastern gate is now in use; the other two being blocked. At the North eastern extremity of the courtyard there is a big well called 'Hati Bauli' (Elephant-well), the water of which was formerly drawn by elephants.

(1) Hadiqatul-Alam.

The 'Khas Bagh,' outside the Sarai is still in a blooming condition and is even now watered by the old 'Hati Bauli.' Outside the Sarai and Khas Bagah there is a subterranean building called 'Tal-Makan,' whose entrance is now blocked by huge pieces of masonry. The upper storey of this 'Tal-Makan,' appears. to have been demolished, and only a mound—the debris of the whole building—and the vaulted subterranean building now remain.

This mosque being a very fine specimen of Qutbshahi architecture should be specially preserved by the State Archæological Department.

No. 19.

(*a*)=The Mosque of Khairiatabad. (New).

(*b*)=In Khairiatabad.

(*c*)=Sarf-i-Khas.

(*d*)=II b.

(*e*)=Sultan Muhammad's reign. 1020 A.H. (1612 A.D.)—1035 A.H. (1626 A.D.)

(*f*)=None.

(*g*)=Fair.

(*h*)=Should be protected.

(*j*)=The mosque has a three-arched opening in front and the length and breadth of the building is (54×30) ft. The Mutawalli of the mosque and the adjoining land, showed me a sanad which bears the 37th regnal year of Aurangzeb. It is mentioned in the sanad that this mosque was built by Khairiatun-Nisa Begum, *alias* Man Saheba, daughter of Sultan Muhammad Qutb Shah, for her tutor Akhund Mulla Abdul Malik. The Akhund had however presented a Quran written by Yaqoot and a Shah Nama, to the King, through the Begum, in return for which the King awarded him 700 Huns and a Khilat (robe of honour) of chehl Nag (40 jewels), but the Akhund declining the award requested that some landed property may be granted to him; consequently 45 Bighas of Inam land was granted to him. The present Mutawalli claims his descent from the late Akhund and is in charge of the mosque and the lands. He holds several other interesting documents which corroborate the facts, an abstract of which has been given above. A reference is also found in the Sanad to the empty domed building which stands close to the mosque. The reason of its being devoid of any grave is thus mentioned in the sanad :— The dome was constructed in the Inam land, north of the mosque by Akhund for self-burial, but owing to his demise in the holy cities (Mecca and Madina) the dome remained vacant.

No. 20.

(*a*)=The tomb of Khairat Khan (New).
(*b*)=Near Gowlipura Gate.
(*c*)=Government.
(*d*)=II a.
(*e*)=1066 A.H. (1655 A.D.)
(*f*)=The following inscriptions are carved on the headstones of the graves :—

۱-بسم الله الرحمن الرحيم -انا انزلناه في ليلة القدر . (تا)حتي مطلع الفجر
وفات مغفرت آثار خيرات خان هجدهم ماه رمضان سنه ۱۰۶۶ ھ
الحكم لله اللهم صل على النبی (تا)و المهدی عليهم السلام

(*Translation*)

On the headstone of Khairat Khan's grave

1. " Quran Chapt. XCVII. "

Khairat Khan.

"The death of Khairat Khan whose sins appear to have been forgiven occurred on 18th of Ramzan 1066 A.H." (1655 A.D.)

2. "The Command is for God." "Shiite Durud."

۱-بسم اللہ الرحمن الرحیم -انا انزلناہ الخ
۲ اللھم صل علی النبی الخ -وفات مغفوری بابا عبد اللہ بن خیرات خان
پنجم ماہ ربیع الثانی سنہ ۱۰۶۶ھ

(*Translation*)

On the headstone of Baba Abdullah's grave.

1. "Quran Ch. XCVII."

2. "Shiite Durud." "The death of pardoned Baba (master) Abdullah son of Khairat Khan (occurred on) 5th of Rabi-us-Sani 1066 A.H.

(*g*)=Requires conservation.

(*h*)=Should be protected

(*j*)=Inside Gowlipura gate in the necropolis of Rifai'e there are two domes. The larger one which is situated on an elevated platform covers the graves of Khairat Khan and his son. The grave of the boy is in the centre of the dome and that of Khairat Khan on its side. The adjoining dome is said to cover that of his wife, but there is no inscription on her grave.

According to Hadiqatus-Salatin, Khairat Khan Sar Naubat, was deputed by Sultan Abdullah Qutb Shah VII, as an ambassador to the court of Shah Abbas Safavi, and was sent from Hyderabad with valuable presents in company with Muhammad Quli Beg son of Qasim Beg, the Persian Ambassador. The Emperor Shah Jahan sent for him from Surat which was the chief port of embarkation at that period and he also gave Khairat Khan a letter to the Shah of Persia. When Khairat Khan reached Bandare-(Port) Abbas, the news of the death of Shah Abbas on 2nd Jamadil-Awal 1037 A.H. (1627 A.D.) and the accession of the Shah Safi were announced. From Port Abbas, Khairat Khan went to Asphahan, which was the capital of Persia at the time, and presented the letters of Shah Jahan and Sultan Abdullah Qutbshah. The new Shah after treating him for several years as a State guest allowed him to return home in 1043 A.H. (1633 A.D.) Khairat Khan returning *via* Qandhar gave the reply of Shah Jahan's letter to him and repaired to Hyderabad on 17th Zil Qadah 1044 A.H. (1634 A.D.) Here he was received with high favour and was promoted to the rank of Minister. In 1047 A.H. (1637 A.D.) when the grandmother of Sultan Abdullah Qutb Shah was proceeding on a pilgrimage to Mecca, Khairat Khan accompanied her as far as Masulipatam. Later in 1050 A.H. (1640 A.D.) several shops and a garden were built by Khairat Khan close to the Northern steps of Musa Burj (No. 62) in the Golconda Fort, and a granary (No. 63) was also constructed under his supervision in 1052 A.H. (1642 A.D.). The headstone of the grave shows that the death of Khairat Khan occured on 18th Ramzan 1066 A.H. (1655 A.D.) and his minor son Abdullah died five months earlier, on 5th Rabius-Sani 1066 A.H. (1655 A.D.); that is why the grave of his son occupies the central portion of the dome. The accompanying plate was copied from the water colour painting of Khairat Khan in the collection of the British Museum Mss.

No. 21.

(*a*)=Kamraki dome. (The dome resembling *Averrhoa carambola*) (New).

(*b*)=On the road to Bhoiguda, opposite Pani Pura near Old Bridge.

(*c*)=Government and Mujawir.

(*d*)=II c.

(*e*)=1070 A.H. (1659 A.D.)

(*f*)=On the balcony of the main gate (Naqarkhana) the following inscription is carved on a black slab in Naskh style and is fixed on the wall facing the road.

قال سلام علیہ انا مدینتہ العلم و علی بابہا ۱۲۳۴ ھ

(*Translation*)

" It has been said, (by the prophet) peace be on him.

" I am the city of learning and Ali is its gate 1234 A.H." (1818 A.D.)

(*g*)=Fair.

(*h*)=Should be protected.

(*j*)=The main porch was built by the clerk of Maharajah Chandu Lal Bahadur, a disciple of the family of the Saint, who is buried in this dome and the inscription was also fixed by him. This dome consists of several graves of the sons and grandsons, of the chief saint Saiyid Miran Khuda Numa Husaini *alias* Miranji Saheb who is buried in the centre. The style of architecture of the dome resembles the fruit of *Averrhoa carambola* and is very graceful. Besides the main porch where the drums are beaten at stated intervals, there is also a Sama' Khana, (a place where a congregation assembles every year on the anniversary-day of the Saint to hear the songs which are recited by master-musicians of both sexes), and a repository for drinking water, but the latter buildings are in a decayed condition. The Miranji Saheb Khudanuma, was formerly employed in the service of Sultan Abdullah Qutb Shah VII, and when he went to Bijapur to carry out some royal mandate, he fell in with Aminuddin A'la there who perfected him in the order of Sufism and after returning to Hyderabad he gave up service and engaged himself in spiritual pursuits. According to

'Gulzari Asafiyah' his death occured on 18th Jamadil-Awal 1070 A.H. (1659 A.D.), during the latter portion of Sultan Abdullah's reign. The same book relates this incident of his life that once Emperor Aurangzeb asked him (by way of criticism) whether he was Khuda Numa (one who leads to God), on which he replied that 'if I do not remain Khuda numa, I shall become Khud Numa,' (vainglorious). The deceased was the author of two books[1] on spiritualism in the old Urdu language of the Deccan[2]. The present dome was constructed by his son and successor Shah Aminuddin II, who died in 1074 A.H. (1663 A.D.) and lies buried under the same roof.

About a furlong from this dome there is a double storeyed dome of Handan Khan, Mandan Khan (Hannan and Mannan Khan). The upper storey is paved with plaster and has no sarcophagus, but in the vaulted lower storey which is comparatively more secure, the central grave is of polished black stone and the other one is of ordinary ashlar stone. In the N. E. direction from the black grave there is another small grave, but none of these bears any inscription. According to the local tradition they were intimate friends of Sultan Abul Hasan Tana Shah, but comtemporary history throws no light on the identity of these brothers,

(1) "Wujudiyah," and "Qurbiyah."

(2) One of the famous disciple of Miranji Saheb was Syed Shah Sohrabuddin Chishti alias "Uryan Shamshir" (Unsheathed Sword), who died on 14th Rabi, I, 1087 A.H. (1676 A.D.) and whose tomb of polished black basalt is situated on the right side of the road, about 1½ furlong after the turn of the road to Sangam (Golconda).

The tomb is covered by a canopy supported by 8 pillars of ashlar masonry. One of these pillars was struck by a cannon ball of the fort in the famous siege of 1098 A.H., with the result that the central portion of the top pillar was fractured, which still stands in the same condition, and locally it is attributed to the miracle of the Saint.

His son Syed Shah Aminuddin Ali Husaini who died in 1150 A.H. is also buried by the side of his father, but his grave is made of concrete.

Ibne Khatoon.

Close to the latter dome there is a three arched mosque which was most probably erected along with this tomb, apparently with the object of securing an abode for the deceased in Paradise. The arched openings have been closed by the Ecclesiastical Department of the State in order to save the mosque from desecration as it is situated in an isolated place.

No. 22.

(*a*)=The mausoleum of Ibne-Khatoon (New).

(*b*)=Near Purani Haveli, Zenani Phatak.

(*c*)=Mutawalli.

(*d*)=II c.

(*e*)=1050 A.H.

(*f*)=The following inscription is carved on the head-stone of the grave of Ibne-Khatoon :—

(١) الحكم لله - اللهم صل على النبی و الوصی و البتول و السبطین و السجاد
والباقر و الصادق و الکاظم و الرضا و التقی و النقی و العسکری المهدی

On the headstone of the grave of the wife of Ibne Khatoon.

(٢) اللهم صل علي المصطفى محمد و علی المرتضی والحسن والحسین و علی
و محمد و جعفر و موسی و علي و محمد و علی . الحسن العسکری و محمد المهدی
صلوات الله علیهم اجمعین سنه ٩٩١ ھ ؟

(*Translation*)

(1) "The Command is for God."

"Shiite Durud."

(2) "Shiite Durud" 991 A.H. (1583 A.D.)

(*g*)=Requires conservation.

(*h*)=Should be protected.

(*j*)=Shaikh Muhammad son of Ali son of Khatun of Toos and Amil, *alias* Ibne-Khatoon, was a nephew of Shaikh Bahai and one of the ministers of Qutb Shah. He is buried within the compound wall of Purani Haveli, opposite to the house of Nawab Qadeer Jung and the other grave belongs to his wife. The citizens often assemble there on Thursdays to recite Fatihah. During the reign of Sultan Muhammad Qutb Shah VI, Ibne-Khatoon held the post of Private Secretary. In 1024 A.H. (1615 A.D.) the King sent him with valuable presents to Shah Abbas Safavi of Persia in company with the Persian Ambassador Husain Beg Qibchachi. He returned from Persia after the death of Sultan Muhammad VI, when Sultan Abdullah was on the throne of Hyderabad. On 9th Ramzan 1038 A.H. (1628 A.D.) he was raised to the rank of Peshwa and Mir Jumla, and was allowed to sit by the side of the Royal throne. The following verses were composed by Nizamuddin Ahmad, author of Hadiqatus-Salatin-Qutbshahi and presented to Ibne-Khatoon on this occasion.

شه یوسف رخ و جمشید حشمت * که حاتم می کند از وی گدائی
ز فرط مرحمت کرده ممکن * محمد را بصدر پیشوائی
بسامان شد مهام ملک و ملت * که بود از بتر آفات سمائی
متاع فضل و دانش بود کاسد * کنون بگرفت در عهدش روائی
جهان معمور گردیده بد انسان * که شد معوا ز خلایق بی نوائی
بالهام آمد این مصراع تاریخ * محمد یافت از حق پیشوائی

(*Translation*)

" The King whose face is as beautiful as that of Joseph and whose dignity is at par with Jamshed, and Hatam goes a-begging before him ; with profound graciousness raised Muhammad to the chair of Peshwa. The maladministration of the country and the people came to an end. The superiority and wisdom of the country, which had hitherto waned became renewed and the whole people passed their lives in peace and tranquility. The following hemistich of chronogram came by intuition. ' Muhammad got ascendancy from God'."

In 1045 A.H. when his good offices averted the invasion of Shah Jahan he was given the honour of coming as far as Dad Mahal and Hydar Mahal, seated in his palanquin. This being his distinctive honour, not enjoyed by previous ministers.

Every morning learned men and priests used to assemble in his school for debates and discussed controversial topics and on every Tuesday poets used to excel in old and fresh poetry. His exact year of death is not given in any contemporary history but the author of Dabistane Mazaheb writes that he died in Mocha in 1050 A.H. while on his way to Mecca. Being of distinguished personality most probably his remains were brought to Hyderabad for interment by the side of his wife who had predeceased him. He was the compiler of Sharhe-Irshad, Arbaeen and foot-notes of Jame'-Abbasi. The last portion of Jame'-Abbasi was also completed by him.

The accompanying photo is a copy of his painting from the British Museum collection.

The loose inscription slab which is lying in the courtyard of Toli Masjid, indicates that a mosque was erected in 1043 A.H. (1633 A.D.) by the endeavours of ' Shaikhe- Peshwa, ' the Shaikhe Peshwa mentioned in this inscription is Shaikh Ibne- Khatoon who was the Peshwa of Sultan Abdullah Qutbshah.

Inscription No. 2 is fixed on the tomb of his wife and the year given is 991 A.H.(1583 A.D.) although the numerals have been much obliterated.

No. 23.

(*a*)=Toli Masjid.

(*b*)=Is situated on the road leading to the Fort from the Old Bridge.

(*c*)=Government.

(*d*)=II a.

(*e*)=1082 A.H. (1671 A.D.)

(*f*)=The following inscription is engraved on the prayer niche (*vide* Plate) :—

لمن الملک الیوم لله الواحد القهار

موسی خان بنا کرد این مسجدش * که شد مستعد دور شاه عبد الله

بتاریخ مسجد چنین شد ندا * بنا کرد مسجد بنام خدا

سنه ۱۰۸۲ ھ

(***Translation***)

"For whom is the Kingdom to-day ? For God,—the One, the powerful.

"Musa Khan built this mosque of his, which was completed in the reign of King Abdulla. For the chronogram of the mosque this (invisible) voice was heard.

"Built the mosque in the name of God" 1082 A.H. (1671 A.D.).

The other inscription on two pieces of black basalt slab is lying close to a grave in the courtyard. This epigraph relates to a mosque which was erected by the endeavours of Shaikh Muhammad Ibne Khatoon, Peshwa of Sultan Abdullah Qutbshah.

The epigraph runs thus (*vide* plate) :—

در زمان شاه خیراندیش گردون بارگاه * یافت اتمام این بنا از سعی شیخ پیشوا

خواستم چون سال تاریخش ز پیر غیب گفت * شد بحکم شاه عبد الله این مسجد بنا

کتبه لطف الله الحسینی التبریزی - سنه ۱۰۴۳ ھ

(***Translation***)

"During the reign of the well-wishing king, of heavenly court.

"This building was completed by the endeavours of Shaik the Peshwa.

"When I asked the invisible inspirer for a chronogram of the building ; he said.

"This mosque was built by the orders of King Abdullah 1043 A.H. (1633 A.D.) written by Lutfullah al-Husaini of Tabriz."

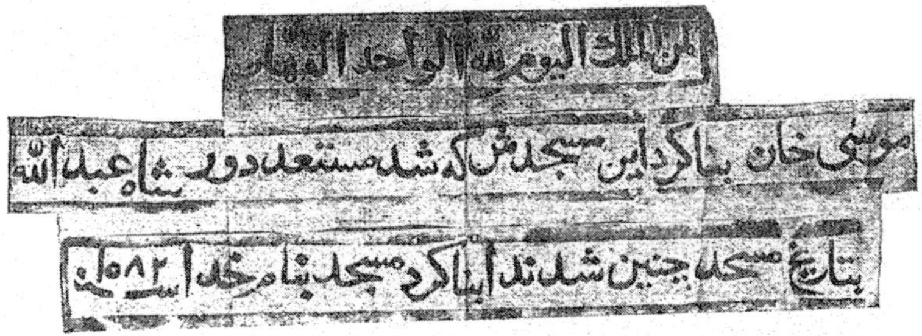

Inscriptions of Toli Masjid (Prayer-Niche).

Inscription slab in the court-yard of Toli Masjid.

Toli Masjid. No. 23.

(g)=Has been repaired.

(h)=Should be protected.

(j)=This mosque was built by Musa Khan Mahaldar (Chamberlain) of King Abdullah Qutbshah. It appears that originally, the courtyard had a large garden. The 6 ft. elevated terrace of the mosque contains flights of steps on all three sides, (North, South and East). This building is divided into two Dalans, the outer hall has five arched openings and the inner only three. Two minarets 60 feet high, flank the building at each side. The Musa Burj of the Golconda Fort was also built by Musa Khan, who was a Minister as well as the General of Abdullah Qutbshah. The author of Gulzare-Asafiyah ascribes the name of " Damri Masjid" to this mosque and writes that, " when Musa Khan held the construction charge of the Mecca Masjid, he was allowed a discount of one Dumri (9 farthings) per rupee out of the building expenditure ; which amount he utilized in building another mosque, at the western side of the Karwan on the road to Muhammadnagar fort." Musa Khan had a hand in the succession of Abul Hasan to the throne of Golconda after the demise of King Abdullah.

No. 24.

(a)=Mausoleum of Syed Muhammad Akbar (New)

(b)=Near Purani Haveli.

(c)=Sarf-i-Khas and Mutawalli.

(d)=III c.

(e)=

(f)=None.

(g)=Fair.

(h)=Unnecessary.

(*j*)=Syed Muhammad Akbar was the son of Mir Muhammad Baqar Damad, whose famous book 'Qabasat,' is well known. During the Qutb-shahi reign he was ranked among the learned men of his time. He is buried by the side of the grave of his wife near Purani Haveli, in a roofed enclosure set with bamboos just opposite the house of the late Nawab Qadeer Jang Bahadur. None of the graves bears any inscription and the correct date of his death is not known but his father[1] died in 1041 A.H.

His anniversary is observed every year on 17th Rabiul-Awwal by the Sarf-i-Khas and the Mujawir, other inhabitants of the vicinity also taking part in it.

No. 25.

(*a*)=Gosha Mahal (New).
(*b*)=Near H. E. H's. Gunnery (**Top Khana**).
(*c*)=Government.
(*d*)=II a.
(*e*)=1083 A.H. (1627 A.D.).
(*f*)=None.
(*g*)=Fair.
(h)=Should be protected.
(j)=A few extensive halls which now remain out of the Gosha palace and other outhouses, are at present used for military purposes. This palace was originally built by Sultan Abdullah, but it was completed by Abul Hasan Tana Shah. It was composed of 1,000 halls and the frontage was considerably high. An expenditure of Rs. 340,000 was incurred on this huge building, but no vestige of it remains now, save a very large reservoir of the same name,

1. Salafatul—'Asr by Syed Ali Khan Madani.

which gives one some idea of what the grandeur of this lofty palace must have been.

In 1097 A.H. (1685 A.D.) on the occasion of the last siege of Golconda, Prince Shah Alam had encamped here. This palace was used as a resort for the Royal ladies ; hence the name of Gosha (Shelter from observation) was appropriately given to this building. It is said that a subterranean passage formerly existed from here to Golconda which is now blocked up. According to the Tarikhe-Zufra (MSS) " the name of " Goshamahal " was given to this palace because it was situated in the village of Gosha and Tana Shah had built a lofty palace 15,000 feet square and 75 feet high. In front of an extensive terrace there was a very large reservoir (1,365 ft.L. 1,230 ft. W. and 12 ft. D.) resembling a tank whose brink was covered with flat stones and the water was supplied to this reservoir from the Husain Sagar tank." According to this history the following inscription was fixed in one of the halls, which is now perhaps buried under the debris of the palace.

شه عالم پناه والا قدر * که رسد فیض او به بحر و بر
رتبه افزای افسر و دیهیم * باد فرمانروای هفت اقلیم
ناهئی ظلم و معنئی دین است * مالک ملک در جهان این است
عالم و فاضل و سخی و کریم * عادل و اشجع و شفیق و رحیم
متشرع چنان که می باید * متورع چنانکه می شاید
با همه مهربان بود این شاه * مظهر لطف هست ظل الله
یار درماندگان مانده زپای * یاورش مصطفی بهر دوسرای
از برای همین کنند دعاء * آدم اندر زمین ملک بسماء
یا الهی تو در امان داری * حافظش باد تا جهان داری
ساخت تالاب شاه دریا دل * که ازو گشته یم و بحر خجل
آبش از آینه مصفا تر * بمذاق همه چو شیر و شکر
حوض و تالاب دیده شد یکسر * کس ندیده چنین بدور قمر
هر کسی آب خورد ازین تالاب * می شود بادشاه عالم آب
این چنین حوض را خضرسا قیست * تا ابد آب اندران باقیست
اندرین نشاء گر خضر ساقیست * آنجهان مرتضی علی ولیست
از خدا خواستم براش دعاء * آمد از غیب اینکه باد بقاء

سال تاریخ این خجسته بناء * با خرد گفتمش که راه نما

گفت با من که شد نجات همه * آب آن با عث حیات همه سنه ۱۰۹۶ھ

قصر فردوس را نمود بدهر * کس ندیده چنین بملک بشهر

سال وماهش مبارک وایام * مرتضی یاورش بحق کرام

سال تاریخ این رفیع اثر * خرد از روی صدق گفت بصر

(۹۴)

شاه بیتے چنین ندیده کسے * باد فرخنده این بشاه بسے

(۱۰۰۴)

It appears from the couplets of this inscription that this building was completed during the years 1096-1098 A.H. in the course of 2 years. The chronogrammatic hemistich (شاه بیتے چنین ندیده کسے ۱۰۰۴) giving the date of its completion (1004) fails in accuracy and the excess of defect is supplemented by (روی صدق) which is (صد) (90+4=94) after the manner of Abjad, thus we have the date required (1004+94) *viz.*, 1098 A.H.

No. 26.

(*a*)=Qutbe-Alam Mosque (New).

(*b*)=Near Baradari of Shamsul-Umara Bahadur.

(*c*)=Government.

(*d*)=II a.

(*e*)=The reign of Sultan Abdullah 1035 A.H.—1083 A. H., (1626 A.D.—1672 A.D.).

(*f*)=The mosque has no inscription. The other 3 inscriptions, two in the courtyard of the mosque and one in a room close to the entrance of the courtyard, are as follows :—

(1) On the headstone of Kalbe Ali's tomb.

۱۰۸۷ ھ - بتاریخ بست ونهم ماه جمادی الاول روز شنبه کلب علی ولد سلیم وفات یافت

(1) " The year 1087 A.H. on twenty-ninth Jamadiul-Awal, Monday. The death occurred of Kalbe Ali son of Saleem."

بسم الله الرحمن الرحيم - اللهم صل على محمد ن المصطفي و على و البتول
فاطمه و الحسن و صل على زين العباد
و محمد ن الباقر و جعفر ن الصادق و الكاظم موسى و الرضا على و التقى محمد
و النقى العسكرى الحسن و امام مهدى صاحب الزمان خليفته الرحمن
سيد الانس و الجان صلى الله عليه و آله و سلم

(*Translation*)

"In the name of the God, the merciful, the compassionate." "Shiite Darud"

(2) On the headstone of a grave (unknown) in the courtyard of Qutbe-Alam Mosque.

اللهم صل على النبى و الوصى و البتول و السبطين والسجاد و الباقر و الصادق
و الكاظم و الرضا و التقى و النقى و الزكى و المهدى سنه ١٠٨٧ ه

"Shiite Darud—1087 A.H."

(3) On the sarcophagus of Syed Miran Bukhari, situated in a chamber.

١- شهد الله انه لا اله الا هو والملائكة و اولوا العلم قائما بالقسط لا اله الا هو العزيز الحكيم
٢- لا اله الا الله محمد رسول الله على ولى الله
٣- بسم الله الرحمن الرحيم الحمد لله رب العالمين الرحمن الرحيم
مالک يوم الدين اياک نعبد واياک نستعين اهدنا الصراط المستقيم صراط الذين
انعمت عليهم غير المغضوب عليهم ولا الضالين - الم ذالک الكتاب
لا ريب فيه هدى للمتقين الذين يومنون بالغيب ويقيمون الصلوة
و مما رزقنا هم ينفقون و الذين يومنون بما انزل من قبلک وبالاخرة
هم يوقنون اولئک على هدى من ربهم و اولئک هم المفلحون-
الله لا اله الا هو الحى القيوم لا تاخذه سنته ولا نوم له ما فى السموت
و ما فى الارض من ذا الذى يشفع عنده الا باذنه يعلم ما بين ايديهم
و ما خلفهم ولا يحيطون بشئى من علمه الا بما شاء وسع كرسيه السموات
والارض ولا يوده حفظهما وهو العلى العظيم-
٤- يسين - والقرآن الحكيم انک لمن المرسلين على صراط مستقيم تنزيل
العزيز الرحيم لتنذر قوما ما انذر اباؤهم فهم غافلون لقد حق القول
على اكثرهم (فهم غافلون لقد حق القول على اكثرهم) فهم لا يومنون انا
جعلنا فى اعناقهم اغلالا فهى الى الاذقان فهم مقمحون و جعلنا من بين ايديهم
سدا و من خلفهم سدا فاغشيناهم فهم لا يبصرون وسواء عليهم ءانذرتهم ام
لم تنذرهم لا يومنون انما تنذر من اتبع الذكر و خشى الرحمن بالغيب
فبشره بمغفرة و اجر كريم - انا نحن نحى الموتى و نكتب ما قدموا و
آثارهم وكل شئى احصينه فى امام مبين-

(*Translation*)

(1) " God hath borne witness that there is no God but He, and the angels and those who are endowed with wisdom profess the same, who executeth righteousness; there is no God but He, the mighty, the wise."

(2) " There is no God but He, Muhammad is his prophet, Ali is the favourite of God." (Shiite creed).

(3) " In the name of the God the merciful and compassionate. Praise be to God, the Lord of all creatures, the most merciful, the King of the day of Judgment. Thee do we worship, and of thee do we beg assistance. Direct us in the right way, in the way of those to whom thou hast been gracious, not of those against whom thou art incensed, nor of those who go astray " (Chapt. I.)

" A. L. M. There is no doubt in this book, it is a direction to the pious who believe in God without seeing Him who observe the appointed times of prayer, and distribute alms out of what we have bestowed on them ; and who believe in that revelation, which hath been sent down into thee, and have firm assurance in the life to come ; these are directed by their Lord, and they shall prosper." (Chapter II.) " Throne Verse."

(4) " Y. S. I swear by the instructive Quran, that thou art one of the Messengers of God, sent to show the right way. This is a revelation of the Most Mighty, the merciful God, that thou mayest warn a people whose fathers were not warned and who live in negligence. Our sentence hath justly been pronounced against the greater part of them (*who live in negligence. Our sentence hath justly been pronounced against the greater part of them*) wherefore they shall not believe, we have put yokes on their necks, which come up to their chins ; and they are forced to hold up their heads ; and we have set a bar before them, and a bar behind them, and we have covered them with darkness ; wherefore they shall not see. It shall be equal unto them whether thou preach unto them, or do not preach unto them, they

shall not believe. But thou shalt preach with effect unto them only who follow the admonition (of the Quran) and feareth the Merciful without seeing him, wherefore bear good tidings unto him of mercy, and an honourable reward. Verily, we will restore the dead to life, and will write down their work which they shall have sent before them, and their footsteps which they shall have left behind them, and every thing do we set down in a plain register." (Chapt. XXXVI). The inscription No. 3, (~) has a repetition of the Quranic verse given in the brackets. Mistakes of this nature very rarely occur in inscriptions. This inscription is engraved in the Thulth script and Tauqi' style of the finest description.

(*g*)=Good.

(*h*)=Should be protected.

(*j*)=This mosque is situated inside Alibad gate, near the Baradari of Shamsul-Umara Bahadur. It comprises three Dalans of stone and mortar on an elevated terrace. Hayath Baksh Begum mother of Sultan Abdullah Qutbshah, built this mosque for her religious head, Qutbe-Alam who died in his 150th year on 4th Shawal, 1163 A.H.[1] (1750 A.D.). The graves of Qutbe-Alam and his brother Hafiz Muhammad are situated in an uncovered enclosure just below the terrace of the mosque. In the Northern direction his father Hafiz Syed Shah Miran Bukhari is buried in a room, whose grave is of polished black basalt and its sarcophagus contains inscription No. 3 (1, 2, 3 and 4) which is one of the most excellent specimens of bold Thulth calligraphy. Shah Bukhari originally came here from Bijapur in company with Emperor Aurangzeb and died in Hyderabad in 1125 A.H. (1713 A.D.)

1. Gulzare-Asafiyah.

The inscriptions Nos. 1 and 2, which belong to the year 1087 A.H. are of unknown people.

No. 27.

(*a*)=The tomb of Hazrat Syed Shah Raju (New).
(*b*)=Out-side Fateh Darwaza, near Ghazi Banda.
(*c*)=Mujawir.
(*d*)=II b.
(*e*)=The reign of Abul Hasan 1096 A.H. (1684 A.D.)
(*f*)=None.
(*g*)=Fair.
(*h*)=Should be protected.
(*i*)=Syed Shah Raziuddin (Shah Razu) alias Shah Raju II, a nephew of Husain Shah Wali (son-in-law of Sultan Ibrahim Qutbshah), came here from Bijapur during the reign of Sultan Abdullah, who conferred a Jagir on him and Abul Hassan had been from the outset his devoted disciple. Through the spiritual provisions of Shah Raju II, he became son-in-law of the King and ascended the throne of Qutbshah.

His father Syed Shah Raju I, a brother of Husain Shah Wali, was the recipient of a Jagir and monthly allowance from Sultan Muhammad Quli, but during the intrigue of Muhammad Khuda Banda for the deposition of his brother Muhammad Quli, Shah Raju I, sided Khuda Banda and the famous secret council was held in his house. The King becoming aware of this plot ordered the imprisonment of all the conspirators, Shah Raju I, in the meantime fled to Bijapur and ended his days there.

His son Shah Raju II, died here in 1096 A.H. (1684 A.D.) during the reign of Abul Hasan Tana Shah, who built a very splendid dome on his grave with extensive Dalans and colonnades of ashlar masonry. It may be safely asserted that none of the domes of the Dominions can compare with this magnifi-

Syed Shah Raju.

cent three storeyed building of finely proportioned arches. Other members of the family of Shah Raju II, are also buried here on either side of the central grave. The western wing of the building was under construction when the Qutbshahi dynasty was overthrown and consequently this portion and the inner plastering is still incomplete. The golden spire above the dome was fixed by Tahniatunnisa Begam (mother of Asaf Jah III) during the reign of Asaf Jah II. The canopy and wooden litters were completed by Asaf Jah IV. The enclosed plate of his photograph is a copy of his painting now in the British Museum collection.

A few furlongs ahead of this building another smaller dome of Syed Shah Shamsuddin, Ali Akbar is situated in an old cemetery. He is said to have been an uncle and spiritual head of Shah Raju II; the present dome was built during the reign of Abul Hasan Tanashah in 1085 A.H. It is profusely decorated with inscriptions and represents fine specimens of excellent Nastaliq and Thulth calligraphy of bold type. The massive entrance doors of the mausoleum are of highly polished black basalt.

The Nastaliq inscriptions are carved on wooden panels fixed on all four sides of the building. (New)

My reading of the lower bands is as under :—

Over the Eastern Dalan, the words (هوا لعلی ا لا کبر) are inscribed in six medallions

۱- شا ہ را جو شہ ستو دہ خصا ل (ھوا لعلی ا لا علی) کہ جز ا و نیست ھیچکس
عا بد (علی)

۲- ھمی شو د شا ہ و سرو ر عالم (ھوا لعلی ا لا علی) ھرکہ د ر د رگہش بو د سا جد

Over the Northern Dalan, the words (ھوا لعلی ا لا کبر) are inscribed in six medallions.

۱- جا نشین علی ا کبر شا ہ (ھو ا لعلی ا لا علی) شد چو مقبو ل د ر گہ ایز د
(محمد علی فا طمہ حسن حسین)

۲- د ر ز ما ن ا بو ا لحسن سلطا ن (ھوا لعلی ا لا علی) گشت حکمش بشش
جہت نا فذ

Over the western Dalan, the words (هو العلی الاکبر) are inscribed in six medallions.

۱- ساخت تا گنبدی بزیر فلک (سال تاریخ این خجسته بنا) شد
بخوبی قرینه مسجد (محمد)

۲- درخیابان صفحه ازره فکر (ها تفی گفت روضه سید) تا ختم تاکمیب خامه بعد
۱۰۸۵ھ

Over the southern Dalan, the words (هوا لعلی الاکبر) are inscribed in six medallions.

۱- ۱............Missing............) (هوا لله)

۲- هرکس که درین روضه درآید بطواف (هوا لعلی الاعلی) از معنی
حج اکبر آگاه شود

The Text of the upper bands which are inscribed on black basalt in bold Thulth is as follows :—

On the top of Eastern Dalan.

۱- اللهم صل علی محمد المصطفی والمرتضی علی والبتول فاطمه والسبطین *

۲- بسم الله الرحمن الرحیم۔

۳- انا انزلناه فی لیلة القدر وما ادریک ما لیلة القدر

۴- لیلة القدر خیر من الف شهر

۵- تنزل الملائکة والروح فیها باذن ربهم من کل امر سلام هی حتی مطلع الفجر

۶- *الحسن والحسین وصل علی زین العباد والباقر محمد والصادق جعفر *۔

On the top of the Northern Dalan.

۱- *والکاظم موسیٰ والرضا علی والتقی محمد والنقی علی والزکی
العسکری الحسن*

۲- الله لا اله الا هو الحی القیوم لا تاخذه سنته

۳- ولا نوم له ما فی السموات وما فی الارض

۴- من ذا الذی یشفع عنده الا باذنه یعلم ما بین

۵- ایدیهم وما خلفهم ولا یحیطون بشی من علمه الا بما شاء+

۶- *وصل علی الحجة القایم الخلف الصالح *

On the top of the Western Dalan.

۱- *والمنتظر المظفر المهدی محمد الهادی صاحب العصر والزمان*

۲- +وسع کرسیه السموات والارض ولا یوده

۳- حفظهما وهوا لعلی العظیم

۴- لا اکراه فی الدین قد تبین الرشد من الغی ومن یکفر بالطاغوت

۵- ویومن بالله فقد استمسک بالعروة الوثقی+

۶- *وخلیفة الرحمن وسید الانس والجان صلوات الله علیه وعلیهم اجمعین

Syed Muzaffar.

On the top of the Southern Dalan.

با نیه سلطان حسین

ابن انبیا قلی خان(۱)

۱- نا د علیاً مظہر العجائب — تجدہ عونا لک فی النوایب*

۲-+لا انفصام لہا واللہ سمیع علیم اللہ ولی الذین

۳- آمنوا یخرجہم من الظلمات الی النور والذین

۴- کفروا اولیاء ہم الطاغوت یخرجونہم من النور

۵- الی الظلمات اولیک اصحاب النار ہم فیہا خالدون

۶- * کل ہم وغم سینجلی بولایتک یا علی

No. 28.

(*a*)=The grave of Syed Muzaffar Mazindarani (New)

(*b*)=Near Hari Baoli.

(*c*)=Sarf-i-Khas.

(*d*)=II c.

(*e*)=The reign of **Abul Hasan Tana Shah**.

(*f*)=None.

(*g*)=Fair.

(*h*)=Should be protected.

(*j*)=He was closely connected with the royal family of Mazindaran (Persia) and became the first Minister of Tana Shah in 1083 A.H.; but shortly afterwards he became unpopular owing to his ill-temper, and the king was also displeased with him, with the consequence that Madanna who was his Peshkar, came into power and Syed Muzaffar was imprisoned and most probably died in confinement. His grave is situated in the house of Fakhrunnisa Begum close to the house of the Chief Qazi of the city near Hari Baoli, the former house at present belongs to the Sarf-i-Khas. His grave is built of mortar and is enclosed by a

1. Ambiya Quli was sent by Sultan Muhammad Qutbshah to receive the Persian Ambassador Husain Beg Qibchachi when he was entering the Dominions in 1021 A.H. (Gulzare-Asafiyah) p. 18.

low wall. According to contemporary history his house and garden were situated near the Mir Jumla tank, once graced by the presence of the king during the illness of Syed Muzaffar and on this occasion he presented to the King his Sultan Shahi Garden, which afterwards the king visited frequently during the rainy season when the Mir Jumla tank was filled to the brim. The enclosed plate is a copy from the British Museum collection.

No. 29.

(*a*)=The mosque of Miyan Mishk.

(*b*)=Mustaidpura, near the Old Bridge.

(*c*)=Government.

(*d*)=II a.

(*e*)=1085 A.H. (1674 A.D.) 1092 A.H. (1681 A.D.)

(*f*)=1. The following Inscription is fixed on an arch-shaped black stone tablet (3′ 2″×7′ 9″) over the western gateway in Naskh style (*vide* plate 1 :—

(۱) نقل فرمان سلطان ابوالحسن قطب شاه

(۲) فرمان جهان مطاع آفتاب (1) ارتفاع ازدیوان همایون خلافت مشحون چنان زینت صدور یافت که عاملان

(۳) متصدیان وکارکنان حال و استقبال و مقاصائیان (2)کتوالخانه تهانه(3) مستعدپور بعنایت شاهانه مستظهر بوده بدانند که مقرب الحضرت الخاقانی ملک مشک سرلشکر

1. This word has been read (آسمان) by Mr. Yazdani (E. I. M. 1917-18 p. 51).

2. The word (مقاصا) is most probably used for (مکاسر) in which a village is held free by a person on condition of his protecting the property of passengers.

3. This has been read (کتوالخانه وتهانه مقاصائیان)(E. I. M. 1917-18 p. 51).

Over Western gateway. No. 1. Mosque of Miyan Mishk.

(۴) کرناتک بعز عرض مقیمان حضور لامع النور رسانیدند که حاصل بازار تعلق
مسجد مشار الیه خارج کرایه (4) سالانه مبلغ هشتاد هون کهره (5) که تفصیل
آن در فرمان گشت پیش جدار (6) ملگیهای محمد نگر
(۵) دوکانهای (7) بازار رد و طرف مسجد با بیک خوشبو فروش و غیره مذکور
از مراحم شاهانه برای (8) اخراجات لنگر
عاشور والاوه و آبدارخانه و فرش و روشنائی مسجد مزبور و اخراجات
دیگر عنایت مرحمت شود لهذا التماس مومی الیه
(۶) بدرجه قبول رسیده هشتاد هون مسطور فوق را با نچه از معموری بازار
مذکور بهم رسد جهت اخراجات لنگر و عاشور
والاوه و اخراجات مسجد عنایت و مرحمت فرمودیم امر عالی صادر
است که سال بسال بلا خلل
(۷) جاری داشته از تغیر تبدیل مصون شناسند (9) وکسیکه از حکم
فرمان (10) عالی تخلف ورزد یا آنکه مبلغ مذکور را متصرف شده
با خراجات مسطوره صرف نه کند بغضب خدا و نفرین رسول خدا و ائمه
هدی گرفتار شود تحریر فی التاریخ شهر محرم ۱ (11) - کتبه حسین بن
تقی فی ۱۰۸۵

(*Translation*)

" Copy of the farman of Sultan Abul Hasan Qutb Shah

" This farman, obeyed by the world and as exalted as the sun, has received the honour of issuing from the auspicious court, filled with imperial dignity, to this effect that the present and future revenue officers, accountants, subordinate establishment and landholders of the Kotwalkhana[12] and police station of Mustaidpur, having been protected by Royal grace should know that the trusted servant of the Imperial court, Malik Mishk, the Commander of the Carnatic troops, has been granted the honour of laying this request before those

---

(4), (5), (6), (7), (8), (9) and (10) All these underlined words have been omitted in E. I. M. 1917:18 (p. 51).

(11) This date, *i.e.*, 1st (Moharram) has been omitted in Mr. Yazdani reading. (*Ibid*).

(12) An Office where transactions of Police, Judicial and revenue laws were regulated.

standing in the resplendent court that the income of the bazaar attached to the mosque of the above mentioned (Malik Mishk), besides the annual rent of 80 pure huns[1], as detailed in the farman in front of the wall of the shop of Muhammadnagar and stalls on both sides of the bazaar of the mosque of Babeg, perfume seller and Narva aforesaid, by royal munificence be graciously awarded and endowed for the expenses to be incurred in connection with the feeding of the poor, the religious ceremonies of the first ten days of Moharrum, and the maintenance of Alawa[2] and Abdar Khana [3] and the carpets and lights of the above mosque as also for other expenses. Accordingly, the request of the aforesaid (Miyan Mishk) having been granted, we have awarded and endowed the eighty huns referred to above, in addition to that which may be collected from the rents of the bazaar, for the expenses to be incurred in feeding the poor, the religious ceremonies of the first ten days of Moharrum and the maintenance of Alawa and the mosque. The august command remains in force that the endowment should be continued without any deviation from year to year and should not be affected by any change, and whoever disobeys the high order of the Farman or appropriates the endowment for such purposes as are not indicated therein, shall be overtaken by the wrath of

---

(1) The pagoda of the Deccan, about 52 grains, worth 4½ Moghal rupees.

(2) Where fire and incense is burnt during the month of Moharrum.

(3) A place where cold drinks are distributed during the month of Moharrum.

Headstone of Miyan Mishk's Tomb
No. 9.

Eastern Gateway (Circular inscription)
No. 2. Miyan Mishk.

Eastern Gateway. No. 3. The Mosque of Miyan Miskh.

God and the imprecation of the Prophet of God and the Imams of the path of righteousness. Written on the 1st of Moharrum. Inscribed by Husain son of Taqi, in 1085 (A.H.)." (1674 A.D.)[1].

2. This circular inscription over the Eastern gateway is composed of the verse which was according to Tarikhi Zufra inscribed in the Royal seal of Tana Shah (*vide* plate II) and his small seal contained (ختمه با لخیر و السعادة).

(۱) یا حضرت فاطمه الله محمد علی (2) علی حسن حسین علی محمد جعفر موسی علی محمد علی حسن محمد (۲) موجود (3) که بتائید حق دکن آست بجان محب علی قطب ابو الحسن است (4)

(*Translation*)

(1) " The names of twelve Imams are arranged in a circle."

(2) " The Deccan is by Divine grace the abode of love, Qutb Abul Hasan is by soul, the lover of Ali."

(3) Below the above inscription another tablet 5′,8″×4′, 8″) is carved in the broken (شکست) or current Persian hand, which is a corruption of the (تعلیق) (*vide* plate III).

(۱) نقل فرمان سلطان ابو الحسن قطب شاه علامتكدرا لخانه و تهانه مستعد پور و موضع طاپور حوالی قلعه عبا زکنه محمد انگر مستظهر بوده (5) بد انند که معتمد اخد مت ملک مشک

(۲) کلید از بعز عرض مقیمان حضور لامع النور رسانید که حاصل بازار مسجد خود و پنت و باغچه و پته (6) قطعه زمین مزرع انعام خود و وظیفه مسجد و غله زمین انعام میر ملک خرید خود کرده موضع

---

(1) This has been freely drawn from the English translation of Mr. Yazdani with necessary alterations. (*Ibid*).

(2) All these names have been omitted by Mr. Yazdani (*Ibid*)

(3) This word is (موید ے) (Zufra MSS.)

(4) This has been read by (Mr. Yazdani) علی ابو الحسن است محب قطب بجان (E. I. M. 1917-18 p. 52).

(5) This word has been read (بوجه) E.I.M. 1917 18 p 52.

(6, This also has been read (سه) (*Ibid*)

(۳) مذکور واقعست بعد از اخراجات ضروری آن سیصد بیست هون و (1)
جهت لنگر عاشورا لاوه و آبدار خانه چهل هون سه لوازجهت لنگر مسجد و
روشنائی و بعضی سالیانه هشتاد هون و غله زمین انعام میر ملک

(۴) مشاهره داران لنگر مسجد و بعضی یکصد و هون وآنرا متولی بیست
هون موذن ده هون فراش شش هون تیل چراغ شش هون فرش
مسجد دو ربع هون مطبخ شش هون سقا شش هون جهت تعمیر مسجد
بعضی دوازده هون

(۵) دیوتی هفت نیم هون دربان دوازده هون دو نفر از (2) جاروکش
شش هون نویسنده بهمن (3) هشت هون و ربع اخراجات حمام و مشاهره
داران سالیانه نود و هشت هون آنرا هیزم سالیانه چهل هون خوراک
گاوان و دنو و ریسمان شانزده و ربع هون پله کاری (4) شش هون

(۶) کیسه مال دو نفر را پانزده (5) هون فراش شش هون تیل چراغ یک نیم
هون حصیر و لنگی وغیره یک ربع هون مالی آب کش دو نفر (6) را دوازده
هون بدین موجب . وقف صحیح شرعی نموده بند حضرات دوازده امام
علیهم السلام نزد یک

(۷) مسجد خود یک حجره تنها و ز ننموده طعام پخته بدرویشان و مستحقین
می خورانیده باشند اخراجات عاشور و حمام و مشاهره چاکران
می رسانیده باشند لهذا التماس موصی الیه بدرجه قبول رسیده امر
عالی عاد راست (7) که برنهج وقف

(۸) نمودن مشار الیه سال بسال بلا خلل جاری داشته از معزال (8)
و تدیل اجتناب نمایند و باغچه از روی معموری باز ارو پنت
و باغچه و مزرعه هرچه (9) اهم رسد بدل اخراجات

(۹) صرف نمایند کسیکه تغافل ورزد یا طمع نماید مسلمان یا هندو هرکه باشد
بغضب وسخط خدای تعالی گرفتار شود و از شفاعت شفیع روز جزا
محمد مصطفی صلی الله علیه و آله و سلم بی نصیب و روسیاه گردد
سنه ۱۰۸۹ ه -

---

(1) This word has been written before (سیصد) by Mr. Yazdani E.I.M. 1917 p. 52.

(2) This word has been read (ار) (*Ibid*).

(3) This word has been read (بهمه) (*Ibid*).

(4) This has been read Palla Kar. (*Ibid.*)

(5) This has been read (شانزده) (*Ibid*).

(6) This word has been entirely omitted (*Ibid.*)

(7) This has been read (شد) (*Ibid*).

(8) This has been read (تغییر آن) (*Ibid.*)

This has been read (زمین چه) (*Ibid*).

(*Translation*)

(1) " Copy of the Farman of Sultan Abul Hasan Qutb Shah. The revenue collectors of the Kutwalkhana and Thana of Mustaidpur and village of Atapur, in the vicinity of the auspicious fort of Muhammadnagar (Golconda) may know that the trusted servant Malik Mishk,

(2) "the keeper of the Royal key has laid this request before those standing in the illustrious presence that the income of the bazaar, attached to his mosque, the market the garden and the lease of the piece of cultivated land of his Inam (freehold), (also) the grant relating to the mosque and the produce of his land.

(3) " situated in the above village (Atapur) originally in possession of Mir Malik, as freehold and afterwards purchased by him, after the deduction of the relevant expenditure amounting to three hundred and twenty huns, and for the provisions of Ashur (ten days of Moharrum), the maintenance of the Alawa and the Abdar Khana, should be apportioned forty huns annually ; for the alms house of the mosque, the lights and other expenses ; eighty huns per annum, in addition to the produce of the freehold land of Mir Malik.

(4) " For the establishment of the almshouse of the mosque and for cognate purposes one hundred and two huns, out of which to the Superintendent of the mosque twenty huns, to the crier of the people to prayers ten huns, the spreader of prayer carpets, six huns ; oil for lamps six huns, carpets for the mosque, two and a quarter huns ; kitchen, six huns, to the water-carrier, six huns ; for conservation and other expenses of the mosque, twelve huns ;

(5) " torch-bearer, seven and a half huns ; door keeper, twelve huns ; two sweepers, six huns ; Brahmin clerk, eight huns and a quarter, for the establishment of the bath and other relative expenditure, ninety-eight huns per annum ; wood for it forty huns per annum ; fodder for oxen

buckets and ropes, sixteen and a quarter huns ; mason for repairing steps, six huns,

(6) " two shampooers, fifteen huns ; the spreader of carpets, six huns ; oil for lamps, one and a half hun; matting and bath sheets, etc., one and a quarter hun; two malees for drawing water, twelve huns. The endowment thus having been made in strict accordance with the Muhammadan law should be spent, near

(7) " the mosque of the aforesaid Miyan Mishk and not the smallest deviation should be made on charities in memory of the twelve Imams—may peace be upon them. Food should be prepared and distributed to the poor and the deserving, and the expenses of the Ashur and the bath and the salary of the establishment be paid. Accordingly the request of the aforesaid (Malik) having been accepted, this exalted order is being issued that according to the terms of the endowment

(8) " made by the above Malik it should be continued without fail from year to year and any alteration and change avoided. And whatsoever be collected from the rents, of bazaar, the market place, the garden and the cultivated land should be utilized to meet the expenditure.

(9) " Whoever will disobey this order or encourage deviation therefrom, whether he be Muhammadan or Hindu shall be overtaken by divine wrath and displeasure and being deprived of the intercession of Muhammad Mustafa, the intercessor of the Day of Judgment—May God bless and assoil him (Muhammad) and his descendants. He (the disobeyer) shall be stricken with misfortune and shall be crestfallen. In the year 1089 A.H." (1677 A.D.)[1].

4. The following inscription is fixed on the inner side of the enclosure wall near the Eastern gateway, in Naskh style

(1) This has been freely drawn from the English translation of Mr. Yazdani with necessary alterations.

Inside Eastern Gateway (Miyan Mishk.) No. 4.

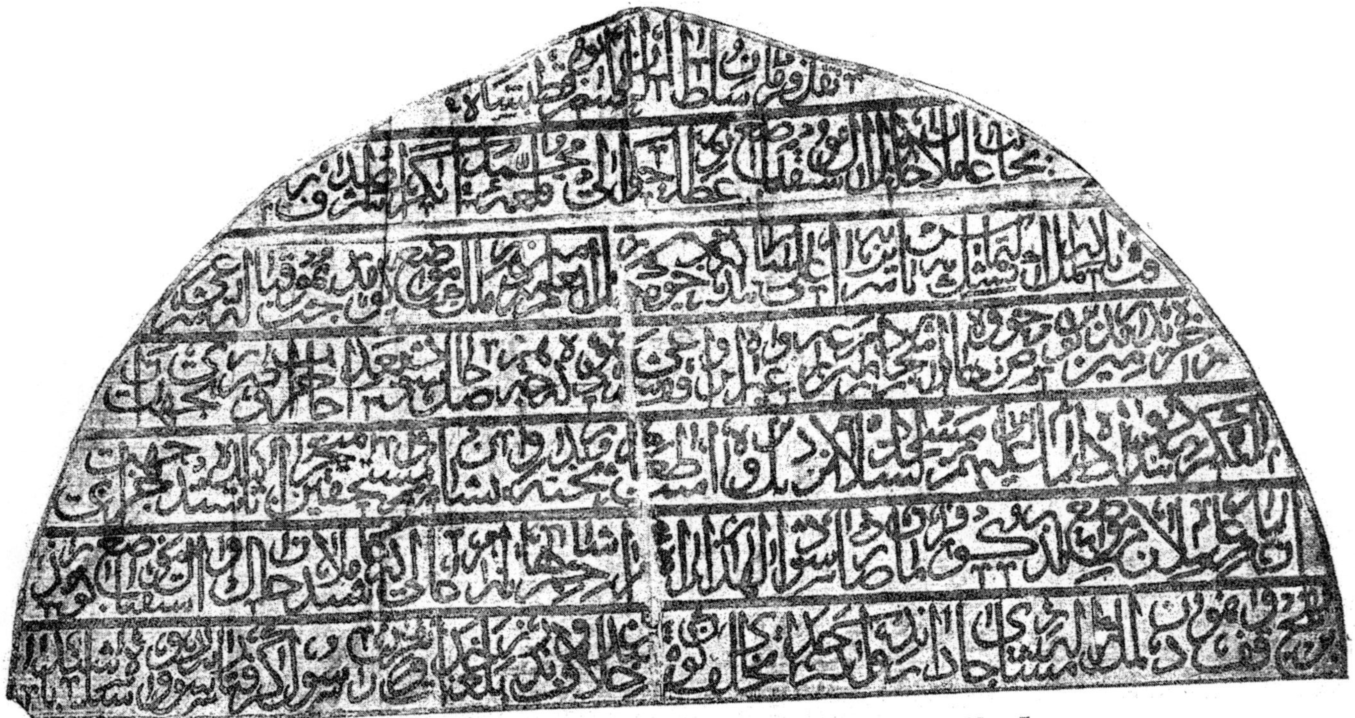

Over the doorway of Miyan Mishk's grave chamber. No. 5.

and Tauqi' script, but this appears to be inappropriate here and pertains to some other building. (*vide* plate VI) :—

الحمد لله و المنه که باتمام رسید این عمارت فایض النور مسمی بجان و خانه
حضور ونا عدار حسب الحکم شاه اعظم خاقان معظم ابوالمظفر سلطان (1)
محمد قطب شاه خلد ملکه ابدا بمبلغ یکهزار چهار صد هون رایج دار السلطنة
سلطان نگر حرسه الله تعالی عن کل شر و الخطر بتاریخ شهر محرم سنه خمس و (2)
ثلاثین بعد الف

(*Translation*)

" All praise and thanks are due to God that this luminous building styled the Magic House of his illustrious Majesty, was completed, by order of the great sovereign and mighty Emperor, Abul Muzaffar Sultan Muhammad Qutbshah, may God perpetuate his Kingdom ; at a cost of fourteen hundred huns, the coin current at the capital Sultan-Nagar. May God, the most High, preserve it from evil and danger. In the month of Moharrum 1035," (1625 A.D.).

5. Inscription over the doorway of the grave chamber of Miyan Mishk (*vide* Plate V).

(۱) نقل فرمان سلطان ابوالحسن قطب شاه
(۲) بجانب عاملان حال و استقبال موضع عطاپور حوالی قلعه محمد انگر شرف اصدار (3)
(۳) یافت که ملک مشک التماس به پایه سریر اعلی رسانید که مکمل زمین
انعام خود (4) میر ملک در موضع مذکور بموجب قباله شرعی
(۴) زخریده میر مزبور بر وجوه خاص و اشجار در زمین مزرعه و غیره آن را (5)
وقف شرعی نموده که هرچه حاصل شود بعد اخراجات ضروری آن بجهت

(1) The word (سلطان) has been omitted by Mr. Yazdani (E. I. M. 1917-18 p. 53).

(2) The word (و) has been written before (سنه) (*Ibid*).

(3) This has been read (صدور) the (الف) of (محمد انگر) has also been omitted (E.I.M. 1917-18 p. 55).

(4) This word has been written before (مکمل) (*Ibid*).

(5) The word (را) has been altogether omitted (*Ibid*).

(۵) لنگر بند ر د وازده امام علیهم السلام بر (6) مسجد نزد نروه (7) است دیگ (8) طعام پخته بد رویشان و مستحقین می دراینده باشند جهت جزای
(۶) آن بنام عاملان موضع مذکور فرمان صادر شود لهذا از راه مراحم شاهانه امر عالی شد که عاملان حال و استقبال موضع مذبور
(۷) بر نهج وقف نمودن ملک مشار الیه جاری دارند واگر احدی تخلف آن کوشند (9) و خلاف ورزند بلعنت خدا و نفرین رسول گرفتار شوند و روسیاه باشند

(*Translation*)

(1) " Copy of the Farman of Sultan Abul Hasan Qutbshah.

(2) " This has gained the distinction of issuing to the present and future revenue officers of Atapur village in the vicinity of Muhammadanagar fort.

(3) " That Malik Mishk has laid this request at the feet of the sublime throne, that the deed of land in accordance with the Muhammadan law, relating to the lands in the above village originally in possession of Mir Malik as Royal award,

(4) " but subsequently purchased from the said Mir for special reasons, as also from trees in the cultivated and other lands,etc., has been endowed by him so that whatsoever be collected after the deduction of necessary expenditure.

(5) " should be spent on almshouse in memory of the twelve Imams, and a caldron of food should be cooked and distributed to the poor and deserving on the mosque which is near Narva. For the observance of

(6) " this a Royal mandate should be issued to the revenue officers of the above village. Accordingly, out of Royal bounty, this exalted order has been issued, that the present and future revenue officer's of the above village,

(7) " should continue to observe the endowment as made by the aforesaid Malik, and those who endeavour to

(6, 7, 8 and 9) These words underlined have been entirely omitted by Mr. Yazdani in his read.ng (*Ibid.*)

disregard or act contrary to it, shall be overtaken by the curse of God and the imprecation of the Prophet and shall be crest-fallen."

6. Inscription on the headstone of Miyan Mishk's tomb. (*vide* Plate VI.)

الحکم لله

۱- بتاریخ بست نهم ربیع الاول

۲- یوم الاحد جنتی میان

۳- مشک برحمت حق پیوست

۴- سنه ۱۰۹۲

Translation)

" All authority is for God.

" On the 29th of Rabi-ul-Awal, Sunday, the blessed Miyan Mishk was taken into the Divine mercy in the year 1092." (1680 A.D.)

(*g*)=Fair.

(*h*)=Should be protected.

(*j*)=The contemporary history contains no account of Miyan Mishk, although the above inscriptions disclose that Malik Mishk held the offices of Secretary, commander and keeper of the Royal key during the reign of Abul Hasan Qutb Shah. His name however shows him to be of African origin. His graveyard is situated near the Eastern end of the Old Bridge in a spacious enclosure. He appears to have been good natured and a philanthropist of no mean order. The karwanserai the mosque and the bath which were built by him are still intact and notwithstanding the lapse of over two centuries are still monuments of public utility. The bath is second to none in the City. On the facades of Eastern and western gateways, inscriptions No. 1,

2 and 3 contain the farmans of Abul Hasan Tanashah, describing in detail the revenues set apart for the maintenance of the tomb, the mosque and the bath. The 4th inscription fixed over the inner enclosure wall, which records the erection of a building (Royal Wardrobe) in 1035 A.H. (1625 A. D.) has no connection with the Malik's tomb. The fifth inscription over the southern doorway of the sepulchre also contains a farman of Abul Hasan. The sixth inscription, bearing the epitaph, is set up at the northern end of the grave. The tomb stands on a platform 5 ft. high, and the grave chamber is entered by three doorways. The epigraphs are in Naskhl Shikasta and Tauqi' script.

A palace was also built by Malik Mishk in the village of Atapur, which is now in ruins.

No. 30.

(*a*)=Cheen Qalich Khan's tomb. (New)

(*b*)=Near Himayat Sagar in the vicinity of Atapur.

(*c*)=Sarf-i-Khas.

(*d*)=II b.

(*e*)=1098 A.H. (1687 A.D.)

(*f*)=None.

(*g*)=Fair.

(*h*)=Should be protected.

(*j*)=The tomb of Cheen Qalich Khan Bahadur is situated to the south of Golconda near Himayat Sagar within an open enclosure. This graveyard, where other members of the Asafiyah dynasty are buried is surrounded by a wall of mud and plaster, and none of the graves bears any inscription. Close to the enclosure there is an incomplete building called the

Baradari of Nawab Nasirud-Dowlah Bahadur son of Asaf Jah I. The central tomb of the enclosure is of Chin Qalich Khan and the other two graves are of Iwaz Khan (right) and Mujahid Khan (left). About half a mile from this place the right hand of Chin Qalich Khan is buried in the village of Qismatpur, (where he fell dead by a canon ball during the siege of Golconda), which was recognised by means of his signet ring after he was buried here. On 28th January 1687 (1098 A.H.) during the last siege of Golconda, Emperor Aurangzeb ordered the fort to be attacked, and Khaja Mir Abid Khan *alias* Chin Qalich Khan Bahadur also took part in the attack as a commander of the Moghal army. Unfortunately a canon ball of the enemy struck and carried away the right shoulder-blade of Qalich Khan, and Qalich Khan was removed to his tent for treatment. When the Emperor sent his Prime Minister Jumdatul-Mulk, Asad Khan, for enquiring after his health, the dresser was found at that time engaged in extracting the broken pieces of bones and stitching his wound, and Qalich Khan with perfect self composure was engaged in sipping coffee with the other hand ; with all the medical aid at the disposal the wound proved to be fatal and three days later Qalich Khan expired. The Emperor Aurangzeb was much distressed over this sad occurance and under the Royal command his body was interred in the vicinity of Atapur where he fell dead during the siege of Golconda. The extreme fortitude with which Qalich Khan faced his death became a household story. He was respectable and of conciliatory demeanour and was held by all in high esteem. On the occasion of Aurangzeb's engagements in Bijapur, Qalich Khan was deputed to Hyderabad for the collection of Peshkash from Abul Hasan. His son, Mir Shahabuddin Khan *alias* Farzande-Be-Reo-Rang, Ghaziuddin Khan Feeroz Jung Bdr., had attained much prominence during the reign of Aurangzeb. He was married to the daughter of Nawab Sa'dullah Khan, the Prime Minister of Shah Jahan, and as a first issue of this union Mir Qamruddin Khan Bahadur, Nizamul Mulk Asaf Jah I, was born. The anniversary of Qalich Khan is observed here annually by the Sarf-i-Khas.

The two graves on either side of the grave of Qalich Khan are that of Iwaz Khan and Mujahid Khan. The full title of the former was Uzdud-Dowlah, Qusoor Jang, Muhammad Iwaz Khan Bahadur son of Uzdud-Dowlah. His original name was Khaja Momin Khan, and he had married the aunt of Asaf Jah I. For a considerable time he held the post of Nazim (Governor) of the province of Berar, later he was transferred from there by Asaf Jah I, in 1153 A.H. as Mutasaddi of Farkhunda Bunyad, Hyderabad, with full powers of dismissal and appointment on the contract of one crore of rupees per annum, and also the title of Muahmmad Iwaz Khan Bahadur was conferred on him. He had quelled the disturbances caused by Ali Qarawal and Loha Pandhrya at Masulipatam and Rajahmandry. He also being a devout and religious man was always bent on preventing intemperate things. The Begum Bazaar, was the property of the (Queen) mother of Nawab Nasir Jung Shahid, and all the toddy shops of that place which were a source of her revenue, were forcibly closed by the order of Iwaz Khan, its use being contrary to the Muhammadan law.

The Begam having been deprived of resourceful income lodged a bitter complaint against him with her husband, (Asaf Jah I), who to conciliate the Begam appointed Anwar-uddin Khan Bahadur (who was the deposed Foujdar of Cikakol and Rajahmandry) in place of Iwaz Khan, as Subadar of Hyderabad[1]. The latter Muhammad Mujahid Khan Bahadur was the brother of Ghaziuddin Khan, Feeroz Jung and a son of Chin Qalich Khan Bahadur. In 1095 A.H. when he had been to Bijapur in company with his brother Feeroz Jung, for supply of provision to the Army of Prince Azam, who was engaged in the siege of Bijapur, both of these brothers had to face enormous obstacles before they joined the Royal army. The Emperor Aurangzeb was extremely pleased when he heard of the valour evinced by these brothers in joining Azam's camp and consequently conferred many Royal bounties and other favours, and the following words uttered on the occasion by the Emperor, will be of special interest :—" As God Almighty has maintained the reputation of the house of Timur by the (untiring) endeavours of Feeroz Jung, May God preserve the honour of his descendants to the day of Judgment.[2]"

No. 31.

(*a*)=Hillock of Mir Mahmood Saheb (New).

(*b*)=On the road leading to Mir Alam's Tank.

(*c*)=Mujawirs.

(*d*)=II c.

(*e*)=1100 A.H. (1688 A.D.)

(*f*)=The grave of Mir Mahmood bears no inscription but on Zanjiri gate some Persian couplets are engraved in plaster which have been much obliterated. Over the facade of the second gate the following quatrain is engraved in plaster.

1) Muntakhabul-lubab and Tarikhe-Zufra (MSS).

2) Muntakhabul-lubab Vol. II.

شاها دل آگاه گدایان دارند * سررشتهٔ عشق بی نوایان دارند
گنجی که مبین و آسمان طالب اوست * تا در نگری برهنه پایان دارند

(*Translation*)

"O king the pauper alone possess an intelligent heart; the helpless bear affinity to love. The treasure which is manifest and which is coveted even by the skies. If you ponder well, is possessed by those who are bare-footed." In the room where Shams-Maula is buried in the red plaster are inscribed a number of Persian couplets and benedictory verses and Shiite Durud, but most of these inscriptions have been effaced.

Over the room of Riza Maula *alias* Ali Raza Husaini the following is fixed on a slab of black basalt:—

اے که از کوچه صاحب نظران می گذری * قدم آهسته ترک نه که صدای نشود
کوه دیدم بلند و اعلی فرش * هست نامش جبل گنج العرش
میر محمود برسر آن کوه * او بحق حق با وست چون در عرش

(*Translation*)

"O who passes the path of those who are pious, put your foot so gently that there may be no noise. I beheld a hillock which is lofty and widespread, its name is hill of Ganjul-Arsh (The teasure of empyrean heaven). Mir Mahmood on the top of that hill, is with God and God is with him as in the empyrean heaven."

(*g*)=Fair.

(*h*)=Should be protected.

(*j*)=This hillock is situated about 5 miles west of the city on the road leading to the tank of Mir Alam, and is the burial place of Syed Shah Imamuddin Husaini *alias* Mir Mahmood Nimat-ullahi, which is situated under a grand dome. He first came to Hyderabad from Najaf (Mesopotamia) during the reign of Sultan Abdullah Qutbshah and stayed on this hillock. Although he had no ostensible means of livelihood yet he lived without accepting the help of anyone. Besides he had several buildings erected on this hill, the masons who worked here were paid over and above the wages and the pregnant women-labourers were paid double the wages, consequently it was a general belief that the Saint had some supernatural means of income. He died on 13th Shaban 1100[1], although the exact date of his demise is not known. The Mujawirs observe his Urs (anniversary) on 11th and 12th Jamadil-awwal. His son Mir Shamsuddin *alias* Shams Moula, who was alive during the reign of Asaf Jah I, and who died on 14th Jamadil-Awal 1155 A.H. (1747 A.D.) in his eightieth year is also buried here. His son, Syed Shah Ali Riza Husaini, was renowned for miracles during the reign of Asaf Jah II. He died in 1215 A.H. (1800 A.D.) and is buried here. Shah Miran, son of Shah Ali Riza Husaini, died in 1230 A.H. (1814 A.D) and is also buried here. It has no grant from the Government. The Khurshid Jahi Paigah contributes a fixed amount for his anniversary.

No. 32.

(*a*)=Mushirabad Mosque.

(*b*)=Near Mushirabad.

(*c*)=Government.

(*d*)=II a.

---

(1) Gulzare-Asafiyah.

According to the" Baghe-Char-Chaman "(Lucknow edition, 1300 A.H.) " No book contains a record of the year of his death, but in a corner of the room where his son Shams-Maula is buried it was inscribed in plaster that Mir Mahmood died on 6th Rabiul-Awwal 1090 A.H. " When the author visited the place in 1345 A.H. the above record had however disappeared owing perhaps to the decadence of the plaster.

(*f*)=None.

(*g*)=Fair.

(*h*)=Should be protected.

(*j*)=This mosque is composed of 5 arches with two lofty minarets on either side and an extensive courtyard in front. The facade has 8 small turrets and the whole mosque is profusely decorated in stucco. One of the minarets which contains iron rods had bent, and it remained in the same position for several years. The state Archæological Department have lately had this minar re-erected and the mosque has also been thoroughly repaired.

No. 33.

(*a*)=The city wall (Intrenchment) (New).

(*b*)=Around the City of Hyderabad.

(*c*)=Government.

(*d*)=III a.

(*e*)=The reign of Subadarship of Mubariz Kha-Imadul Mulk and Asaf Jah I.

(*f*)=None.

(*g*)=After the floods of 1326 A.H. (1908 A.D.) the ramparts have been washed away in several places.

(*h*)=Except certain portions its protection is unnecessary.

(*j*)=The city wall was erected after the extinction of Qutbshahi Kingdom in the last days of the Subadarship of Mubariz Khan, Imadul Mulk, during the reign of the Moghal King Farrukh-Siyar. It was built from Chadderghat gate to the gate of Dabirpura, of uneven stone and mortar without turret-parapets. The rest of the wall which is surmounted by turret parapets was done by Asaf Jah I. The circumference of the entire wall is 6 miles and the area is about 4½ miles; the bastions still hold cannons of the old pattern. A century after the erection of the wall it was extensively repaired by Bahadur Dil Khan Shujauddowlah, a governor of Hyderabad, during the reign of Asaf Jah II. On either sides of the river Musi the parapet wall and battlements have been tastefully renovated by the Hyderabad Improvement Trust-Board under the command of His Exalted Highness the Nizam, Asaf Jah VII, which has added considerably to the excellent view of the city.

The city wall had 13 gates and 13 doors as follows :—

1. Chadderghat gate.
2. Delhi gate.
3. Afzul gate.
4. Champa gate.
5. Old bridge (Narva) gate.
6. Dudh Bauli gate.
7. Ghazi Banda or Fateh gate.
8. Aliabad gate.
9. Lal gate.
10. Gawlipura gate.
11. Mir Jumla gate.
12. Yaqootpura gate.
13. Dabirpura gate.

(1) Borah Khirki (door) (2) Mir Jumla Khirki (3) Matha Khirki (4) Rangeli or Rangali Shah Khirki (5) Bodla Khirki (6) Darushshifa Khirki (7) Kalala Khirki (8) Dhobi Khirki (9) Hasan Ali Khirki (10) Champa gate Khirki (11) Char Mahal Khirki (12) Dudh Bauli Khirki (13) Khirki of Kahar.

No. 34.

(*a*)=Kali Masjid and graves of Jan Supar Khan and Rustam Dil Khan (New).

(*b*)=Outside Yaqootpura gate.

(*c*)=Government.

(*d*)=II a.

(*e*)=1114 A.H., (1702 A.D.)

(*f*)=Over the central arch of Kali Musjid the following inscription is fixed on black basalt :—

بخدا بانئی این بیت خدا * خان (دل رستم) رستم دل عالیجاه است
بکشا لب بمناجات و بگو * مسجد ثانی بیت الله است

۱۱۱۴

کتبہ محمد علی الحسینی -

(*Translation*)

(1) " By God the founder of this abode of God (mosque) is the Exalted Khan Rustam Dil,

" Open your lips for prayers and say,

" This mosque is the prototype of Kaaba, 1114 (A.H.) written by Muhammad Ali Husaini."

(2) On the polished black basalt prayer niche of the mosque the following verses are painted in colours :—

عجلوا بالصلوٰة قبل الفوت * عجلوا بالتوبة قبل الموت
(دایره) نصر من الله و فتح قریب * نصر من الله و فتح قریب

(*Translation*)

(2) " Hasten to say prayers lest ye miss them."

" Hasten in penitence (vowing to sin no more) lest ye perish."

(In circles) " The help is from God and the success is close by."

(*g*)=Fair.

(*h*)=Should be protected.

(*j*)=After the fall of Hyderabad in 1098 A.H. the deposed King Abul Hasan was sent by the

Emperor Aurangzeb to Daultabad in company with Mir Bahadur Dil titled Jan Supar Khan of Sabzwar who was the third son of Syed Muhammad titled Mukhtar Khan Sabzwari. After the return of Jan Supar Khan from Daulatabad he took charge of the Subadarship of Hyderabad from Roohullah Khan. He got the title of Jan Supar Khan after he successfully fought against Dara Shikoh ; later he was appointed Kiladar of the fort of Bidar by Aurangzeb and ultimately he got the Subadarship of Hyderabad in which capacity he died in 1113 A.H. and was buried near Imli Mahal where his house was situated.

After his death his son Rustam Dil Khan was appointed Subadar of Hyderabad as a deputy of Prince Kam Baksh, later he was given Foujdarship of the Carnatic, (Bijapur) in 1116 A.H., and again in 1117 A.H., he was made Subadar of Hyderabad. After the demise of Emperor Aurangzeb in 1118 A.H., when Prince Kam Baksh came to Golconda from Bijapur, he was given an ovation by Rustam Dil Khan although the former's position had greatly diminished owing to the succession of Bahadur Shah to the throne of Delhi. Some of his confidants ill-advised him that Rustam Dil Khan, Saif Khan, Ahmad Khan and Ahsan Khan (Mir Malang) had plotted to imprison him. He became very suspicious and sent a note to Rustam Dil Khan to the effect that he should call on him the following morning together with his pen-case for writing a reply to a letter of Bahadur Shah. On Rustam Dil Khan's arrival Kam Bakhsh excused himself for breakfast and went inside asking him to wait in the chaplet. Immediately Rustam Dil Khan was taken prisoner and after 3 days he was mercilesly trampled to death by tying his body to the feet of an elephant. His body was interred close to his own house near Imli Mahal by the side of the grave of his father, where he had built his tomb in his lifetime. Rustam Dil Khan's tomb is situated in the centre of a raised terrace and is made of black basalt. It is covered by a pierced trellised covering of black basalt. On the same terrace the grave of his father Jan Supar Khan is made of Ashlar on the Western side, but it has no covering. The central portion of both these graves is filled with loose soil. The descendents of Rustam Dil Khan still inhabit these quarters and it has been related by one of them that an inscription slab was fixed over the covering of the grave of Rustam Dil Khan, which has since fallen. At present none of these graves bears any inscription. The only inscription which is fixed over the central arch of Kali Masjid, indicates that this mosque was built by Rustam Dil Khan one year after the demise of his father Jan Supar Khan. This small mosque is composed of 3 massive arches of Qutb Shahi style of architecture, but it contains no architectural beauty. On the Eastern end of the courtyard there is a small cistern for ablution which is enclosed by an iron railing. Beyond this railing the graves of Jan Supar Khan and Rustam Dil Khan are situated on a terrace.

No. 35.

(*a*)=Husaini Alam (New).

(*b*)=Is situated in the lane of the same name.

(*c*)=Government.

(*d*)=II a.

(*e*)=During the reign of Sultan Muhammad Quli.

(*f*)=Over one of the rooms of the inner dalan the year 1151 A.H. (1738 A.D.) is inscribed.

(*g*)=Fair.

(*h*)=Unnecessary.

(*j*)=During the reign of Sultan Muhammad Quli Qutbshah one Ali Agha had brought to Hyderabad an Alam (standard) from Arabia over which was fixed double edged sword of Imam

Jafare-Sadik. The King honouring this standard ordered it to be stored in the present house and Ali Agha after being handsomely rewarded was put in charge of this house. This standard is up to this day opened from 1st to 10th Moharrum every year. The adjoining mosque and the well were built by Ali Agha. Formerly the building was only on the western side, but Darab Beg, grandson of Ali Agha, built the eastern wing and an inscription bearing 1151 A.H., was fixed over one of the rooms. Darab Beg is buried in one of these rooms and a Jagir of Rs. 4,000 per year was granted by the Asafiya Kings for the expenses of Husaini Alam. Naubath (Kettle-Drum) and clock was furnished here by Maharajah Chandu Lal Bahadur, the then Prime Minister.

No. 36.

(*a*)=Bam (Reservior) of Ruknud-Dowlah (New).

(*b*)=Near Mir Alam Tank.

(*c*)=Sarf-i-Khas.

(*d*)=II b.

(*e*)=1184 A.H., (1770 A.D.)

(*f*)=A slab bearing the following inscription is fixed on the foundation stone of the spring :—

خوش آن رکن دوله بنام حسین * بنا کرد این چشمهٔ فیض عام

پی سال تاریخ گفته خرد * بخور آب سردی بیاد امام

سنه ۱۱۸۴ ھ

(*Translation*)

"That fortunate Ruknud-Dowlah founded this spring of public utility in the name of Husain (Imam). The genius spoke for its chronogram 'Drink cold water in Memory of the Imam'. 1184 A.H."

(*g*)=Good.

(*h*)=Should be protected.

(j)=In those days when pure and sweet water was scarce in the city this reservoir was built by Nawab Mir Musa Khan, Ruknud Dowlah, the Martyr,[1] who was Prime Minister of Asaf Jah II, and owing to his good intentions its water proved to be excellent and agreeable to such a degree that besides the public and aristocracy the Asafiyah Kings reserved it for their own use. Whenever the Kings of Hyderabad went out of the Dominions this water was despatched every day to the Royal camp as far as Delhi and Simla. The other name of this reservior is Musa Bam or Husaini Nahr (stream).

No. 37.

(a)=Kali Kabr (The black grave) (New).

(b)=Inside Chadderghat gate, on the roadside.

(c)=Mujawirs.

(d)=II b.

(e)=1197 A.H. (1782 A.D.)

(f)=The following inscription is engraved over the sarcophagus :—

۱- شہد اللہ انہ لا الہ الا ہو و الملائکۃ و اولوا العلم قائما بالقسط و ہوا لعزیز الحکیم

۲- تاریخ وفات حضرت سید شاہ اللہ دوست قدس سرہ سوم شوال سنہ ۱۱۹۷ ہجری

(*Translation*)

(1) " God hath borne witness that there is no God but He, and the angels and those who are endowed with wisdom profess the same, who executeth the righteousness there is no God but He, the Mighty, the Wise.

2. " The date of the demise of Hazrath Syed Shah Allah Dost, May his tomb be sanctified (is) 3rd Shawwal, the year 1197 A.H."

---

(1) For the burial place of Ruknud-Dowlah please refer to No. 2.

(*g*)=Fair.

(*h*)=The inscription should be preserved.

(*j*)=This grave is situated on a small terrace. The inscription No. 1 is in Thulth script and Tauqi' style and bears affinity to the inscription of the grave of Miran Bukhari (No. 26). The inhabitants of the vicinity perform the Urs of the deceased every year.

No. 38.

(*a*)=The tombs of Shamsul-Umara (New).

(*b*)=Near the Mousoleum of Barahna Shah Saheb.

(*c*)=Paigha.

(*d*)=I b.

(*e*)=1205 A.H. (1790 A.D.)

(*f*)=The following inscription is engraved on the grave of Tegh Jung Bahadur, the founder of the family of Shamsul Umara Bahadur :—

۱- اشهد ان لا اله الا الله و اشهد ان محمد ارسول الله - الله - محمد-علی
فاطمہ-حسن-حسین-مرقد حضرت محمد ابوالفتح خان مغفور-بتاریخ
۲۵ شهر ربیع الاول سنہ ۱۲۰۵ هجری-مقبرہ جناب محمد ابوالفتح خان
صاحب مرحوم مغفور-گزرانیدہ محمد محی الدین خان خورشید جاہ
بهادر ماہ محرم الحرام سنه ۱۳۰۸ ھ

(*Translation*)

1. " I witness that there is no God but the Almighty and that Muhammad is the Prophet of God, Allah, Muhammad, Ali, Fatima, Hasan, Husain. The grave of Hazrath Muhammad Abul Fateh Khan, whose sins are pardoned (expired) on 25th Rabiul Awwal in the year 1205 A. H. The mausoleum of Muhammad Abul Fateh Khan Saheb, the deceased and pardoned ; presented by Muhammad Mohyuddin Khan, Khurshid Jah Bahadur, in the month of Moharram-ul Haram 1308 A.H." (1890 A.D.).

2. Inscription over the grave of Haji Almas .

۲- وفات مرحومی مغفوری حاجی الماس بابت مرحومی صدل قای
تقریش(؟) بتاریخ هفدهم شهر محرم الحرام ۱۰۸۵ هزار و هشتاد و پنج

(*Translation*)

" The death of deceased and pardoned Haji Almaos on 17th Moharram-ul-Haram 1085 A.H. (1674 A.D.) one thousand and eighty five."

3. Inscription on the mausoleum of Hazrat Barahna Shah Saheb.

۳ درگاه حضرت سید حسن برهنه صاحب اولیاء قدس سره بارہ دری
گزرانیده محمد محی الدین خان خورشید جاه بهادر رماه
جمادی الاول ۱۳۱۷ ھ

(*Translation*)

" The mausoleum of Hazrat Syed Hasan Barahna Saheb the Saint, May his grave be sanctified. This Baradari was presented by Muhammad Mohiyuddin Khan Khurshed Jah Bahadur in the month of Jamadilawwal 1317 A.H."

۴- درود شریف(قبر مالک پرست خان)
۵- درود مختصر(نا معلوم)

(*Translation*)

4. The inscription slab on the grave of Malik Parast Khan (which is outside the grave of Baranha Shah Saheb bears 'Durud' in Naskh Script.

5. 'Durud' on the grave of an unknown man.

(*g*)=Good.

(*h*)=Should be protected.

(*j*)=Two miles north of Sururnagar is situated the mausoleum of Syed Hasan Barahna Shah Saheb, which contains the family vault of Nawab Shamsul Umara Bahadur. By the side of the grave of the founder of the family, Nawab Tegh Jung Shamsul Umara Bahadur his successors and other members of the family are buried in the graveyard. Notably Nawab Sir Asman Jah Bahadur (Prime Minister); Nawab Sir Khurshed Jah Bahadur; Nawab Sir Vikarul Umara Bahadur (Prime Minister) Nawab Zafar Jung Bahadur, (Military Minister) are also buried here. The graves of Nawab Shamsul Umara III and of Lady Khurshid Jah Bahadur have been finished in exquisite styles. Several graves are of marble, covered by pierced marble screens, and finished in mother o'pearl, mosaic and other decorations. All these graves are situated in an extensive courtyard and the central gate of the enclosure has a Naubat Khana (place for beating drums at proper intervals). Hazrat Syed Hasan Barahna *alias* Barahna Shah Saheb, Majzoob (saint) came to Hyderabad from Northern India during the reign of Sultan Abdullah Qutbshah. He was a Khalifa and disciple of Sufi Sarmad of Delhi, and died here on 6th Jamadi-Sani 1064 A. H. (1653 A.D.) His chief disciple Malik Parast Khan built a small dome over the grave of Barahna Shah Saheb and he himself was buried here together with his sons.

Malik Parast Khan was one of the ministers of Sultan Muhammad Quli and Muhammad Qutb Shah, and later, Commandant of the Royal body guard of Sultan Abdullah and also Havaldar of Golconda fort. He died in Zilhej 1064 A.H., six months after the death of his spiritual head Barahna Shah Saheb. He left sixty sons and daughters out of whom five elder sons and eight sons-in-law were provided for by Sultan Abdullah in his household and for the rest of his family a salary of 4,000 huns was granted[1]. The inscription No. 2 relates to the grave of Malik Almas

(1) Muhammad Qutbshahi (MSS).

who was a steward of Sultan Muhammad Qutb Shah and who was appointed for the management of the City after the death of Muhammad Quli, and during the reign of Sultan Abdullah he was made Superintendent of buildings. His massive Almas Masjid is situated just inside the Chaderghat gate and is in the best state of preservation.

No. 39.

(*a*)=Gunfoundry (Top-ka-Sancha)
(*b*)=Near Fateh Maidan.
(*c*)=Government.
(*d*)=III a.
(*e*)=Asaf Jah II.
(*f*)=None.
(*g*)=Dilapidated.
(*h*)=Should be protected.
(*j*)=Monsieur Joachim Raymond had built here a foundry in which guns were manufactured. A number of guns of the city especially those which at present may be seen in front of the Town Hall in the Public Garden, were manufactured here and several of them bear inscriptions to the same effect.

No. 40.

(*a*)=The grave of Monsieur Raymond.
(*b*)=Near Osman-Garh on the road to Sururnagar.
(*c*)=Government.
(*d*)=II a.
(*e*)=1213 A.H., (1798 A.D.)
(*f*)=In the centre of the high obelisk, (tombstone) the words (J. R.) are inscribed.
(*g*)=Fair.
(*h*)=Should be protected.

(j)=The French General Mons. Michel Joachim Marie Raymond who held the command of a regular regiment, 15,000 strong, was held in high esteem at the court of Nawab Asaf Jah II, and his pet name at the court was Moosa Rahmoo. He was born in France in 1755 A.D. (1169 A.H.) and died in Hyderabad on 25th March 1798 A.D. (1213 A.H.) Thus he was only 43, at the time of his death. His grave is situated at the back of Osmangarh on an elevated terrace 33 ft. high 180 ft. long and 85 ft. wide, and commands a nice birdseye view of the city. It has a conical tombstone (obelisk) 23 ft. high. The Hindus considering him to be Musa Ram and Muhammadans taking him to be Musa Rahim hold his grave in great veneration and perform his anniversary with great pomp. There is another grave close by whose inscription indicates that one Anne Jane Elizabeth Jenkins died at the age of 21 years and 6 months on 26th November 1809 A.D. (1224 A.H). About half a mile from this hillock is situated that French garden where Raymond and his army were stationed and traces of the military barracks may also be seen here. The one dream of Raymond's life was to develop the schemes of Dupleix and Lally and acquire ascendancy over the English. According to Malleson, "No European of mark who preceded him, no European of mark who followed him in India, ever succeeded in gaining to such an extent, the love, the esteem, the admiration of the natives of the country." About 25 ft. beyond the grave of Raymond there is a small building of Grecian style of architecture where the paraphernalia of Raymond's Urus is stored

No. 41.

(*a*)=Mir Alam Bund (New).

(*b*)=Near Mir Alam lake.

(*c*)=The Estate of Nawab Salar Jung Bahadur.

(*d*)=II b.

(*e*)=Asaf Jah III's reign 1221 A.H. (1806 A.D.)

(*f*)=On the reservoir stone of black basalt the following inscription is set :—

بسم الله مجریها و الحمد الله مرسیها سنه ۱۲۲۱ ھ

(*Translation*)

"In the name of God it flows and thank God it stands firmly. In the year 1221 A.H."

(*g*)=Good.

(*h*)=The inscription should be protected.

(*j*)=This bund which is a unique piece of architecture was constructed near Kotwal-gurah close to Isa river (Sankal) by Mir Abul Qasim Khan, Mir Alam Bahadur, the Prime Minister of Nawab Sikandar Jah Bahadur (Asaf Jah III). It was constructed under the superintendence of Saidud-Dowlah Bahadur and Mir Muhammad Ali Khan, sons of Khalilullah Khan and grandsons of Mir Alam Bahadur. The tank and the bund was completed at a cost of Rs. 8,00,000. After the completion of this tank the whole city of Hyderabad abounded in underground canals of running drinking water and the suffering of inhabitants from the scarcity of water were diminished. The inscription above referred to is set on one of the reservoirs wherefrom the water is distributed. Owing to the construction of Osman Sagar the importance of this tank has been greatly reduced. Mir Alam led the forces of the Nizam during the war with Tippu Sultan in 1799, and built this tank and several other buildings, out of the prize money which fell to his share after the fall of Seringapatam. The tank is about 8 miles in circumference. The bund is 1,120 yards in length and is formed of 21 large granite arches with semi-circular projections.

No. 42.

(*a*)=Chauck Mosque (New).
(*b*)=Near Shah Ganj.
(*c*)=Government.
(*d*)=II a.
(*e*)=1233 A.H. (1817 A.D.).
(*f*)=None.
(*g*)=Fair.
(*h*)=Should be protected.
(*j*)=This mosque was constructed by Khaja Abdullah Khan which has an elevated plinth and in front of this mosque a big clock tower is situated. The expenses of this mosque are met by the income of the shops which are situated in the lower storey of the mosque. The mosque and the shops are under the management of the State Ecclesiastical Department. A small Madrasah is also attached to the mosque.

PART II.

No. 43.

(*a*)=Golconda fort.

(*b*)=2 miles due west of Old bridge.

(*c*)=Sarf-i-Khas.

(*d*)=II c.

(*e*)=The reign of Rajahs of Warangal and Qutb Shahi Kings.

(*f*)=The inscriptions inside the fort are enumerated from No. 44.

(*g*)=Fair.

(*h*)=Certain portions are worth preserving.

(*j*)=According to the Maathire-Alamgiri the old name of Golconda fort was ' Mankal ' and the ancestors of Deo Rai, Rajah of Warangal had built this fort with walls of mud. During the reign of Sultan Muhammad Shah Bahmani (1358-1375 A.D.) this fort was made over by means of a sanad by the Rajah of Warangal to the Bahmani Kings. Later in 1518 A.D. (924 A.H.) this was ranked among the important forts of the Bahmani kingdom, and in the same year after the death of Sultan Mahmood Shah Bahmani when other Governors had cast down the yolk of the Bahmani Kings and ' Barid Shahi ' was established at Bidar, Sultan Quli, the Governor of Telingana also proclaimed his independence and made Golconda his capital. Sultan Quli after constructing the boundary wall of the fort, the Jamay Masjid (Safa Mosque), and the Royal palace, (Dawlatkhanae 'Ali) and other buildings, named this fort, as Muhammadnagar. During Ibrahim Qutbshah's reign the ramparts of the fort were strengthend by stone and mortar. When this impregn-

Bird's-eye view of Golconda Fort.

able stronghold of the Deccan was attacked by the Moghal forces under Prince Muhammad Azam a strong bastion called Musa Burj was erected close to the northern boundary. The elevation of this fort is 400 ft. and the circumference of the fort wall is 4 miles containing 87 semi-circular bastions, 50 to 60 ft. high. Certain blocks of granite which have been used in the wall must weigh at least a ton each, they are firmly cemented together and some are bound with clamps. The fort contains the following 8 huge gates which are studded with sharp iron knobs, intended to prevent elephants from battering them in.

1. Fatah Gate (2) Makka gate (3) Patancheroo gate (4) Banjara gate (5) Jamal gate (6) Moti gate (7) Bahmani gate (8) New fort gate.

At present Nos. 1, 2, 4 and 5 are open to the public. The name of Fatah gate was given by the Emperor Aurangzeb because through this gate the Moghal forces entered the fort. Outside the ramparts of the fort there exists a trench 50, ft. wide and at present the main entrance gate of the fort is Fatah gate. Inside this gate may be seen the ruins of Royal palaces, mosques, bazaars, arsenals, gunpowder magazines and Madanna temple. Cultivated fields and water tanks may also be seen within the fort wall and in times of danger the major portion of the population of the city used to be accomodated inside the fort. At present the assembly mosque (Masjid Safa), Madanna temple,[1] Ibrahim Qutb

(1) This temple most probably belongs to the early Dravidian and the later Warangal Rajahs, Madanna being a powerful Minister of Tanashah, it was called after him and as the king resided in the fort this was being used by his Hindu Courtiers. This temple is a striking proof of the toleration of Islamic Kings, who allowed its existence in close proximity to their own residence and the Assembly Mosque. Madanna and Akanna were Brahmins of the Carnatic and it is also asserted by some historians that their father was Kulkarni of Maisram. They had built a temple in the vicinity of Anantgiri where they used to go with their retinue in great pomp.

Shah's mosque, the Bala Hisar and the Baradari, (citadel) are in the best state of preservation. In one of the corners of this Baradari there is a secret subterranean passage which goes to Gosha Mahal, a distance of 5 miles, which was used by Qutb shahi Kings on occasions of emergency and danger. Halfway up the ascent of the fort is situated a small mosque which was built by Sultan Ibrahim Qutb Shah, this has been of late thoroughly repaired by the State Archæological department. On the northern outskirts of the fort at a distance of about 1¼ mile, on the road to Sholapur, those historic hillocks may be seen, where the camp of Emperor Aurangzeb was pitched during the last siege of Golconda. A thousand paces ahead of Patencheroo gate are situated the tombs of Golconda Kings. A detachment of His Exalted Highness the Nizam's Regular forces still resides in the military barracks, inside the fort wall. In the vicinity of the fort is situated, the mausoleum of Hazrat Husain Shah Wali who built the Husain Sagar tank[1] in 970 A.H.(1562 A.D.) and was a son-in-law of Sultan Ibrahim Qutb Shah. He died on 14th Jamadi Sani 1030 A.H. (1620 A.D.), during the reign of Sultan Abdullah Qutb Shah. The present dome and the mosque was built by the same King.

No. 44.

(*a*)=Jamay Masjid (Masjid Safa)

(*b*)=Near Bala-Hissar entrance gate.

(*c*)=Sarf-i-Khas.

(*d*)=I c.

(*e*)=924 A.H., (1518 A.D.)

(*f*)=Over the gateway of this Assembly mosque the following inscription on black basalt, measuring (2 ft. × 10·3) is fixed :—

۱- بناء هذا المسجد الجامع فی زمان السلطان الاعظم المتوکل علی الله
الغنی ابی المغازی محمود شاه بن محمد شاه البهمنی

۲- خلد الله ملکه و سلطانه و بانیه المبتهل الی الله مالک الملک سلطان
قلی المخاطب بقطب الملک فی سنه اربع و عشرین و تسعمایة

---

(1) It is 1 mile 2,280 feet long and costs Rs. 2,54,636.

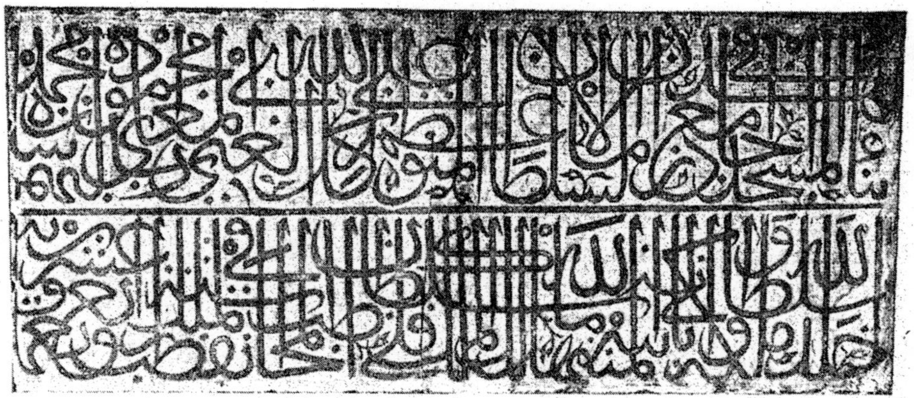

Over the doorway of Masjid Safa (Golconda.)

Over the Sarcophagus of Sultan Quli I. No. 45.

(*Translation*)

(1) " This Assembly mosque was built during the reign of the great King, trusting in the Independent God, Abil Maghazi Mahmood Shah son of Muhammad Shah Bahmani.

May God perpetuate his Kingdom and sovereignty, and its builder the humble suppliant of God, the Lord of The Universe is, Sultan Quli, entitled Qutbul Mulk. In the year 924 (A.H.)." (1518 A.D.) (*Vide* enclosed plate).

(2) Over the above inscription the following is engraved in Persian enamel. It shows that the calligrapher Abdul Karim inscribed it in 927 A. H. (1520 A. D.) (New).

قا ل ا لله تعا لے و ا ن ا لمسا جد لله فلا تد عوا مع ا لله ا حد ا

قل کل یعمل علی شا کلته * ال کل یعمل علی شا کلته

نو کلي علی خا لقی - ۶ ا له ا لا ا لله محمد رسول ا لله علی و لی ا لله - کتبه

عبد ا لکریم سنه ۹۲۷

(3) The following is fixed in the prayer niche of the mosque (New).

هنا لک د عا زکر یا ر به قا ل رب هب لی من لد نک ذ ریة طیبة ا نک

سمیع ا لد عاء فنا د ته ا لملا ئکة و هو قا یم یصلي فی ا لمحر ب ا ن ا لله یبشرك

بیحیی مصد قا بکلمة من ا لله و سید ا و حصورا و نبیا من ا لصا لحین -

صد ق ا لله ا لعلی ا لعظیم و بلغ رسوله ا لکریم (۱)

Quran Chap. III Verses 33 & 34.

This benedictory verse is quite appropriate for the first Qutbshahi mosque, in which a hope is cherished by the founder of the kingdom that his descendents would be honourable, chaste and righteous.

(*g*)=Good.

(*h*)=Should be protected.

(*j*)=This Assembly mosque was built by Sultan Quli Qutbul Mulk when he resided at Golconda in the capacity of a Bahmani Governor of Telingana. This mosque is composed of a large hall divided into four aisles and five arches and the courtyard is paved with slabs of granite.

---

(1) The above inscriptions Nos. 2 and 3 have been entirely omitted by Mr. Yazdani (E. I. M. 1915-16).

In this Mosque 25 years after its erection Sultan Quli the 1st King of Golconda, while he was in the act of prostration, was assassinated by Mir Mahmud Hamadani, Qiladar of Golconda at the instigation of the heir apparent Yar Quli Jamshid.

No. 45.

(*a*)=The dome of Sultan Quli, Qutbshah I.
(*b*)=Among the tombs of Qutbshahi Kings.
(*c*)=Sarf-i-Khas.
(*d*)=I c.
(*e*)=950 A.H., (1543 A.D.)
(*f*)=The following inscriptions are engraved in three bands, on his tomb of highly polished black basalt. They are in Naskh style and Tauqi script of the finest quality.

١- صدق الله العظيم وصدق رسوله النبي الكريم ونحن على ذلك من
الشاهدين والحمد لله رب العالمين

٢- اللهم صل على المصطفى محمد والمرتضى علي والبتول فاطمة
والسبطين الحسن والحسين وصل على زين العباد علي والباقر محمد
والصادق جعفر والكاظم موسى والرضا علي والتقي محمد والنقي علي
والزكي العسكري الحسن وصل على الحجة القائم الخلف الصالح الامام
الهمام المنتظر المظفر محمد المهدي صاحب الزمان وخليفة الرحمن
ومظهر الايمان وسيد الانس والجان صلوات الله وسلامه عليه
وعليهم اجمعين في سنه ٩٥٠

٣- آية الكرسي - قرآن سوره ٢ - آيات ٢٥٦ - ٢٥٩

٤- (١) انتقل صاحب هذه الروضة الرضية وهو الملك المغفور
(٢) السعيد الشهيد الغازي لوجه الله و(١) المجاهد في سبيل الله
الملك سلطان قلي
(٣) المخاطب بقطب الملك المشهور به بر(2)ملک انار الله برهانه
الى جوار رحمة الله في يوم الاثنين ثاني شهر جمادى الثانيه سنه ٩٥٠

---

(1) In line 2 Mr. Yazdani has left out the letter (و) between (الله) and (المجاهد) (E.I.M. 1915-16 p. 27).

(2) Mr. Yazdani's reading is (برے ملک) although the word used in the inscription is only (برملک). (*Ibid*).

(*Translation*)

1. " True is God, the great, true is his Apostle, the benevolent Prophet, and we bear witness to that, praise be to God, the Lord of all creatures."

2. *The Shiite Darud* :—

" O God, bless the chosen Muhammad, the Murtuza (agreeable) Ali, the chaste Fatima, the two offsprings Hasan and Husain and bless Zainil Ibad (the ornament of holy persons) Ali, the Baqir (learned) Muhammad, the Sadiq (truthful) Jafar, the Kazim (forbearing) Musa, the Riza (submissive) Ali, the Taqi (pious) Muhammad, the Naqi (pure) Ali, the virtuous Hasan Askari, and bless the standing proof, (of God) the worthy son, the noble leader, the expected, the victorious Muhammad Mahdi, the Lord of the time, the viceregent of God, the manifestation of the faith, the lord of mankind and genii, May God's blessing and peace be upon him and upon them all. In the year 950 (A.H.). "

3. " The Throne Verse. Quran Chapter II, verses 256-259. "

4. *On the foot of the grave.*

" The occupant of this chosen shrine, is the blessed monarch, the felicitous, the Martyr, the warrior for God's sake and the striver in God's path, the King Sultan Quli, entitled Qutbul Mulk, known as Bar (great) Malik, May God illumine his argument ; marched to the neighbourhood of God's mercy on Monday, the 2nd of Jamadi II, 950 (A.H.)." (September 2, 1543 A.D.) (*vide* plate).

(*g*)=Good.

(*h*)=Should be protected.

(*j*)=According to the Tarikhe Qutbshahi, Sultan Quli died in his ninety-ninth year thus his year of birth comes to 849 A. H. Although his year of birth is not given in any contemporary history. After the death of his master Mahmood Shah Bahmani in 924 A.H. Sultan

Quli declared his independence, and this may be reckoned as his first regnal year, although other Governors of Bahmani provinces had declared their independence in the lifetime of their Royal master. Ferishta and other historians considering that Sultan Quli must have also followed suite, have erroneously recorded Sultan Quli's assumption of regal title in 917 or 918 A.H. Sultan Quli who was born at Sadabad (Hamadan) descended from the ruling family of Qara Yousuf, Turkomans and his lineage ends with Amir Tara Beg son of Aghaz Khan son of Yafis son of the prophet Noah.[1] When he first came to the Deccan from Persia, he was taken into Royal favour by Sultan Mahmood Shah Bahmani. In recognition of his valour and devotion he first received the title of Khawas Khan and then Qutbul-Mulk and was appointed Governor of Telingana. After the declaration of independence his territories extended in the North as far as the Godavari, in the East as far as Orissa and the sea coast and in the South as far as river Kistna. He was very fond of architecture; besides the Golconda fort a big city was constructed there by him which was composed of fine buildings. He was the originator of that style of architecture, called the Qutbshahi Style, which is a combination of Persian, Hindu, and Pathan styles of Archi-

(1) On a manuscript copy of Kanzul-lughat which is at present in the library of Nawab Salar Jung Bahadur, the following is written in the handwriting of Sultan Muhammad Qutbshah, which deals with the pedigree of his house. "Muhammad Qutbshah son of Mirza Muhammad Amin son of Ibrahim Qutbshah son of Sultan Quli Qutbul Mulk son of Uwais Quli son of Peer Quli son of Alwand Beg son of Mirza Iskandar son of Qar Yousuf son of Qar Muhammad Turkoman."

tecture. When he attained the ripe age of 99, and his heir-apparent Yar Kuli Jamshed became tired of the length of his father's reign, on Sunday, the 2nd Jamadi Sani 950 A.H. (1543 A.D.) he instigated Mir Mahmud Hamadani, the Qiladar, who murdered the King while he was in the act of prostration in the Assembly Mosque of the fort. According to the Tarikhe Zufra the Qiladar inflicted 23 wounds on the king while he was engaged in evening (Asr) prayers. The chronogram of his death is "Faiyaze Hind" (950 A.H.) and the following Quatrain also gives the date of his death :—

قطب شاه جهان چوا زتقدیر * از جهان جست سوی جنت راه
گوا بوا لفضل سال وصلش نیز * معدن جود قطب شاهنشاه
۹۵۰ ھ ۹۵۰ ھ

This dome was erected by Sultan Quli during his life time for his own internment according to the prevalentc ustom. It is situated on an elevated square terrace, 100 ft. each way, and internally it is octagonal and the inner dimensions of the hall are 30 ft. 10 inches each way. It is crowned by a circular dome and externally, on account of the terrace, it appears to be a square building, the walls of the basement storey being 20 ft. high. In the inscription No. 4 the word (شہید) corroborates the incident of his assassination which occured in 950 A.H. in the assembly mosque of the fort. The word Bar Malik (the great Malik) which occurs in this inscription was according to 'Tarikeh Farkhunda,' 'Muhammad Qutbshahi' and 'Zufra,'"[1] a pet name of Sultan Quli, by which all the high and low inhabitants of the Deccan used to call him. This dome contains 3 graves and on the outside terrace 21 graves of polished black basalt, all

(1) Mr. Yazdani says that "the pet name of Bare Malik is not to be found in any contemporaneous writings" E. I. M. 1915-15 p. 27.

uninscribed, are situated. These domes of Golconda Kings were held in such veneration that whenever any criminal took refuge there, he was given amnesty and during the Qutbshahi period the tombs were always furnished with expensive carpets and lamps and a number of Qurans were kept on supports, which were recited by the readers at appointed intervals. The domes of ruling kings were, distinguished by spires of golden crescents fixed above the centre of the dome and those of other members of the family and of Khaja-Sara's had no such sign and were built on comparatively lower terraces, and in those days it was not possible for every layman to have access to these tombs. Owing to years of neglect the condition of these tombs had become deplorable and Sir Salar Jung the great, after getting them thoroughly conserved had a nice garden laid out and a compound wall built, and posted a guard over the main gate. These tombs are now constantly repaired by the Sarf-i-Khas Mubarak, and the garden is well kept. In the Qutbshahi days this place was called " Langar-e-Faiz Athar, " (A place for the bountiful entertainment) where the poor were entertained every afternoon and this custom of entertaining the poor in this place was also observed during the lifetime of Sultan Quli.

No. 46.

(*a*)=The Mortuary Bath (New).

(*b*)=Opp : to the dome of Muhammad Quli V.

(*c*)=Sarf-i-Khas.

(*d*)=III c.

(*e*)=The reign of Sultan Quli I.

(*f*)=None (several broken inscriptions of different tombs have been stored here).

(*g*)=Requires conservation.

(*j*)=This bath was built by Sultan Quli I, in the course of the erection of his own tomb, for the purpose of washing the bodies of the dead.

It has several apartments and appears to have been built on a masterly model as it is one of the best specimen of the old Persian and Turkish Baths. It contains a number of cisterns for hot and cold water, with running pipes of mortar for the supply of water, and the shrouding platforms are decorated with Mosaic. The dead bodies of Kings and of Royal family used to be taken out of the fort through Banjara gate and brought to this bath for ablution after which they were carried to the last resting place with requisite pomp attended by a great retinue.

No. 47.

(*a*)=The tomb of Jamshed Quli II (*vide* plate).

(*b*)=Near the dome of Sultan Quli I.

(*c*)=Sarf-i-Khas.

(*d*)=I c.

(*e*)=957 A.H., (1550 A.D.)

(*f*)=None.

(*g*)=Good.

(*h*)=Should be protected.

(*j*)=The date of the birth of Jamshed Quli could not be ascertained but he ascended the throne soon after the Martyrdom of his father in 950 A.H. (1543 A.D.) and after a reign of 7 years died of cancer in 957 A.H. (1550 A.D). He was the 2nd son of Sultan Quli I, Hyder Quli and Abdul Karim his elder and third brothers respectively, had predeceased Sultan Quli. His fourth brother Qutbuddin who was made heir-apparent was blinded by Jamshed soon after he ascended the throne. The fifth brother Daulat Khan known as Diwana-

Malik (The mad Malik) was a maniac. He died in the reign of Ibrahim Qutbshah IV, who was the sixth and last brother of Jamshed.

Jamshed Quli was a brave and diplomatic king, whose soundness of diplomacy was repeatedly manifested in the wars between Ali Barid, Ibrahim Adilshah and Burhan Nizam Shah. At the outset he fought against these kings, and broke up this triple alliance and ultimately assuming the position of an arbitrator he liberated Ali Barid from the confinement of Adil Shah and re-established him in the kingdom of Bidar, as a result of which Ali Barid remained his staunch friend and supporter to the end of his life. The dome of Jamshed contains two more graves none of which bears any inscription. His own tomb not being of black basalt and its external form being a little dissimilar to that of his family, there is a difference of opinion as regards the identity of Jamshed's tomb, but according to the authorities of 'Tarikhe-Farkhunda' and 'Muhammad Qutbshahi' which, distinctly lays down that "Jamshed was buried in the neighbourhood of the dome of his father," there remains very little doubt as to its identity owing to its close proximity to the dome of Sultan Quli. The following Quatrain gives the chronogram of the death of Jamshed :—

شه جمشید جم دولت شه دهر * ز دنیا برد رخت خود بجنت
وصال پاک او میر بهشت است * دگر قطب الحسن میر ولایت
۹۵۷ ه   ۹۵۷ ه

Jamshed was fond of poetry some specimens of which are given below.

بی لب لعل بتان باده حرام است مرا * لب میگون شما چون سر جام است مرا (۱)
با سر زلف تو سودای سیاهی دارم * این چه سوداست که با زلف چو شام است مرا
ترک این کار نخواهم من بیدل کردن * من که جمشیدم و این کار تمام است مرا
و له - در ره عشق هر که پا نه نهاد * آخرا و سر کشد بر سوای
من بدیوانگی شدم مشهور * تو بخوبی و عالم آرای
تو همان آفتاب بی همتا * من همان عاشق تماشائی

(۱) لب میگون چو سر جام حرام است مرا

وله - اشکها ز دیده بهر نیل که چون می آید * کوکب بخت منست اینکه برون می آید
ان نه اشکست که از دیده روان می آید * قاصدی گوی که از شهر برون می آید
چند در عشق بتان شهره شوی ای جمشید * گرکند غیر تو این کار ز بون می آید
وله - سرو روان خویش را کردم روان دیده جا
تا پرورش باید دگر آن سرو ز آب چشم ما

No. 48.

(*a*)=The dome of Subhan Quli Qutbshah III.

(*b*)=Is situated in the centre of the domes of Sultan Quli and Jamshed Quli.

(*c*)=Sarf-i-Khas.

(*d*)=I c.

(*e*)=Unknown.

(*f*)=None.

(*g*)=Good.

(*h*)=Should be protected.

(*j*)=After the death of Jamshed Quli Qutbshah his courtiers placed his seven year old son Subhan Quli on the throne in 957 A.H., and Saif Khan 'Ainul-Mulk[1] son of Fathi Khan, an uncle

(1) The Mausoleum of Saif Khan is situated close to the Lal Tekri or Fateh Maidan of Golconda, where the victorious forces of Aurangzeb had assembled after the fall of the Fort and which is said to have been the Parade ground of Qutb Shahi forces. The grand dome which is built of ashlar and concrete, stands on an elevated square terrace. The sarcophagus of the tomb of Saif Khan which is in the centre of the dome, is of highly polished black basalt and bears the following inscription in Naskh script. (New).

قال الله سبحانه تبارک و تعالے قل یا عبادی الذین اسرفوا علی انفسهم
لا تقنطوا من رحمة الله ان الله یغفر الذنوب جمیعاً انه هو الغفور الرحیم -
صدق الله العلی العظیم و صدق رسوله النبی الکریم و نحن علی ذلک
من الشاهدین و الحمد لله رب العالمین و صلی الله علی خیر خلقه محمد
و آله اجمعین -

It appears that the original tomb is situated in the subterranean vault which is however closed. The terrace is surrounded with several other tombs of unknown personages. The general condition of this building deserves the attention of the State Archæological Department.

According to "Muhammad Qutbshahi," after the advent of Ibrahim Qutbshah, Saif Khan had to quit the country in 957 A.H. (1550 A.D.). He fought many battles in Berar and Ahmadnagar and was ultimately suffocated to death by the orders of Husain Nizam Shah in 964 A.H. The

of Jamshed Quli Qutb Shah, was made Vakil-us-Sultan (Plenipotentiary). But owing to the high-handedness of Saif Khan the nobles of the court invited Ibrahim Quli, the sixth son of Sultan Quli, (who after the accession of Jamshed Quli, had sought refuge with Ramraj of Vijyanagar), and ultimately with the assistance of Naigwars, Ibrahim Quli was proclaimed King of Golconda on 12th Rajab 957 A.H. (1550 A.D.). It is not recorded in the contemporary writings what became of Subhan Quli and when and where his days ended, but midway between the domes of Sultan Quli and Jamshed Quli there exists a dome of " Chhote Malik" which is said to contain the remains of Subhan Quli although it bears no inscription.

No. 49.

(a)=Makka Gate.

(*b*)=Golconda.

(*c*)=Sarf-i-Khas.

(*d*)=II c.

(*e*)=967 A.H., (1559 A.D.) The reign of Sultan Ibrahim Qutbshah.

(*f*)=On the facade of Makka Darwaza the following inscription is engraved in Naskh script and Tughra style. Notwithstanding the boldness of the letters the style is graceful and masterly. The inscription is 46 ft. 2 inches long and 1 foot 6½ inches wide.

---

present dome of Saif Khan was kindly brought to my notice by Col. the Nawab Hashim Nawaz Jung Bahadur, Commdt. Golconda forces, who stated that for the last so many decades this dome was locally acknowledged to be that of Saif Khan. Recently the author came across History of the Deccan, (Silsila-e-Asafiyah) Vol. III, p. 416-18, which lays down that Saif-Khan was buried in the village of Tikapur in the Purgannah of Man (Ahmadnagar District), although it fails to give any reference as regards the source of this information.

The dome of Jamshed Quli II.

The author's reading of the text is as under :—

بسم الله الذی جعل کلمة توحیده حصناً حصیناً و اصابنا فتح ابوابه بالرحمة
فمن دخله کان آمنا و الصلوة علی المصطفی الذی تمت به حصون النبوة
و شعابها و هو مدینة العلم و علی بابها و علی آله التی ارتفعت بهم بروج
الولایة و الامامة و اصحابه الخازنین الخصال الصدق و السلامة
و بعد فهذا من (1) درب الدولة و حصن السعادة قد بنی فی ایام
خلافة اعظم السلاطین اکرم الخواقین قهرمان (2) الماء و الطین فاتح
ابواب البرکة علی العالمین رافع بناء شریعة سید المرسلین معمار الدولة
و الدین ظل الله فی الارضین سمی خلیل الله همایون اعظم قطب شاه
لا زال حصون دولته محفوظة عن التزلزل و بروج خلافته عن وصمة التغیر
و التبدل بمساعی جمیله رکن دولته القاهره و عماد سلطنته الباهره جامع الکتب
و مفرق الکتایب الذی ینوء لحسباً و نسباً الی مظهر العجایب المسمی فی البین
بکمال الدین حسین و المخاطب بعلو الشان بمصطفی خان شکر الله مساعیه
و یسر دواعیه فی شهور سنه ۹۷۲ ه کتبه محمد اصفهانی -

(*Translation*)

"In the name of God, who made the word of His unity an impregnable fort, the gates of which have been opened to us through his mercy, and whoever entereth therein shall be safe; and blessings be upon Mustafa, in whose person the forts and defences of prophecy have been completed, and he is the town of learning and Ali is the gate of the town and upon his descendents through whom the towers of Viceregency and religious leaderships have arisen, and upon his friends the custodians of the qualities of truth and integrity. After that, this gate which is of fortune and fort of felicity was, verily, built during the days of the administration of the greatest of sovereigns, and the noblest of kings who is an invincible hero on sea and land, the opener of the gates of benevolence to all creatures, the elevator of the edifice of the law prescribed by the Chief of Apostles, the builder of state and religion, the shadow of God in the world, the namesake

1. Mr. Yazdani has omitted the word (من) before (درب) E.I.M. 1913-14 p. 48.

2. Mr. Yazdani's decipherment is (فهو اهمان) and the translation is "who is the refuge." (*Ibid*).

of Khalilul-lah (the Friend of God) (Prophet Ibrahim), Humayooni Azam Qutbshah, may the forts of his sovereignty ever remain safe from trembling and the towers of his kingdom from the clefts of change and alteration! By the noble efforts of the pillar of his powerful empire, and the prop of his bright kingdom, the collector of books and the disperser of armies, whose qualities and pedigree are related to Mazharul Ajaib the (manifestation of wonders in mankind) Ali, better known among the people by the name of Kamaluddin Husain and entitled Mustafa Khan on account of his high rank, may God accept his efforts and mitigate his misfortune! In the months of the year 967 A.H. (1559 A.D.) written by Muhammad of Isphahan." (*vide* plate).

(*g*)=Good.

(*h*)=Should be protected.

(*j*)=Makka Darwaza is one of the 8 gates of the fort, it is so named because it faces the Mecca. It is a strong and spacious gate, made of strong teakwood fixed with sharp iron spikes with a view to protect the gate from the battering of elephants. In the inscription the name of the reigning sovereign Sultan Ibrahim Qutb shah has been metaphorically referred to as "Khalilul-lah" which is the *nom-de-plume* of the Prophet Ibrahim. The battlements and gates of Golconda which form a circumference of 8,000 yards were completed in the course of 9 months, under the supervision of Syed Kamaluddin of Ardastan, entitled Khane-Azam, Mustapha Khan, at the expense of 20 lacs, and Mustapha Khan was also appointed a Peshwa and Vakil. According to 'Muhammad Qutbshahi' Mustapha Khan was closely related to Mir Maqsood Ali Tabataba who was maternal grandfather of Sultan Muhammad

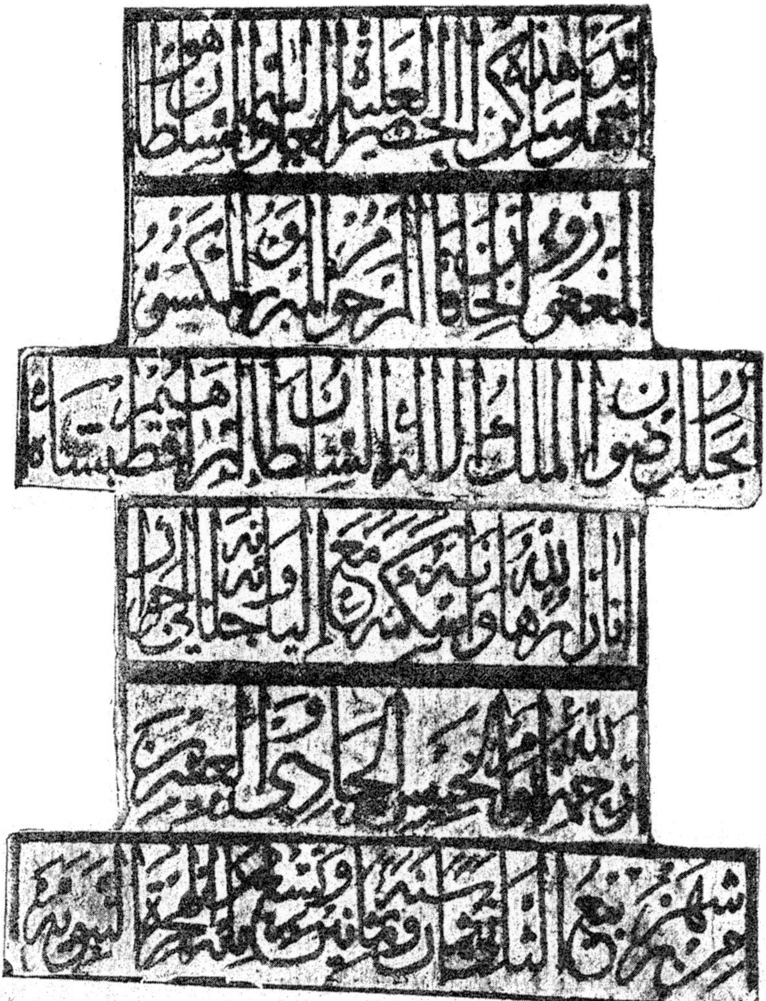

On the Head and Footstones of Ibrahim Qutbshah's grave.

Qutbshah. In 972 A.H. he helped Ibrahim Qutbshah a great deal in the overthrow of Ramraj but, soon after, Ibrahim charged him of being in league with Ali Adilshah and consequently he joined Ali Adilshah and accepted the post of Peshwa under him. After the assassination of Ali in 988 A.H. he met the same fate at the hands of the rebels.

No. 50.

(*a*)=The dome of Sultan Ibrahim Qutbshah IV.
(*b*)=Golconda Tombs.
(*c*)=Sarf-i-Khas.
(*d*)=I c.
(*e*)=988 A.H. (1580 A.D.)
(*f*)=The tomb proper is of polished black basalt measuring 9 ft. 4 inches × 6 ft. 2 inches. On its head and foot stones the following inscription is engraved in Thulth script :—

١- (١) قد انتقل ساكن هذه الحضيرة العلية العالية وهو السلطان
(٢) المغفور والخاقان المرحوم المبرور المكرو (٣) بحلل رضوان
الملك الاله سلطان ابراهيم قطب شاه (٤) انار الله برهانه واسكنه مع
اوليائه جنانه الى جوار
(٥) رحمة الله يوم الخميس الحادي والعشرين (٦) من شهر
ربيع الثانی سنه ثمان وثمانين وتسع مائته من الهجرة النبويه

On the top slab of sarcophagus.

٢- لا اله الا الله محمد رسول الله علی ولی الله حقا حقا شهد الله انه
لا اله الا هو والملائكته واولوا العلم قائما بالقسط لا اله الا هو العزيز الحكيم
فی سنه ٩٨٨ ھ

On the right hand slab.

٣- صدق الله العظيم وصدق رسوله النبی الكريم ونحن علی ذلک من
الشاهدين والحمد لله رب العالمين

On the left hand slab of sarcophagus.

٤- نادن عليا مظهر العجائب تجده عونا لک فی النوايب كل هم وغم سينجلی
بولايتک يا علی يا علی يا علی قال محمد بنی الكونين المومن حی فی
الدارين المومنون لا يموتون بل ينتقلون من دار الی دار

(*Translation*)

1. " The occupant of this high and grand tomb, and he is the Sultan whose sins have been forgiven and the king whom God has taken into His mercy, the pious defunct, who is clad with the garment of Divine acceptence ; the Sultan Ibrahim Qutbshah, may God illumine his arguments and cause him to dwell with his friends in His Paradise ; marched to the neighbourhood of Divine mercy on Thursday, the 21st of Rabi II, 988 years after the flight of the Prophet." (June 5-1580 A.D.)

2. (*The Shiite creed and Quran, verse* 16,*Chap. III.*)
" There is no god but God, Muhammad is the apostle of God and Ali the friend of God, Verily, verily ! God hath borne witness that there is no god but He ! and the angels and those who are endowed with wisdom profess the same who executeth righteousness ; there is no God but He, the mighty, the wise. In the year 988 (A.H.). "

3. (*Quran —Verse* 256-59 *Chap. II*).

" True is god, the high, the great ; true is His apostle, the benevolent prophet, and we bear witness to that, praise be to God, the Lord of all creatures."

4. (*Nade Ali*)

" Invoke Ali, the manifestation of wonders, thou wilt find him succour in misery. All grief and sorrow will soon disappear, by thy friendship (with God) O Ali ! O Ali ! O Ali ! Muhammad the prophet of both the worlds has said : The true believer is alive in both the worlds. Believers do not die, but they move through from one abode to another."

(*g*)=Good.

(*h*)=Should be protected.

(*j*)=After the ephemeral reign of Subhan Quli, Ibrahim, son of Sultan Quli I, succeeded to the throne of Golconda with the help of Naigwars and in acknowledgment of the same, Jagdeva Rao, the leader of Naigwars was made his Vizier by Ibrahim but soon afterwards he devised a plan to dethrone Ibrahim in favour of his brother Daulat Khan *alias* Diwana Malik (the Maniac Malik) who was then a prisoner in Bhongir fort.

Ibrahim became aware of this intrigue at the nick of time and Jagdeva Rao fled precipitately first to Burhan Nizamshah in Berar and later to Ramraj at Vijyanagar and contemporaneously Ibrahim had to fight a decisive battle in company with the Kings of Bijapur and Ahmadnagar against Ramraj of Vijaynagar, at Talicotta, in 952 A.H., which marked the death of Ramraj and the complete overthrow of the Vijyanagar Kingdom. Afterwards Shitab Khan one of the officers of Ibrahim conquered Warangal and annexed it to Golconda. Sultan Ibrahim was a capable and vigilant ruler, during his reign a number of mosques karwanserais, hospitals, and tanks were constructed, and the fort of Golconda[1] was strengthened. Several palaces, gardens, the Langar or Katura Hauz and Kala Chabutra of Golconda, the town and tank of Ibrahimpatan and the Katwa (bund) of Budwell bear testimony to his philanthropic actions to the present day. His territories extended from Rajahmandri and Cassimcotta to the sea-cost, encircling the whole of the Western part of India within his Kingdom. The three famous calligraphists of his time were Muhammad of Isphahan, Ismail, son of Arab[2] of Shiraz, and Taqiuddin Muhammad Salih of Bahrien. Most of the Naskh and Thulth inscriptions on the Qutbshahi edifices and tombs are the pro-

(1) During the reign of this King 8,000 yards of the fort wall with 404 bastions, etc., were constructed at a cost of 20 Lacs of rupees. (Tuzuke Qutb Shahi MSS).

(2) Mulla Arab of Shiraz was a calligraphist of the Royal library. He wrote with such expedition that 1,000 or 1,500 couplets were written by him per diem. He was also well versed in ornamental writings and inscriptions (Hadiqatus-Salatin Qutbshahi. MSS)

ductions of these masters, who have left a store of Naskh, Thulth, and Nastaliq inscriptions with Tauqi' and Tughra styles of the highest order in this city. During the reign of this King Golconda had become a central market for the Turkish, Persian and Arab traders. After a benign reign of 30 years Ibrahim died in 988 A.H., leaving behind him three daughters and six sons all of whom had attained their majority, besides some minor ones. His first son Abdul Qadir *alias* Shah Saheb died in his 21st year at Devarkonda fort, wherefrom his remains were brought to Golconda to be interred in the Langare-faiz athar (the Tombs). His second son was Mirza Husain Quli, who was an authority in Medicine and Logic, and who met a watery grave while swimming in the Nampalli tank in 994 A.H., and was buried in the tombs. The third son was Muhammad Quli Qutbshah (No. 52). The fourth son was Mirza Abdul Fattah, who died in 1003 A.H., in his 28th year, of epilepsy. He was a good Qari, (a reciter of the Quran in proper manner). The fifth son was Mirza Muhammad Khuda Banda, who died in 1020 A.H., as a prisoner in the Golconda fort. The sixth was Mirza Muhammad Amin[1] (No. 51).

The dome of Sultan Ibrahim is larger in comparison with that of Sultan Quli, and it was once decorated with Persian enamelled tiles, traces of which are still to be seen on the southern wall. The square terrace on which the dome stands is 117 ft. each way. Inside the dome there are two tombs and the outside terrace contain 16 tombs of black basalt all of which are uninscribed. The following quatrain contains the chronogram of Sultan Ibrahim :—

چون زد نیا سوی عقبی رخت بست * شاه ابراهیم شاه اهل جاه
سال وصل او ست فیاض زمان * نیز زیبا تاج ابراهیم‌شاه‌سنه ۹۸۸ھ

۹۸۸ ھ

(1) Muhammad Qutbshahi MSS.

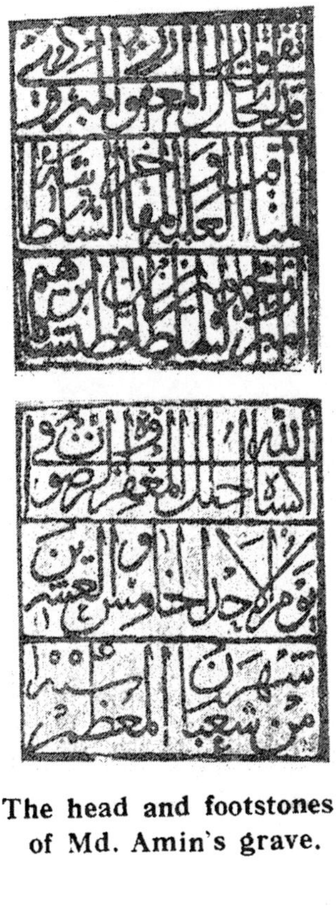

The head and footstones of Md. Amin's grave.

Over the Sarcophagus of Md. Amin's grave.

The 3rd band of Muhammad Amin's grave.

No. 51.

(*a*)=The tomb of Prince Mirza Muhammad Amin.

(*b*)=This dome is situated on the same terrace on which the dome of his father Sultan Ibrahim Qutbshah stands.

(*c*)=Sarf-i-Khas.

(*d*)=I-c.

(*e*)=1004 A.H., (1596-A.D.)

(*f*)=On the top slab of the sarcophagus Surae Ikhlas (*vide* plate) (Chap. CXII Quran), is written in the Kufic script and is important as being the only specimen of this script in Golconda or the city of Hyderabad. The following verse 16 Chap. III of the Quran is written in Tauqi style :—

شهد الله انہ لا آ الہ الا هو وا لملائکته و ا و لوا لعلم قا ئما با لقسط لا ا له آ لا هو
ا لعز یز ا لحکیم فی ۱۰۰۴ ھ

(*Translation*)

1. "God hath borne witness that there is no god but He, and the angels, and those who are endowed with wisdom, profess the same, who executeth righteousness there is no God but He, the Mighty, the wise. In 1004 A.H. *Vide* plate).

The first band along the sides of the grave contains the Throne verse (Chap. II Verse 256), and the second band the (Nadi Ali). The third band contains the following Arabic poem in best Thulth style and the fourth band the Shiite creed, as carved on the top slab of Sultan Ibrahim (inscription No. 2) :—

The poem.

یا قا هر آ با لمنا یا کل جبا ر * بنور و جهک ا عتقنی من ا لنا ر
ا لیک اسلمنی من کان یعضدنی * من ا هل و د ی و اصحابی وانصا ر
فی قعر مظلمة قفرا ء موحشة * فر د آ غریباً وحیداً تحت ا حجا ر

امسیت ضیفک یا ذا الجود مرتهنا * وانت اکرم منزول به قار

فاجعل قرای بفضل منک مغفرة * انجوا لیک بها یا خیر غفار

ان الملوک اذا شابت عبیدهم * فی رقهم اعتقوهم (1)عتق ابرار

وانت یا سیدی اولیهم کرما * قد شبت فی الرق فاعتقنی من النار

(*Translation*)

" O controller of the deaths of all the haughty, through the light of Thy countenance save me from the fire (of Hell).

" To thee he entrusted me, he who helped me, was from among my friends, companions and supporters;

" In a pitch dark pit, desolate, dreadful, under the stones, all alone, a stranger and solitary.

" O Benevolent Lord, being mortgaged to Thee, I am Thy guest and Thou, O entertainer, art the most hospitable host.

" So with Thy grace, entertain me with forgiveness so that I may obtain refuge near Thee, O most Merciful.

" Verily the Kings when their slaves get old in their service liberate them with the magnanimity of noblemen. and Thou, O my Lord art preferentially generous. I have grown old in Thy service, therefore set me free from the fire (of Hell)." (*Vide plate*)

At the head and foot of the sarcophagus the following is inscribed in Naskh script :—

(۱) قد اتفق ارتحال المغفور المبرور ذی (۲) المناقب العلیه و المفاخر

السلاطنیه (۳) میرزا محمد امین ابن السلطان ابراهیم قطب شاه (۴) اسکنه

الله حلل المغفرة و الرضوان فی (۵) یوم الاحد الخامس و العشرین

(۶) من شهر شعبان المعظم سنه ۱۰۰۴

(*Translation*)

" The death of the departed into His Mercy, the purified, the possessor of high virtues and Royal glories, Mirza

(1) Mr. Yazdani has read this word as (عتقوهم) without the prefix (الف). (E.I.M. 1915-16 p. 30).

Muhammad Amin, son of Sultan Ibrahim Qutbshah, May God clothe him with the garments of pardon and acceptance, occurred on Sunday, the 25th of the month of Shaban-ul-Muazzam, in the year 1004." (2, March 1596 A.D.). (*Vide* Plate).

(*g*)=Good

(*h*)=Should be protected.

(*j*)=Prince Mirza Muhammad Amin was the sixth son of Sultan Ibrahim Qutbshah and father of Sultan Muhammad Qutbshah VI. His small dome is situated on the same terrace where his father's dome stands. Muhammad Amin was a learned and a literary man. He died at the early age of 25, on 25th April 1596 A.D. (1004 A.H.) His dome contains two more graves which may belong to his 2nd and fourth brothers who died in 994 and 1003 A.H., respectively, but none of these bears any inscription.

No. 52.

(*a*)= The dome of Sultan Muhammad Quli.

(*b*)=The tombs.

(*c*)=Sarf-i-Khas.

(*d*)=I-c.

(*e*)=1020 A.H., (1602 A.D.)

(*f*)=The tomb is of polished black basalt on which the Shiite creed and chapter III verse 16, the Throne Verse and verses 286 and 258 chapter II and verses 97, 109, 112 and 114, chapter III, and the Shiite Durud (the same as inscription No. 2 of Sultan Quli No. 45), are inscribed in best Tauqi' style. The following inscription is engraved in Persian language and Naskh script :—

(۱) اعلحضرت جنت مکانی عرش آشیانی محمد قلی قطب شاه بن ابراهیم قطب شاه انار الله برهانهما

(۲) بتاریخ روز شنبه هفتدهم ماه ذی القعده الحرام سنه ۱۰۲۰ هـ(۱) عشرین والف هجری برحمت حق واصل شد

(۳) سن شریفش چهل و نه سال و مدت سلطنتش سی و یک سال رحمة الله تعالی رحمتم کامله

(*Translation*)

" His Exalted Majesty, whose abode is Paradise and whose resting place is Heaven, Muhammad Quli Qutbshah son of Ibrahim Qutb Shah, May God illumine the arguments of both, was joined to God's mercy on Saturday, the 17th of the sacred month of Zil-Qadah, in the year 1020 A.H. one thousand and twenty Hijri (January 11, 1612 A.D.). His age was forty nine years and the duration of his reign thirty one years; may the Supreme God have perfect mercy on him." (*Vide* plate).

(*g*)=Good.

(*h*)=Should be protected.

(*j*)=Sultan Muhammad Quli was the third son of Ibrahim Qutbshah who ascended the throne in his fifteenth year after the demise of his father in 988 A.H. (1580 A.D.). He was born on Friday the 14th Ramzan 973 A.H. and the chronogram of his birth is[2] (با عشرت روزی اهل عالم). During his reign the Qutbshahi Kingdom was at its zenith. He was very fond of architecture, inasmuch as the city of Hyderabad is the outcome of his Architectural instinct and the Char Kaman, Char Minar, Jamay,

(1) The indication of Hijri (ھ) has been omitted after (سنه ۱۰۲۰) E. I. M. 1915-16 p. 31.

(2) Muhammad Qutbahahi.

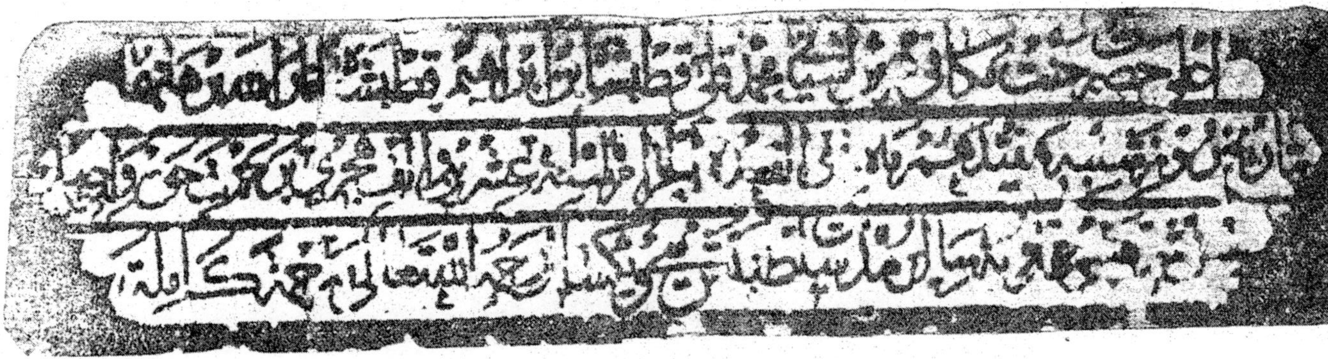

Over the Sarcophagus of Muhammad Quli V.

Muhammad Quli V.

Masjid (City) and Darush-Shifa were also built during his reign. According to the Tarikhe-Zufra the following buildings were also constructed during his reign and about 70 lacs Huns were spent over them : Ilahi Mahal, Baghe Muhammadi, Banat Ghat, Kohe Toor, Naddi Mahal, Hina Mahal, Dad Mahal, Khudadad Mahal, Langar Khana and Ashur Khana. The dome in which his remains rest was built during his lifetime. His relations with Shah Abbas I. Safavi of Persia became very friendly and consequently a Persian Embassy first came to the Deccan during his regime. Muhammad Quli was a philanthropic ruler, and had remitted a number of taxes to his subjects. After a peaceful reign of 31 years he died in his 49th year in 1020 A. H. (1611 A.D.). His grand dome with extensive double terraces is second to none among the Tombs. The elevation of the terrace is 13 ft. 6 in. The upper terrace is 200 ft. each way and the lower 126 ft. 3 inches. The outer dimensions of the dome are 71 ft. 3 inches each way and the height of the colonnades is 22 ft. There are two entrance doors to the dome on the southern and eastern sides and the dimension of the inner dome is 33 ft. 3 inches each way. A flight of steps leads to the tomb-proper which is situated in a vault below the terrace, the vaults of other Kings being closed. The year of his death may be had from the following quatrain, the last two verses of which bear the chronogram :—

محمد رفت چون از دار فانی * وصال آن شه دین سال فانی
ز قطب فضل و فضل عام جستم * دگر بار ه ز عالی جاه فیاض

سنه ۱۰۲۰ھ سنه ۱۰۲۰ھ

He was also fond of Persian and Urdu poetry and "Qutbshah" was his pen-name. The following are a few of his Persian poems :—

با شمع بگو گرم نمی دیوانه خود را * کاتش زند از رشک تو پروانه خود را
مستان محبت بد و عالم نفروشند * کیفیت نه جرعه پیمانه خود را
ای قطبشه آخر ره مردان ره عشق است * مردانه همی رو ره مردانه خود را
وله - از التفات دلبر عالی مقام ما * گردون زده است سکه شاهی بنام ما
وله - ساقی بیار باده که فصل بهار شد * صحن چمن ز آب و هوا لاله زار شد
ما اقتدا بشرب مدام تو کرده ایم * پر کن پیاله که زمان خمار شد
چشم فلک ز رشک حریفان بزم تو * چون دیده صراحئی می اشکبار شد
هر جرعه زهر غضب نوش کرده ام * از دست آن نگار مرا سازگار شد
بر وعده وصال دلش خوش کن ای حبیب * چون قطبشه ز هجر رخت بیقرار شد
وله - گهی تغافل و گاهی سلام می سوزد * چگویمت که دلم را کدام می سوزد
وله - تکیه گه قطبشاه چون دگران نیست * جز کرم دوست تکیه گاه ندارد
وله - ای قطبشه از درد دل خویش چه گویم * مشتاق تر از خویش ندیدیم و ندیدیم
وله - قطبشه دوش که در گلشن کوی بودم * ذوق کیفیت مرغان سحر دانستم
وله - اگرچه نیست زیبنده به ز عدل و داد شاهان را * ازان زیبنده تر ماند به عاشق از تو بیدادے
بملک عشق از سد سکندر کس نمی گوید * درین ملک مبارک روند اردست بنیادے
خرابی ها که دل از ترکتاز غمزه دارد * فدای آن خرابی باد معموری و آبادے
غم یارے که در دل قطبشه دارد عجب نبود * گر از خاک درش سر بر ندارد یک نفس شادے

The accompanying plate of the king was copied from the **British Museum** collection.

No. 53.

(*a*)=The dome of Muhammad son of Qutbuddin Ahmed (New).

(*b*)=In the neighbourhood of the dome of **Hakims**.

(*c*)=**Sarf-i-Khas.**

(*d*)=**II-b.**

(*e*)=**1021** A.H., (1612 A.D.).

(*f*)=**The** following inscription is engraved over the sarcophagus :—

محمد بن قطب الدین احمد سنه ۱۰۲۱

"Muhammad son of Qutbuddin Ahmad in the year **1021** H. (A. H.)"

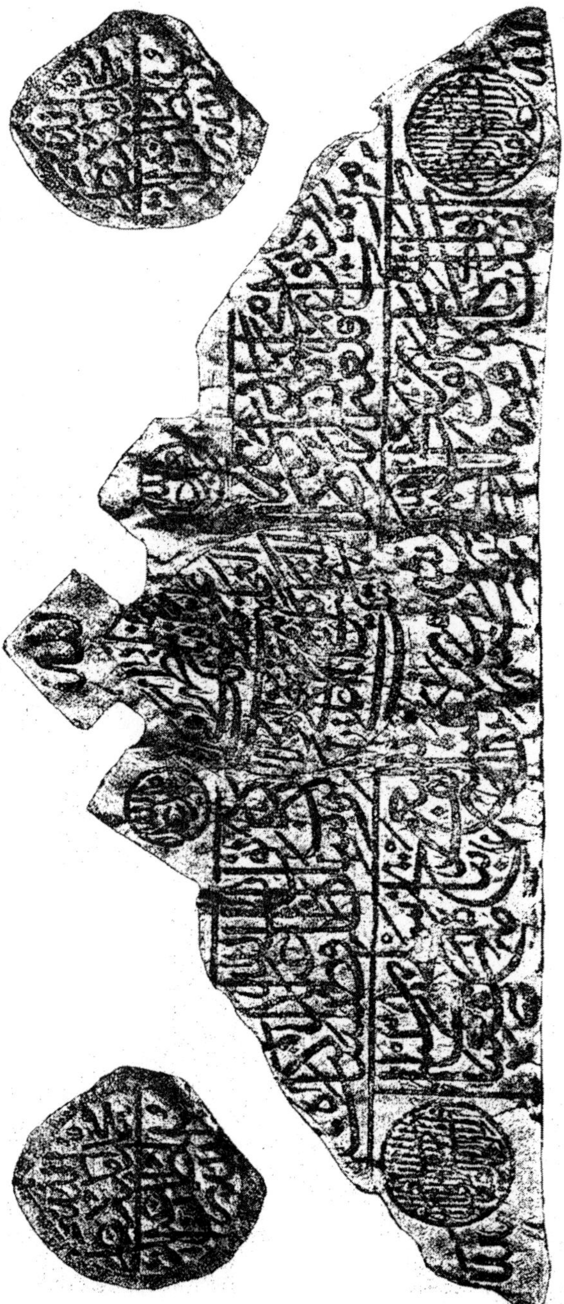

Over the Western wall of the Fort.

(*g*) = Good.

(*h*) = Should be protected.

(*j*) = This tomb belongs to Muhammad, the son of Qutbuddin, the fourth son of Sultan Quli I, who was blinded by his brother Jamshed Quli II, after his accession, and according to "Hadiqa," Qutbuddin also died in 1021 A.H.

No. 54.

(*a*) = The Western wall of the Fort.

(*b*) = Golconda fort.

(*c*) = Sarf-i-Khas.

(*d*) = II-c.

(*e*) = 1029 A.H., (1619 A.D.) 1038 A.H., (1628 A.D.)

(*f*) = The following inscription is engraved in Naskh script and Tughra style in the form of medallions. The slab on which it is inscribed measures 5 ft. 11 in. It contains two dates, the former belongs to the year of conservation of the wall and the latter to the year when the inscription was fixed.

(۱) لله

(۲) ا لله محمد علی

(۳) ا لله محمد علی مد د سلطا ن عبد ا لله ر ا

(۴) مر مت د یو ا ر قلعه محمد ا (۱) نگر د ر کا رکر د سلطا ن نوا ب عبد ا لله
قطبشا ه گشت

(۵) ملک یو سف (2) کا رگر فته ملک نور محمد شهور سنه تسع عشرین و ا لف
بتا ریخ سلخ ما ه شعبا ن سنه ۱۰۳۸ ھ

(۶) نا د علیا مظهر العجا ئب تجد ه عو نا لک فی النوا یب کل هم و غم سینجلی
بو لا یتک یا علی

(۷) لا فتی ا لا علی لا سیف ا لا ذ و ا لفقا ر

(۸) لله -

---

(1) Mr. Yazdani has read this (محمد نگر) (E.I.M. 1913-14 p. 50).

(2) Malik Yousuf a Khajasara (Steward) of Sultan Abdulla Qutbshah, was in his service from the latter's childhood. (Hadiqatus-Salatin Qutbshahi).

(*Translation*)

1. " Unto God."

2. " Allah, Muhammad, Ali."

3. " O God ! O Muhammad ! O Ali ! help Sultan Abdullah."

4. " The wall of Muhammadnagar fort was repaired under the superintendence of Sultan Nawab Abdullah Qutbshah."

5. " By Malik Yousuf a deputy of Malik Noor Muhammad during the months of the year one thousand and twenty nine. On the last day of Shaban 1038 A.H. " (1628 A.D.).

6. (Nade Ali) " Invoke Ali the manifestation of wonders Thou wilt find him a refuge in Misery.

All grief and sorrow will soon disappear.

By thy friendship (with God) O Ali."

7. " There is no soldier like Ali, and no sword like Zulfiqar."

8. " Unto God."

(*Vide* plate).

(*g*)=Fair.

(*h*)=Should be protected.

(*j*)=The weak points of this fort were strengthened from time to time with a view to sufeguard it from the dangers of Moghal attacks. The Western wall on which this inscription is fixed, was repaired during the reign of Sultan Muhammad Qutbshah, by his son Nawab Abdullah Mirza, as in the year 1029 A. H., which is given as the date of the conservation of the wall, Muhammad Qutbshah VI, was on the throne of Golconda, and at the end of Shaban 1038 A.H. whenthis inscription was

Over the Sarcophagus of Khanum Agha.

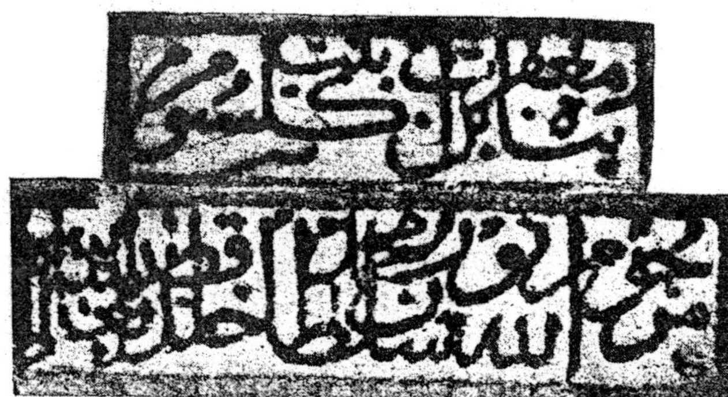

Over the grave of Kulthoom. No. 60.

fixed, Sultan Abdullah, VII, had ascended the throne.

No. 55.

(*a*)=The tomb of Khanum Agha.

(*b*)=Inside the dome of Sultan Muhammad Qutb-shah VI.

(*c*)=Sarf-i-Khas.

(*d*)=I-c.

(*e*)=1031 A.H., (1635 A.D.).

(*f*)=The following inscriptions are engraved on the sarcophagus :—

۱ لا اله الا الله محمد رسول الله علی ولی الله حقا حقا ۔ سورہ ۳ ۔ آیتہ ۶ .
سنہ ۱۰۳۱ ھ

۲ آیۃ الکرسی

۳ سورہ ۲ ۔ آیات ۲۸۵ ۔ ۲۸۶

۴ ناد علی

۵ سورہ ۹ ۔ ۱۰۹ ۔ ۱۱۲ ۔ ۴ :

۶ درود شریف

۷ علیا حضرت خدیجہ مرتبت مریم مکانی بلقیس زمانی صالحہ عفیفہ رابعہ
راکعہ ساجدہ صائمہ خانم آغا (۱)

(*Translation*)

1. (*Shiite Creed*) " There is no god but God and Muhammad is the prophet of God and Ali is the favourite of God, without any doubt." and " Quran Chap. III verse 16, The year 1031 A.H."

2. " Throne verse, Quran (chap. II verse 256) ".

---

(1) Mr. Yazdani does not seem to have followed the construction of the epitaph and consequently he has named this lady as (صائمہ خانم) instead of (خانم آغا), further he could not prove her identity, as in his opinion she was " probably a princess of the family." The word (آ) after (خانم) is the abbreviation of (آغا), as according to the Persian technology the proper name (آغا میرزا) is spoken as well as written (آمیرزا) According to the Hadiqa-tus-salatin it is proved that (آغا خانم) was buried in the dome of Muhammad Qutbshah (E.I.M. 1915-16, p. 32).

3. " Chap. II. verses 285-286."

4. " Nadi Ali."

5. " Chap. XCVII, CVI and CXII-CXIV."

6. " Shiite Durud."

7. " Her Highness in rank like Khadija, in position like Mary, the Bilqis of the age, the pious and chaste (like) Rabia, the bower of her head in prayer, the prostrator with the forehead touching the ground, the observer of fast, Khanum Agha." (*Vide* plate).

(*g*)=Good.

(*h*)=Should be protected.

(*j*)=The tomb of Khanum Agha daughter of Mir Maqsud Ali—Tabataba and wife of Prince Mirza Muhammad Amin, is of polished black basalt and is situated within the dome of her son Sultan Muhammad Qutbshah. She was buried here during the reign of her son; and wielded much influence during his regime. The Tank of Ma-Saheba was built by her; for further details please refer to Nos. 15 and 61.

No. 56.

(*a*)=Baradari of Pemmati.

(*b*)=On the southern side of the Golconda fort.

(*c*)=Sarf-i-Khas

(*d*)=II-b.

(*e*)=1035 A.H., (1625 A.D.)

(*f*)=None.

(*g*)=Requires conservation.

(*h*)=Should be protected.

(*j*)=On the South-Western side of the fort on the road to Osman Sagar, on two elevated terraces nearly 150 ft. square each way are situated the Baradari of Pemamati and Taramati of arched corridor and a small mosque with decagonal minarets on the opposite terrace. These girls were concubines of Sultan Abdullah Qutbshah and Sultan Muhammad Qutbshah. The Baradari and the mosque may be reached by climbing three storeys containing about 70 steps. On careful investigation of the precincts it was found that Ibrahim Bagh of Sultan Ibrahim Qutbshah (d. 988 A.H.), terminates at the base of the mosque and it extends as far as "Mahallat," (the Royal Palaces), which are situated a few furlongs behind the mosque and where ruins of lofty palaces may still be seen. It is interesting to note that the garden with a few mangoe trees is still called Ibrahim Bagh. It may therefore be inferred that the Baradari and the mosque were built later, during the reigns of Sultan Abdullah and Muhammad Qutbshah, on the outskirts of the garden and served as the main entrance to Ibrahim Bagh and during the construction of these lofty edifices the garden must have been in a bloomy condition and a favourite royal resort.

No. 57.

(*a*)=The dome of Fatima Sultan.

(*b*)=Golconda tombs.

(*c*)=Sarf-i-Khas.

(*d*)=II-c.

(*e*)=1035 A.H., (1665 A.D.)

(*f*)=The following inscriptions are engraved on polished black basalt :—

۱- لا اله الا الله محمد رسول الله علی ولی الله حقا حقا سنه ۱۰۳۵ ه

۲- آیتہ الکرسی

۳- سورہ ۲ - آیتہ ۲۸۵ - ۲۸۶

۴- نا د علی صیغر-علیا حضرت مریم مکانی خدیجہ مرتبت زهرا ی(۱)
ثا نی (2)نا طمہ سلطا ن بنت سلطا ن محمد ا مین

۵- سورہ ۹۷ - ۱۰۹ - ۱۱۲ - ۱۱۵

۶- د ر و د شریف

(*Translation*)

1. " Shiite creed. In the year 1035 A.H. "
2. " Throne verse."
3. " Chap. 2 Verses 285—286."
4. " Nande Ali."
5. " Her Highness of Mary's position and Khadija's station, next in rank to Zahra, Fatima Sultan daughter of Sultan Muhammad Amin." (*vide* plate).
6. " Shiite Durud."

The next grave is also inscribed as follows although it bears no name :—

۱- نا د علی - کلمه طیبه

۲- آیتہ ا لکرسی

۳- سورہ ۱ - آیا ت ۱۱۲ - ۱۱۴

(*Translation*)

1. " Nade Ali "—" Shiite creed."
2. " Throne Verse."
3. " Chap. 1 Verses CXII, CXIV."

(*g*)=Fair.

(*h*)=Should be protected.

=This dome, which belongs to Fatima Sultan who was the daughter of Prince Muhammad Amin and Khanum Agha and sister of Sultan Mu-

---

(1) Although this tomb belongs to (نا طمہ سلطا ن) but instead of (زهرای) which is a commendatory phrase. Mr. Yazdani reads it (زهرا بی) and takes her to be the wife of Md. Amin, while this tomb belongs to the daughter of Md. Amin. The appendage (بی) was not customary in the Qutbshahi days, Nowadays (بی) is a debased form of the old word (بی بی) which was in vogue in the Qutbshahi period.

(2) Mr. Yazdani's reading of this word is (بانی) meaning builder. (E.I.M. 1915-16, p. 34).

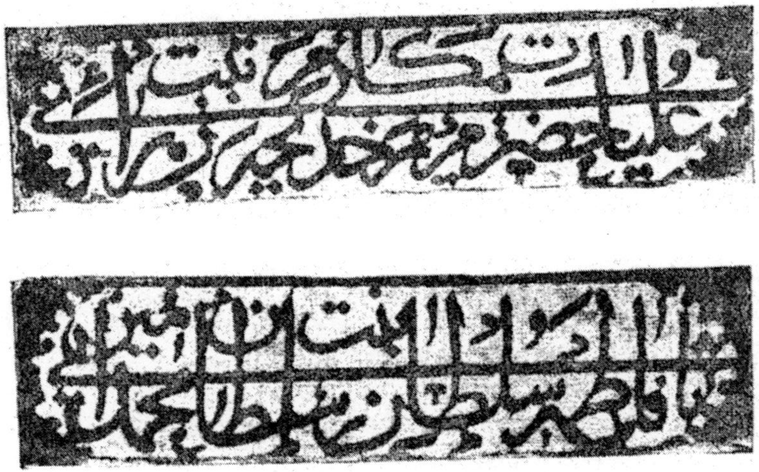

Over the grave of Fatima Sultan. No. 57.

Sarcophagus of Muhammad Qutbshah VI. Nos. 1 & 2.

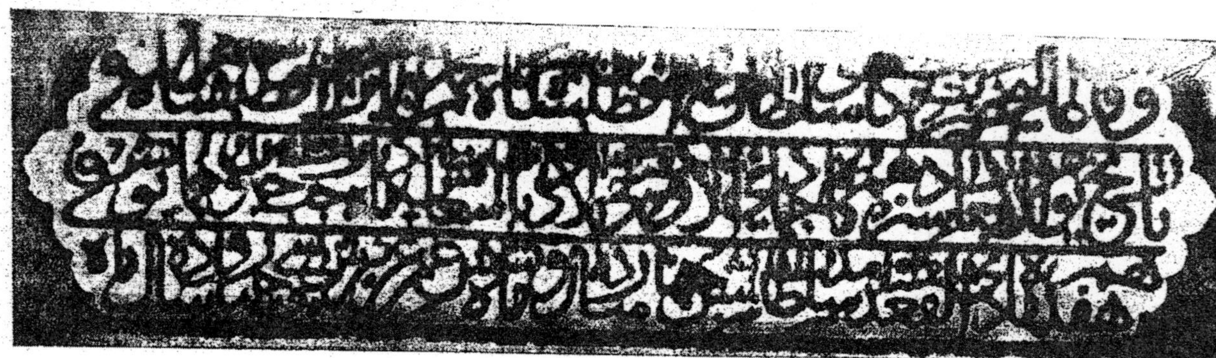

Md. Qutbshah's Tomb. No. 7.

hammad Qutbshah VI, is situated to the left of the entrance of the Tombs; it contains several graves, two of which are inscribed, one belonging to Fatima Sultan and the other bearing no name. It has a disproportionately large dome.

No. 58.

(*a*)=The Mousoleum of Sultan Muhammad VI.
(*b*)=The Tombs.
(*c*)=Sarf-i-Khas.
(*d*)=I-c.
(*e*)=1035 A.H., (1626 A.D.).
(*f*)=The following inscription is engraved on a sarcophagus of polished black basalt in Tulth and Naskh styles :—

۱- لا اله الا الله محمد رسول الله علی ولی الله حقا حقا
۲- شهد الله انه لا اله الا هو والملائکة واولو العلم قائما بالقسط لا اله الا هو العزیز الحکیم فی ع ۱۰۳ (۱)
۳- آیة الکرسی
۴- سورة ۲ - آیات ۲۸۵-۲۸۶
۵- سورة ۹۷ - ۱۰۹ ۱۱۲ - ۱۱۴
۶- درود شریف
۷-
(۱) وفات عالی حضرت جنت مکانی سلطان محمد قطب شاه ابن (2) میرزا محمد امین ابن (3) ابراهیم قطبشاه فی
(۲) تاریخ یوم الاربعا سیزدهم جمادی الاولی سنه ۱۰۳۵ ولادت باسعادتش در ماه رجب سنه ۱۰۰۱ جلوس همایونش فی
(۳) هفدهم ماه ذی القعد سنه ۱۰۲۰ مدت سلطنتش چهار ده سال و شش ماه عمر عزیزش سی وچهار سال و ده ماه۔

---

(1) Mr. Yazdan has read this as 1035. It must however be borne in mind that in Persia the numeral 6, is written in this way (ع ع) and in Egypt and Constantinople the numeral 4 is written thus (ع) (E.I.M. 1915-16 p. 32).

(2) and (3) The word (الف) has been omitted before (ابن). (E.I.M. 1915-16 p. 32).

(*Translation*)

1. " Shiite creed."
2. " Quran Chap. III. Verse 16., In 1036 (A.H.)." (*vide* plate).
3. " Throne Verse (Chap. II. verse 256)."
4. " Chap. 2 Verses 285-286."
5. " Chap. 97, 109, 112, 114."
6. " Shiite Darud."
7. " The death of his exalted Majesty, of heavenly abode Muhammad Qutbshah, son of Mirza Muhammad Amin, son of Ibrahim Qutbshah, occurred on Wednesday, the 13th of Jamadi I, 1035 (Feb. 1-1626 A.D.). His felicitous birth in the month of Rajab 1001 (April 1593 A.D.). His auspicious accession on the 17th of Zil-Qada 1020 (January 11, 1612 A.D.). The duration of his reign was fourteen years and six months and the period of his honoured life thirty-four years and ten months." (*vide* plate).

On the top slab the years (۱۰۳ع) 1036 A.H. in line (2) and 1035 in line (7) represent the dates of fixing the slab and the death of the King respectively. Hadiqatus-Salatin also corroborates this fact and lays down that "on the forenoon of Wednesday the 13th Jamadil-Awal 1035 Hijri Sultan Muhammad Qutbshah expired in the Daulatkhanae Ali (Royal Palace), (which was situated near the Kali Kaman), and in the afternoon his remains were removed to Golconda in the Langare-Faiz-Athar, to be interred in the dome which he had built for this purpose in his lifetime."

(*g*)=Good.

(*h*)=Should be protected.

(*j*)=Sultan Muhammad Qutbshah was born on 23rd Rajab 1001 (1593 A.D.). He was the only son of Prince Mirza Muhammad Amin and Khanum Agha and a nephew and son-in-law of Muhammad Quli Qutbshah. According to the Tawarikhe-Farkhunda (MSS) on the day of his birth the reigning sovereign Sultan Muhammad Quli Qutbshah, prevailed upon his brother Prince Mirza Muhamamd Amin, to let him adopt the boy as he had no male issue, asserting that he being young would have many more sons ; but Prince Amin procrastinated until four years later after the death of Prince Amin, Muhammad Quli took the boy in his own charge and appointed Qazi Muhammad Samnani for his tuition and also Yousuf Saheb, a famous soldier who used to teach swordsmanship, archery and horse-riding to the whole city, was appointed to teach these arts to the young prince, who had also become the heir-apparent to the throne. This Yousuf Saheb died in 1028 A.H. and was buried near Nampalli where his tomb, is held in great veneration. When the young prince reached the age of 14, the daughter of Sultan Muhammad Quli was given in marriage to him in 1015 A.H. One Mirak Moin of Sabzwar composed a quatrain on this occasion, the last hemistich contains the year of marriage ۱۰۱۵ ھ (مہر و مہر عید مولودی و بزم شہ و عقد). When he attained his majority he ascended the throne of his uncle in his 21st year. Mir Muhammad Momin of Subzwar composed a long poem, a few couplets of which are given below. The eighth hemistich gives the year of the accession.

با محبت باز بستم عہد وپیمان نوے * کہنہ جا می می فشانم پیش جانان نوے
سر مرشد خاک تلنگانہ زفرخ پای تو * ای فدای خاک پایت هر زمان جان نوے

گر صفاهان نو شد از شاه جهان عباس شاه * حیدر آباد از تو شد شاها صفاهان نوے
خواستم تاریخ فرخنده جلوست عقل گفت * جمله عالم نو بهاری شد ز سلطان نوے (۱۰۲۰ھ)
از دعا گوئی چو مومن هم دعا بهتر که هست * او کهن داعی و تو شاها جهان بان نوے

Sultan Muhammad was a great friend of learning and was a very pious King. He used to recite one chapter of the Quran every morning and invariably used to finish the recitation of the whole of the Quran every month. Most of his time was spent in the company of learned men. He was the founder of the famous Mecca Masjid, and an initial amount of 40,000 huns[1] was spent by him on this stately edifice. The histories of this period were first written during his reign, notably the Tarikhe-Sultan Muhammad Qutbshahi (MSS) which, contains an exhaustive and authoritative account of the inauguration of Qutbshahi dynasty until 1020 A.H. and the Hadiqatus-Salatin Qutbshahi (MSS) which is really a compendium of the above history, was written by Nizamuddin, during the reign of his son Sultan Abdullah VII. His contemporary Moghal Emperor was Jahangir, and during his reign Hyderabad was for the first time visited by a Prince of the Moghal blood in 1025 A.H. When Khurram (Shah Jahan) made Muhammad Qutbshah pay him a Peshkash of 14 lacs of rupees for his father, as an indemnity for the hostile assistance rendered by him to Nizam Shah of Ahmadnagar, against Jahangir[2].

This pious king died after a short reign of 15 years in 1035 A.H., (1625 A.D.). This Chronogram was composed by Ibne-Khatoon (No. 22) on this occasion (لب باد سنه ۱۰۳۵ھ حشرش به علی بن ابیطا). He left four sons and one daughter. The first issue was Prince Abdullah Mirza (Qutbshah VII) the second was a daughter who was married in 1042 A.H. to Sultan Muhammad Adil Shah of Bijapur. The third was Prince Ibrahim Mirza, who was born of the daughter of Sultan Ibrahim Adilshah of Bijapur and who died in the

(1) Hadiqatus Salatin (MSS).

(2) Hadiqatul-Alam.

second regnal year of Sultan Abdullah Qutbshah and was buried in the dome of Muhammad Qutbshah. The author of Hadiqatus-Salatin relates this curious incident that on the day of Ibrahim Mirza's birth, the Ilahi Mahal, Muhammadi Mahal and Hydar Mahal which were built in seven spacious storeys by Sultan Muhammad Quli, caught fire and the whole building was burnt to ashes. The fourth and fifth were Prince Sultan Quli Mirza and Prince Mirza Kamal born of his favourite wife Khurshid Bibi, who had predeceased her husband and was buried close to the dome of Sultan Abdullah. The above mentioned Prince Sultan Quli Mirza had attempted to commit suicide by taking powdered diamond in 1047 A.H. but owing to the timely succour of Sultan Abdullah the Royal physicians administered antidotes and he was recovered. He died a natural death in 1052 A.H. and was buried in the dome of Muhammad Qutbsh ah VI. The Mousoleum of Sultan Muhammad Qutbshah VI, ranks next in grandeur to the tomb of Muhammad Quli. It comprises a square hall, 63′ 4″ each way and the width of the colonnade is 19′ 8″. The facade of this dome had enamelled tiles, traces of which still exist. Besides the tomb of Sultan Muhammad Qutbshah there are five more[1] graves in this dome, two of which have been cracked by the effects of lightning. Of these graves the two, which bear inscriptions are herein noticed in their chronological order (*vide* 55 and 61) and the rest are uninscribed. Sultan Muhammad Qutbshah was also fond of poetry like his uncle, his *nom-de-guerre* was " Urooji " and " Zillul-lah ," a selection of his poems is given below.

---

(1) In the Western sofa are buried Shah Khundkar and Khanum Agha, the third tomb belongs to Prince Sultan Quli Mirza son of Sultan Muhammad Qutbshah who died in Zil Qada 1052 A.H.

Among the small graves of childern one belongs to the young Prince Ibrahim Mirza, son of Muhammad Qutbshah, who died in the 2nd regnal year of Abdullah Qutbshah and the other is the tomb of the seven-month old son of Abdullah Qutbshah who expired on 29th Jamadi II 1042 Hijri. (New) (Hadiqatus-Salatin).

در حضرتت یقین وگمان را چوراه نیست * حیران وصف تست یقین وگمان ما
ظل الله از شر و زبدان در پناه تست * ای درگه جلال تو دار الامان ما
وله تعالی الله چه حسن است این بنازم صنع یزدان را * که در آینه روی تو دیدم صورت جان را
وله دماغ وطبع عروجی چه دلکشا چمن است * چنین مگو که خود آسمان فر هنگ است
وله عز وجاه هم ز عشق و دولت او ست * این همه حشمتم بهمت او ست
مست از باده نیست ظل الله * سرخوش از باده محبت او ست
وله مدعی گرد عوی دارد مسلم داشتیم * روشنست باداکه ظل الله عوید ار نیست
وله تا تو در دل آمدی غیرے ندارد در درو * در حریم خاص شه نامحرمان را بار نیست

No. 59.

(*a*)=The dome of Kulthoom Begam (New).

(*b*)=To the south of the dome of Sultan Muhammad Quli Qutbshah, on the Western side.

(*c*)=Sarf-i-Khas.

(*d*)=II-c.

(*e*)=The reign of Sultan Muhammad Qutbshah.

(*f*)=None.

(*g*)=Fair.

(*h*)=Should be protected.

(*j*)=This dome contains three uninscribed tombs, the one to the West is said to be of Kulthoom Begam, the second and third are said to be those of her husband and daughter. Through the main road leading to Golconda near Mustaidpura, there exists a bye-lane which is called Kulthoompura, named after this lady where there is a nice mosque built by her which is in an excellent state of preservation. The main gate of the mosque bears the following inscription :—

(الله محمد علی)

No. 60.

(*a*)=The pavilion of Kulthoom.

(*b*)=West to the Golconda tombs.

(*c*)=Sarf-i-Khas.

(*d*)=II-b.

(*e*)=1037 A.H., (1627 A.D.)

(*f*)=The following inscriptions are engraved in Thulth :—

۱- سورہ ۳ - آیت ۱۶ ؛ - ۱۹ سنہ ۱۰۳۷ ہ

۲- لا الہ الا اللہ محمد رسول اللہ علی ولی اللہ حقا حقا

۳- آیتہ الکرسی

۴- درود شریف

۵- کلثوم (۱) بنت ابن مغفرت پناہ مرحومی نور اللہ سلطان قطبشاہ
خلداللہ تعالی

(*Translation*)

1. "Chap. 3 verse 16—The year 1037 A.H." (Top slab).

2. "Shiite creed."

3. "Throne Verse."

---

(1) Mr. Yazdani's decipherment of this inscription does not stand the historical test. He reads it thus
(مغفرت پناہ ابن کلثوم بنت مرحومن نور اللہ سلطان محمدقطبشاہ خلد اللہ تعالی)
and he describes the grave to be that of an infant grandson of Muhammad Qutbshah by his daughter Kulthoom. But according to the Hadiqatus Salatin, Muhammad Qutbshah had only one daughter and she was given in marriage to Muhammad Adil shah of Bijapur, where she remained as the Queen of that realm ; consequently this grave cannot be that of his grandson, by his so-called daughter Kulthoom. In the author's humble opinion this tomb belongs to Kulthoom, who was the grand-daughter of Muhammad Qutbshah, and the father of this child was the son of his favourite wife Khurshid Bibi and who according to "Hadiqa," died in 1052 A.H. Moreover if Mr. Yazdani's decipherment is taken to be correct there remains no alternative but to attribute the suffix of (خلد اللہ تعالی) towards Muhammad Qutbshah, in 1037 A.H. which is the year of the epitaph *vide* the top slab), although he had expired in 1035 A.H. and the words (خلد اللہ تعالی)) according to the Arabic philology being patent words for the living Kings and Princes, cannot be assigned to a dead body. It therefore follows that the suffix of (خلد اللہ تعالی) relates to the (ابن) son of Muhammad Qutbshah, whose name was Sultan Quli Mirza and who was alive at the time: and the prefixes of (مغفرت پناہ) and (نور اللہ مرحومن) are quite appropriate for Muhammad Qutbshah in 1037 rather than (خلد اللہ تعالی). (E.I.M. 1915-16 p. 34.).

4. " **Shiite Durud.'**

5. Kulthoom daughter of the son of Sultan Muhammad Qutbshah, whose sins have been forgiven (and who is), expectant of the light of God. May God keep him (the son) for ever." (*vide* plate).

(*g*)=**Fair.**

(*d*)=**Should be protected.**

(*j*)=This small pavillion which is open on all sides contains a small grave of an infant girl who was the grand-daughter of Sultan Muhammad Qutbhsah. The word (کلثوم) has been wrongly spelt with (س) instead of (ث) in this inscription.

No. 61.

(*a*)=**The tomb of Shah Khundkar.**

(*b*)=**Inside the dome of Sultan Muhammad Qutbshah.**

(*c*)=**Sarf-i-Khas.**

(*d*)=**I-c.**

(*e*)=**1045 A.H., (1635 A.D.)**

(*f*)=The following inscriptions are engraved on the sarcophagus in Thulth style and Tauqi' script :—

۱- لا آلہ الا اللہ محمد رسول اللہ علی ولی اللہ حقا حقا - سورہ ۳۶ - آیتہ
۱۶ سنہ ۱۰۴۵ ھ

۲- آیتہ الکرسی

۳- سورہ ۲ - آیات ۲۸۵ - ۲۸۶

۴- ناد علی صغیر

۵- سورہ - ۹۷ - ۱۹۱ - ۱۱۲ - ۱۱۴

۶- درود شریف

۷- عالیحضرت سیادت و نجابت پناه مغفرت و مرحمت دستگاه شاه خوندکار(1)
ابن سیادت پناه شاه محمد الحسینی (2)

(*Translation*)

1. " Shiite creed—Chap. 3 Verse 16, the year 1045 A.H."

2. " Throne Verse."

3. " Quran Chap. 3 Verses 285-86."

4. " Nadi Ali."

5. " Chap. XCVII, CIX, CXII and CXIV."

6. " Shiite Durud."

7. " His Highness, the refuge of the Sayyids and persons of noble birth, enjoying Divine forgiveness and mercy, Shah Khundkar, son of the refuge of Sayyids, Shah Muhammadul-Husaini." (*vide* Plate).

(*g*)=Fair.

(*h*)=Should be protected.

(*j*)=Shah Khundkar was the grandson of Kahnum Agha and a cousin of Abdullah Qutbshah. His father Shah Muhammad son of Shah Ali Arabshah, had married the sister of Muhammad Qutbshah and daughter of Prince Muhammad Amin and Khanum Agha. According to the " Hadiqa" in the 1st regnal year of Sultan Abdullah, Shah Muhammad held the post of Peshwa for a period of two years on 1,000

---

(1) Mr. Yazdani has described (شاه خوندکار) as " the spiritual guide of the royal family, " although he was closely related to the Royal family as being the grandson of Khanum Agha, and his mother having been (according to the Hadiqa) the sister of Muhammad. Qutbshah. (E.I.M. 1917-18 p. 33).

(2) Mr. Yazdani instead of identifying this gentleman, says that "this was the name of the famous saint of Gulburga." In fact this gentleman had married the (according to the Hadiqa) sister of Muhammad Qutbshah and the daughter of Khanum Agha and held the post of Peshwa during the reign of Abdullah Qutbshah, on 1,000 huns per month. Thus he was closely related to the Royal family. (E.I.M. 1917-18 p. 33)

huns per month, but as he did not prove equal to the task, the post of Peshwa was conferred on Ibne-Khatoon (No. 22). Shah Kundkar was the recipient of an annuity of 7,000 huns during the reign of Sultan Abdullah and had the honour of sitting on the right side of the Royal throne. The Tank of Ma-Saheba (No. 16) was given as a freehold to the same Shah Khundkar (No. 61).

No. 62.

(*a*)=Inscription of Musa-Burj.

(*b*)=Close to the steps of Musa Burj.

(*c*)=Sarf-i-Khas.

(*d*)=II-c.

(*e*)=1050 A.H., (1640 A.D.).

(*f*)=To the North of Musa Burj close to the steps, the following inscription in Nastaliq script is fixed. It measures (2′ 8″×2′ 6″).

۱- در زمان دولت پادشاه والاجاه
۲- سلطان عبد الله قطب شاه
۳- بنده دولتخواه خیرات خان
۴- بنای این ملگیها وچاه آب وباغ
۵- نمود فی شهر رجب سنه ۱۰۵۰

(*Translation*)

" During the regime of the exalted King Sultan Abdullah Qutbshah, the well-wishing servant of the State, Khairat Khan built these shops, well and garden, in the month of Rajab 1050 (A.H.) " (November 1602 A.D.).

(*Vide* Plate).

(*g*)=Fair.

(*h*)=Should be protected.

(*j*)=The inscription records the building of shops, etc., by one Khairat Khan, whose grave was discovered by me by chance, while I was engaged in finding out the grave of Syed Muzaffar

North of Musa Burj.

Ambar Khana. No. 63.

Once Khairat Khan had the honour of taking a letter and presents from Sultan Abdullah to the Emperor Shah Jahan. For his full description please refer to No. 20.

No. 63.

(*a*)=Ambar Khana (Granary).

(*b*)=Close to the Citadel (Baradari) of Golconda Fort.

(*c*)=Sarf-i-Khas.

(*d*)=II-c.

(*e*)=1052 A.H., (1642 A.D.).

(*f*)=This inscription which measures (2′ 9″×1′ 11″) is carved on black stone in Nasta'liq script.

۱- در عهد دولت پادشاه جمجاه
۲- ملایک سپاه سلطان عبد الله
۳- قطبشاه بسعی بنده درگاه خیرات خان
۴- این انبارخانه باتمام رسید
۵- بتاریخ شهر رجب المرجب سنه ۱۰۵۲ ه

(*Translation*)

During the regime of the King Sultan Abdullah Qutbshah, equal in rank to Jamshed, whose army is the heavenly host, this storehouse (granary) was completed by the endeavours of the slave of court, Khairat Khan, in the month of Rajab, the year 1052 A.H." (October 1642 A.D.). (*Vide* Plate)

(*g*)=Fair.

(*h*)=Should be protected.

(*j*)=Halfway up the ascent towards the Baradari (citadel) of the fort may be seen the ruins of some chambers, called Ambar Khana where a stone slab is fixed in a slanting position. Its original place had been over the front door.

No. 64.

(*a*)=The twin domes of Hakims. (New).

(*b*)=Golconda Tombs.

(*c*)=Sarf-i-Khas.

(*d*)=II-c.

(*e*)=1062 A.H., (1651 A.D.).

(*f*)=One of the tombs of these twin—domes contain the following inscription which is engraved in Thulth script and Tughra style. The other grave is uninscribed.

۱- هوا لعالی ا لعظیم سنه ۱۰۶۲ ھ

۲- نا د علی

۳- آیتہ ا لکرسی

۴- د رود شریف

(*Translation*)

1. (Top slab) " He is eminent and magnificient. In the year 1062 A.H."

2. " Nade Ali. "

3. " Throne Verse. "

4. " Shiite Durud. "

(*g*)=Good.

(*h*)=Should be protected.

(*j*)=The twin pavillions of the Hakims are situated side by side and are open on all sides. The sarcophagus of these domes are of highly polished black basalt. Bats have made their nests in the roof as a result of which it is always filled with filth and offensive smell. Although the names of these Hakims are not mentioned on the grave, but they are said to have been favourite physicians of Sultan Abdullah. The author is inclined to assign these tombs to

Hakim Nizamuddin Ahmad Gilani, Hakimul Mulk, who was appointed a Royal physician [1] in 1045 A.H., by Sultan Abdullah in place of Hakim Gabriel, on 6,000 huns per annum, and to Hakim Abdul Jabbar Gilani, who also became a favourite Hakim of the Court in 1045 A.H., and being very handsome, he was also appointed to read Hadith in the presence of the King during the month of Moharrum[2].

About 2 miles North of Tolichauki over the top of the hill of Hakim Pet, are situated a small Baradari and a dome with a mosque. The dome contains grave of an unknown Hakim[3] of the reign of Abdullah; the sarcophagus is one peice of oblong black basalt measuring (4′ 3″ × 2½′) with the following inscription.

الحکم لله سنه ۱۰۵۹

"The command is for God. The year 1059 (A. H.)"

In the tower of a tank below the Baradari some Persian couplets were engraved in plaster, which have now become hopelessly obliterated. Out of many I could with much difficulty, decipher the following of Hafiz.

چه گویمت که بمیخانه دوش مست و خراب * سروش عالم غیبم چه مژدها داد است
که ای بلند نظر شاهباز سدره نشین * نشیمن تو نه این کنج محنت آباد است
ترا ز کنگره عرش می زنند صفیر * ندانمت که درین خاکدان چه افتاد است
نصیحتی کنمت یاد گیر و در عمل آر * که این حدیث ز پیر طریقتم یاد است
مجو درستی عهد از جهان سست نهاد * که این عجوزه عروس هزار داماد است

(1) and (2) *Vide* Hadiqatus Salatin (MSS) and Muhammad Qutbshah (MSS). (3) I am inclined to assign this to Hakim Gabriel.

The hill commands a fine birdseye view, but it could only be reached after walking about a mile and a half in the uneven paddy fields.

No. 65.

(*a*)=The Domes of Pemmati and Taramati.

(*b*)=Golconda tombs.

(*c*)=Sarf-i-Khas.

(*d*)=II-c.

(*e*)=1073 A.H., (1662 A.D.).

(*f*)=The following inscriptions are engraved on the grave of Pemmati, in Nasta'liq :—

۱- سورہ ۳-آیتہ۱۶

۲- سورہ ۲-آیتہ۲۵۶

۳- درود شریف مختصر

۴- بود از ازل گل جنتی پیم متی سنہ ۱۰۷۳

۵- گل جنتی بود از ازل پیم متی سنہ ۱۰۷۳ (1)

(*Translation*)

1. (Top Slab) " Chap. 3, verse 16. "
2. Chap." 2 Verse 256, and Chap. CXII. "
3. " Shiite Durud. "
4. " From eternity Pemmati was a rose of Paradise 1073." (1662 A.D.).
5. " A rose of Paradise was from eternity, Pemmati 1073." (*Vide* Plate).

(1) Inscription No. 5 has been entirely omitted in his reading by Mr. Yazdani. (E.I.M. 1915-16 p. 36).

(*g*)=Good.

(*h*)=Should be protected.

(*j*)=The names Bhagmati, Pem Mati and Tara Mati occur frequently in the Qutbshahi history. The present dome belongs to Pemmati who was a concubine of Sultan Abdullah Qutbshah and the dome was erected by the same king. The inscription No. 4 is engraved on the opposite side of the sarcophagus (*vide* No. 5) with a little verbal alteration.

Another twin dome next to that of Pemmati, is said to be that of Tara Mati who also was a concubine of Sultan Muhammad but it contains no inscription.

No. 66.

(*a*)=**Musa Burj.**

(*b*)=**Golconda fort.**

(*c*)=**Sarf-i-Khas.**

(*d*)=**I-c.**

(*e*)=**1077 A.H., (1666 A.D.).**

(*f*)=At present the following Persian inscription is fixed on the wall of the first storey west of the flight of stairs. Apparently this is not in its original position, but was fixed here after the renovation of the steps. The upper portion of the tablet has been slightly broken, as a result of which the first line of the inscription is missing, it measures (3′ 9½″ ×1′ 4½″). A translation of this Persian inscription is also fixed on the southern wall in Telugu script, a transliteration of which is given below after the Persian text. The author considers it a piece of singular good fortune for having been able to trace this inscription in a book[1] in which it has been completely reproduced, thus the missing link of the first line, which owing to obvious reasons was omitted by Mr. Yazdani (in E. I. M. 1913-14 p. 52) has now been completed. The Telugu text fully corroborates the name of Mir Miran which has been now deciphered in the first line of the Persian text.

My reading of the Persian text in addition to the first line which has been borrowed from the Tarikhe Farkhunda is as follows :—

۱- به میرمیران (2)حکم عالی صادر گردید که شما قایم بوده مورچه و نقب را (۱)
۲- (ر) انزدیک این برج تا بخندق رسانید چون درینجا
۳- برج کوچک بود اما حکم جهان مطاع عالم مطیع خسرو
۴- زمان شهنشاه دوران السلطان العادل ظل الله
۵- ابو المظفر ابو المنصور ابو الغازی سلطان عبد الله
۶- قطبشاه به دستور (3) الوزراء فی الزمان مقرب
۷- الحضرت السلطانیه معتمد الدوله الخاقانیه
۸- خان ذی شان سپه سالاری موسی خان
۹- چنان شرف صدور یافت که خود درینجا
۱۰- بوده به دفع غنیم مشغول باشد بر آن خان
۱۱- عالیشان شب و روز بهشیاری تمام در دفع
۱۲- غنیم بودن (4) از قضاء ربانی غلوله توپ بروجون
۱۳- میرمیران چنان خورد که در همان مورچه
۱۴- هلاک گشت و بعد از فوت او بسه روز صلح
۱۵- شد و بعد از گذاشتن محاصره به خان
۱۶- مشار الیه حکم عالی شد که برج عظیم درینجا بنا
۱۷- باید کرد تا غنیم را فرصت نقب مورچه کندن
۱۸- مجال بنا شد بنا بر حکم همایون اعلی

(1) Tawarikhe Farkhunda (MSS).

(2) Out of the first line only the following was deciphered by Mr Yazdani (قایم کرده مورچه و نقب را) (E.I.M. 1913-14 p. 52.)

(3) Mr. Yazdani's reading is (بدستور) (*Ibid.*)

(4) Mr. Yazdani's reading is (بوده) and according to the construction it ought to have been (بودند) (*Ibid.*)

Musa Burj.

Sarcophagus of Pemmati. No. 65.

Sarcophagus of Shah Khundkar. No. 61.

۱۹ باندک زمانی این برج عظیم بسعی خان موصوف

۲۰ اتمام رسید در سال سنه هزار و هفتاد و هفت (1)

۲۱ و اسم معمار دهرما چار

(*Translation*)

" The exalted order (of Emperor Aurangzeb) was issued to Mir Miran that he should establish himself and carry the intrenchment and mines to the ditch, as at this place was a small bastion. But the order—obeyed by the world and respected in the universe, of the Lord of the time, the emperor of the period, the just Sultan, the shadow of God, Abul Muzaffar, Abul Mansur, Abul Ghazi, Sultan Abdullah Qutb-shah, to the wazir of the wazirs of the time, the confidence of the Royal court, the trust of the State, the Khan of high rank, the commander-in-chief, Musa Khan, had the honour of issuing to this effect, that he himself be at the spot and occupy himself in repelling the enemy day and night. Thereupon the exalted Khan with all caution was engaged day and night in checking the enemy. In the meantime by the divine decree a gun shot struck the body of Mir Miran in such a manner that he expired in that very intrenchment, and three days after his death peace was concluded. When the siege had been raised the supreme orders were issued to the above named Khan that a large bastion be built at this place, so that the enemy might not get an opportunity to dig intrenchments and mines. In obedience to the auspicious, exalted order, through the efforts of the aforesaid Khan, this large bastion was completed within a short time, in the year one thousand and seventy seven (A.H.) and the architect's name (is) Dharmachar."

TELUGU TEXT.[2]

(*Piece I.*)

1. " Svasti, Sri Jay—abhyudaya —Saliva (ha)
2. na-Saka-varshalu 1578 Manmatha—nama—sa

(1) In Tarikhe Farkhunda this date is mentioned as 1080 A.H.

(2) Deciphered and translated by Rao Saheb H. Krishna Sastri of Madras.

3. mavatsara—Magha-sudha Budhavaram na
4. du Sulutanu Auramgujebu Kha
5. Saru (sa) haji Sangina laskaruto va-
6. chchi kile mubaraku Mahamada-
7. (na) garu bedavesi vumdamganu va-
8. ri padushahi—vajilalo pedda va-
9. Jirudu—Miru—Mira ani atani A-
10. varamgujebu touttu yi durgam
11. Mudu-dinalku puchchukomttunnan-a-
12. ni mocha—ratri-pagalu chhala netu-

(*Piece II*)

13. —Ram deggir aledu—Juka—
14. —Jahamati Hajarati Suluta—
15. nu Abdulla-kutu—Shahagaru tana (ve)
16. gulu dodda Vajirudu Mokarrabu
17. Hajratu Amusakhanunigariki
18. hukum yichchi nivu a buruju -va (d) da vu (m)
19. di para-dandu ko (t) tu anduku cha (la)
20. Jagrata-kaligi vumadalen-ani ala-
21. ge khanu Masarnulahegaru ratri-pa-
22. pagalu jagratato ganimulu daphe che-
23. se panilo mukhyulai vumdamganu (kho)
24. daraja (tto) phirumgi-gumdu Ami
25. ru Mira (ku) tagilitenu a Mocha-
26. (lo) ne Mayatu ayi poyanu a-
27. (tlu) (Mri) tam-aina Mudu-dinalku (pa)
28. —na ayanu mocha————
29. —m (pa) nahagari hukum a
30. yite alage yelinavari
31. hukumu chopuna Khanu Musa-
32. rnulahegaru Komchemu diva-
33. salalo vuppara-Dharmacharya-
34. lachata tamamu Mus (t) aidu
35. cheyinchenu Avaramgujebu va-

36. chchina salu su sna settu kha ma-
37. senu alapu
38. tamamu mustaidu aiyna-
39. di su sna samanu setaigu ala-
40. pu 1078 Salivaha (na) Saka-va (rsha)
41. lu 158 (9)."

(TRANSLATION).

(Ll. 1-7) " Hail ! on Wednesday, the 7th day of the bright half of Magha in the (cyclic) year called, Manmatha,

" (corresponding to) the prosperous, victorious and increasing salivahana Saka years. 1578 (23rd January 1656 A.D.). His Majesty the King Sultan Aurangzeb having come with stony army was laying siege to the blessed fort of Muhammadnagar.

(Ll. 7–12) " The brother of Aurangzeb that he would capture this fort in three days (ordered) the person named Mir Miran, the Chief Minister among his imperial Ministers ———at a battery, very ably day and night.

(Ll. 13–20) " Hazrat Sultan Abdullah Katu Shah (Qutub Shah)

(Ll. 20–23) " Accordingly the above named Khan was the foremost in the work of checking the enemies carefully day and night.

(Ll. 23–26) " May God's will (be done)—A cannon shot having struck Amiru Miran (he) met his death at that very battery (morcha).

(Ll. 26–35) Three days after (his) death in this manner....

" By the order of..mpanaha and in the same manner as ordered by His Majesty, the above named Khan got (the bastion) completely made by the bricklayer Dharmacharya within a few days.

(Ll. 35–37) " The year (salu) in which Aurangzeb came (in) Susna setta Kha ma senu alapu (1057 A.H.).

(Ll. 37–41) " The complete doing (up of the bastion) took place (in) su sna samanu setaigu alapu 1078 A.H. Salivahana Saka years 1589 (1667 A.D.)"

(*g*)=Fair.

(*h*)=Should be protected.

(*j*)=This bastion is associated with several historical incidents of the period. The author will endeavour to deal with each of them categorically. It is well known that Mir Muhammad Saeed of Isphahan, the Mir Jumla of Sultan Abdullah Qutbshah had become arrogant by obtaining abnormal influence over the king. His young son, Mir Muhammad Amin, one day came to the Court in a drunken state and in violation of all etiquette and decency fell asleep on the Royal Masnad (Throne) and vomited there, which intensely offended the King, who ordered him to be kept in confinement. His father being much annoyed and heart-broken went to Prince Aurangzeb (Viceroy of the Deccan) at Aurangabad in the 29th regnal year of the Emperor Shah Jahan, and was received into royal favour by the recommendations of the Prince. He was soon elevated to the rank of Panjhazari (Commander of five thousand horse) and his son Muhammad Amin (then in confinement at Hyderabad) got the rank of Dohazari, and a Farman was despatched through Qazi Muhammad Kashmiri to Sultan Abdullah Qutbshah to the effect that the family of Mir Jumla should not be molested. The King having been much irritated by this pressure at once confiscated all the property of Muhammad Amin and placed a stronger guard over his household. When the news of the utter disregard of the Royal Farman reached Aurangzeb, he sent to Hyderabad his elder son Sultan Muhammad as advance guard on 8th Rabi-ul-Awal 1066 A.H., and he himself left his head-quarters on 3rd Rabi-us-Sani 1066 A.H. On hearing this Sultan Abdullah released Muhammad Amin and his mother and sent them to Sultan Muhammad who had encamped 24 miles off the city, but as their property was not returned, Sultan Muhammad making this a pretext advanced towards the city and Sultan Abdullah fled to Golconda on 5th Rabius-Sani. Sultan Muhammad pitching his camp near Husain Sagar tank sacked the city. Sultan Abdullah tried his best to evade the invasion by sending valuable presents of jewellery and elephants, but as Aurangzeb had joined his son it was resolved to attack the fort, till at last after a siege of a few days, occurred the incident of the death of Mir Miran as related in the above inscription and Sultan Abdullah besides furnishing the arrears of Peshkash sent all the confiscated property of Muhammad Amin and in addition sent his elder son-in-law Mir Ahmed in company with his own mother to Aurangzeb. The old woman settled all differences by agreeing to the marriage of the daughter of Sultan Abdullah with Sultan Muhammad and after the wedding ceremony had the Princess sent from Golconda to the camp of Aurangzeb with a dowry of

10 lacs of rupees. After this settlement Aurangzeb with his son and daughter-in-law returned to Aurangabad on 7th Rajab 1066 A.H., and Sultan Abdullah ordered Musa Khan to erect the Musa Burj by the inclusion of the small hillock in the fortification of the fort[1].

The following peace treaty, executed in 1066 A.H. by Sultan Abdullah, throws a flood of light over the issues of the conclusion of peace and is a record of considerable historical importance. It also fully corrobarates the version of Khafi Khan that owing to straitened circumstances Abdullah Qutbshah was forced to open negotiations for peace, by promising to pay the arrears of tribute and giving his own daughter in marriage to Prince Sultan Muhammad. The undermentioned treaty also lays down that Abdullah Qutbshah had designated his newly made son-in-law, the heir-apparent to the throne of Golconda after his own demise. The original Persian treaty is reproduced here from the Tarikhe-Zurfa (MSS) of Girdhari Lal.

" فدوی درگاه سلاطین پناه مرید بلا اشتباه بطوع و رغبت خود چندین "
" تقبل و تعهد نمود که بعد از ای عفو جرایم و تقصیرات (2) و عنایت "
" مملکت قدیم که درینولا نواب اعلیحضرت سکندر شوکت فریدون حشمت "
" جمشید ابهت ادام الله اقباله مجدداً باین مرید موروثی عطا فرموده "
" اند شروط مذکوره ذیل را بتقدیم رساند و هیچ جهد را دادی وظایف "
" انقیاد و اطاعت و لوازم دولتخواهی و فدویت تهاون نورزد و دقیقه از "
" دقایق اتفاق و یکرنگی مهمل و نامرعی نه گذارد -
" اول اینکه برای کسب مباهات و افتخار و تحصیل شرف و اعتبار خود "
" صبیه صلبیه خویش را بحباله ازدواج تازه نهال بوستان سلطنت و اقبال "
" گزیده ثمره ریاض عظمت و جلال جوان بخت دولت بی زوال جوانی "
" بخش سعادت لایزالی مرشد زاده حقیقی والاگهر سمو المکان محمد سلطان "
" خلف الصدق اعز اعظم صاحب عالمیان و عالم متع الله المهیمن بطول "

---

(1) Tawarikhe-Farkhunda (MSS) by Ghulam Qadir Khan Bidri.

(2) Here the words " faults and offences " relate to the disregard of the Farmans of Shah Jahan regarding the non-molestation of the family of Mir Jumla.

" حیاتها الی انصرام زمان در آورده که بعد از مرید موروثی ایالت "
" این مملکت بان بیدار بخت متعلق باشد و دیگر آنکه سوای پیشکش "
" مقرری مبالغ ده لک روپیه هزار هون قلعه رامگیر (1) را با ولایات "
" متعلقه سابق آن حواله وکلای سرکار فیض آثار نماید اگر حاصل ـ "
" آن ولایت کم از مبلغ مذکور شود از پیش خود وجه تتمه را نقد جواب "
" گوید و مبلغ بیست لک هون را بطریق نذرونیاز از نقد و جواهر نفیسه "
" و از فیلان که بهتر از ان پیش مرید موروثی بنا شد برسانند و بیست لک "
" روپیه مطالبه سرکار خاصه شریفه از ین مبلغ محسوب باشد و اگر چیزی "
" از جواهر و فیلان پنهان دارد خاین باشد و برابر عنایات و امداد "
" هرگاه لشکر بجای تعین فرمایند بعد از صدور حکم طلب پنجهزار سوار "
" از ممالک متعلقه این عقیدت مند داخل عساکر منصوره باشد التماس "
" و استدعا از مکارم علیه و مراحم متعالیه آنست که در باب اعانت "
" و حمایت این مرید موروثی دقیقه فرو نگزارند که از مردم اطراف "
" و جوانب آسیبی و مضرتی باین ملک نرسد و اگر ضرور شود افواج "
" قاهره بکومک و امداد این فدوی عقیدت کیش و رفع فساد معاندان "
" بد اندیش تعین فرمایند و عهد نامه والا بمهر و دستخط خاص و نشان "
" خجسته عنوان مجلی با پنجه مبارک مرحمت فرمایند که بطناً بعد بطن "
" حرز بازوی طمانیت باشد ـ "

Another version of this famous siege (1655 A.D.) related by the French traveller Bernier, who had come to India in 1655 A.D. and visited Golconda in 1667 A.D., *i.e.*, eleven years after this siege, is reproduced below.

Besides corroborating many facts which have been enumerated above, it throws a flood of light on certain political aspects of the period. It also lays down that the surprise visit of Emperor Aurangzeb to Golconda was a result of negotiations of Mir Muhammad Saeed, the Qutbshahi Mir Jumla,[2] and that the important stipulation of the peace treaty was the marriage of the daughter of Sultan Abdullah to Sultan Muhammad, the son of Aurangzeb, with a heavy indemnity and a promise of making the newly made son-in-law his successor; and the introduction of Shah Jahan's arms on the coins of Golconda.

" During the time that Aurangzeb was in Deccan, the

---

(1) These territories were made over as dowry. (Zufra).

(2) After leaving the service of the king of Golconda he went over to the moghals and died as Governor of Bengal.

King of Golkonda had for his Vazier and General of his armies this Emir Jumla, who was Persian by nation, and very famous in the Indies. He was not a man of great extraction, but beaten in business, a person of excellent parts, and a great captain. He had the wit of amassing great treasures not only by the administration of the affairs of this opulent Kingdom, but also by navigation and trade, sending ships into very many parts, and causing the diamond mines, which he alone had farmed under many borrowed names, to be wrought with extraordinary diligence. So that people discoursed almost of nothing but of the riches of Emir Jumla, and of the plenty of his diamonds, which were not reckoned but by sacks. He had also the skill to render himself very—potent and considerable, entertaining, besides the armies of the King, very good troops for his particular, and above all a very good artillery, with abundance of Franguys and Christians to manage it. In a word, he grew so rich, and so puissant, especially after he had found a way to enter into the Kingdom of Karnates (Carnatic) and to pillage all the ancient churches of the idols of that country, that the King of Golkonda became jealous of it, and prepared himself to unsaddle him; and that the more, because he could not bear what was reported of him, as if he had used too great familiarity with the Queen his mother, that was yet beauteous. Yet he discovered nothing of his design to any, having patience, and waiting till Emir came to the court, for he was then in the kingdom of Karnates with his army. But one day, when more particular news was brought him of what had passed between his mother and him he had not power enough to dessemble any longer, but was transported by choler to fall to invectives and menaces; whereof Emir was soon made acquainted, having at the court abundance of his wife's kindred, and all his nearest relations and best friends possessing the principal offices. The Kings' mother also, who did not hate him, had speedy information of the same; which obliged Emir, without delay, to write to his only son Mahmet Emir (Amin) Kan, who then was about the King, requiring him to do the best he could to withdraw with all speed from the court, under some pretence of hunting or the like, and to come and join with him. Mahmet Emir Kan, failed not to attempt divers ways; but the king causing him to be narrowly observed, none of them all would succeed. This very much preplexed Emir, and made him take a strange resolution, which cast the king in great danger to lose his crown and life; so true it is, that he who knows not to dissemble, knows not how to reign. He writ to Aurangzeb, who was then in Daultabad, the capital of the Deccan, about fifteen or sixteen day's journey from Golkonda, giving him to understand, that the king of Golkonda did intend to ruin him and his family, notwithstanding the signal services he had done him, as all the world knew; which was an unexampled injustice and ingratitude, that this necessitated him to take his refuge to him, and to entreat him, that he would receive him into his protection; that for the rest, if he would follow his advice, and confidence him he would so dispose affairs, that he would at once put into his hands both the King and Kingdom of Golkonda. This thing he made very easy, using the following discourse " you need but take four or five thousand horse, of the best of your army, and to march with expedition to Golkonda spreading a rumour by the way, that it is an ambassador of Chah—(Shah) Jehan that goes in haste, about considerable matters, to speak with the King of Bag-nageur (Bhag-Nagar).

" The Dabir, who is he that is first to be addressed unto, to make anything known unto the King, is allied to me and my creature, and altogether mine; take care of nothing but to march with expedition, and I will so order it, that without making you known, you shall come to the gates of Bag-Nageur; and when the King shall come out to receive the letters, according to custom, you may easily seize on him, and afterwards of all his family, and do with him what shall seem good to you, in regard that his house of Bag-Nageur, where he commonly resides, is unwalled and unfortified." He added, that he would make this enterprise upon his own charges, offering him fifty thousand rupies a day (which is about five and twenty thousand crowns) during the whole time of the march.

"Aurangzeb, who looked only for some such occasion, had no mind at all to lose so fair a one. He soon undertook the expedition, and so fortunately managed his enterprize, that he arrived at Bag-nageur without being otherwise known than as an ambassador of Chah-Jehan. The King of Golkonda being advertised of the arrival of this pretended ambassador, came forth into a garden, according to custome, received him with honour, and having unfortunately put himself into the hands of his enemy, ten or twelve slaves, gurgis, were ready to fall upon and to seize his person, as had been projected; but that a certain Omrah, touched with tenderness, could not forbear to cry out, though he was of the party, and a creature of the Emir, "Doth not your Majesty see that this is Aurangzeb? Away or you are taken." Whereat the King being frightened, slips away, and gets hastily on horseback, riding with all his might to the fortress of Golkonda, which is but a short league from thence. Aurangzeb seeing he was defeated in his design, yet was not therefore discomposed; but seized at the same time on the royal house, taketh all the rich and good things he finds there; yet sending to the King all his wives, (which over all the Indies is very religiously observed), and goeth to besiege him in his fortress. But as the siege, for want of having brought along all necessaries, held on long, and lasted above two months, he received order from Chah-Jehan to raise it, and to retire into Deccan again; so that although the fortress was reduced to extremities, for want of victuals and ammunition of war, he found himself obliged to abandon his enterprise. He knew very well, that it was Dara (Shikoh (and

Begam (Jahan Ara) that had induced Chah-Jehan to send these orders, from the apprehension they entertained that he would become too powerful; but in the meantime he never discovered any resentment of it, saying only, that he ought to obey the orders of his father. Yet he withdrew not, without causing underhand payment to be made to him of all the charges of his expedition; besides, he married his son Sultan Mahmood, to the eldest daughter of that King, with a promise that he would make him his successor, causing him also to give for a dowry the fortress and the appurtenances of Bamguyre (Ramgir). He also made the King consent that all the silver money, that should be coined for the future in that kingdom, should bear on one side the arms of Chah-Jehan; and that Emir Jumla should withdraw, with his whole family, all his goods, troops, and artillery[1]."

The bastion is semi-circular in shape and consists of three storeys. The solid blocks of granite employed in its construction, which must weigh over a ton each, are firmly cemented together. The expenses of the erection of this bastion amounted to Rs. 5,94,000[2]. The inscription states that a shot from the guns of the fort hit the Moghal Commander and Bakhshi Mir Miran (Asadullah Khan Bukhari) as a result of which he expired on the spot and three days after his death peace was concluded. Another historical personage mentioned in the inscription is Musa Khan (mahaldar) who had played the role of a Commander in the seige. Toli Masjid (No. 28) was built by the same Khan in 1082 A.H., and after the death of Abdullah Qutbshah when the question of his succession arose, he voted in favour of Abul Hasan Tanashah.

---

(1) (Bernier's Voyage to the East Indies pp. 65-67. A general collection of voyages, travels in all parts of the world. By John Pinkerton. vol. 8. London Edition 1811).

(2) Tuzuke Qutbshahi (MSS).

No. 67.

(*a*)=The great mosque of the Golconda Tombs (*vide* plate).

(*b*)=The Tombs.

(*c*)=Sarf-i-Khas.

(*d*=I-c.

(*e*)=1077 A.H. (1666 A.D.).

(*f*)=Over the prayer-niche the following inscription is carved :—

۱- اعوذ بالله من الشیطان الرجیم سیقول السفهاء من الناس ما ولیهم
عن قبلتهم التی کانوا علیها قل لله المشرق والمغرب یهدی من یشاء
الی صراط مستقیم

۲ وکذلک جعلناکم امة وسطا لتکونوا شهداء علی الناس ویکون
الرسول

۳- علیکم شهیدا وما جعلنا القبلة التی کنت علیها الا لنعلم من یتبع الرسول
ممن ینقلب علی عقبیه وان کانت لکبیرة الا علی الذین هدی الله وما کان
الله لیضیع ایمانکم ان الله بالناس لروف رحیم - ۱۰۷۷ -

۴- کتبه تقی الدین محمد بن شیخ ما لم البحرانی

(*Translation*)

1. "I seek the asylum of God from the Satan who is an outcast." "The foolish men will say, what hath turned them from their Qiblah, towards which they formerly prayed. Say, unto God, belongeth the East and West, he directeth whom he pleaseth into the right way."

2. "Thus have we placed you, an intermediate nation, that ye may be witnesses against the mankind, and that the apostle may be—"

3. "A witness against you, we appointed the Qiblah towards which thou didst formerly pray, only that we might know him who followeth the apostle, from him who turneth back on his heels, though this seem a great matter, unless unto those whom God hath directed. But God will not render your faith of no effect; for God is gracious and merciful unto men. 1077 (A.H.)

The Great Mosque of Golconda Tombs.

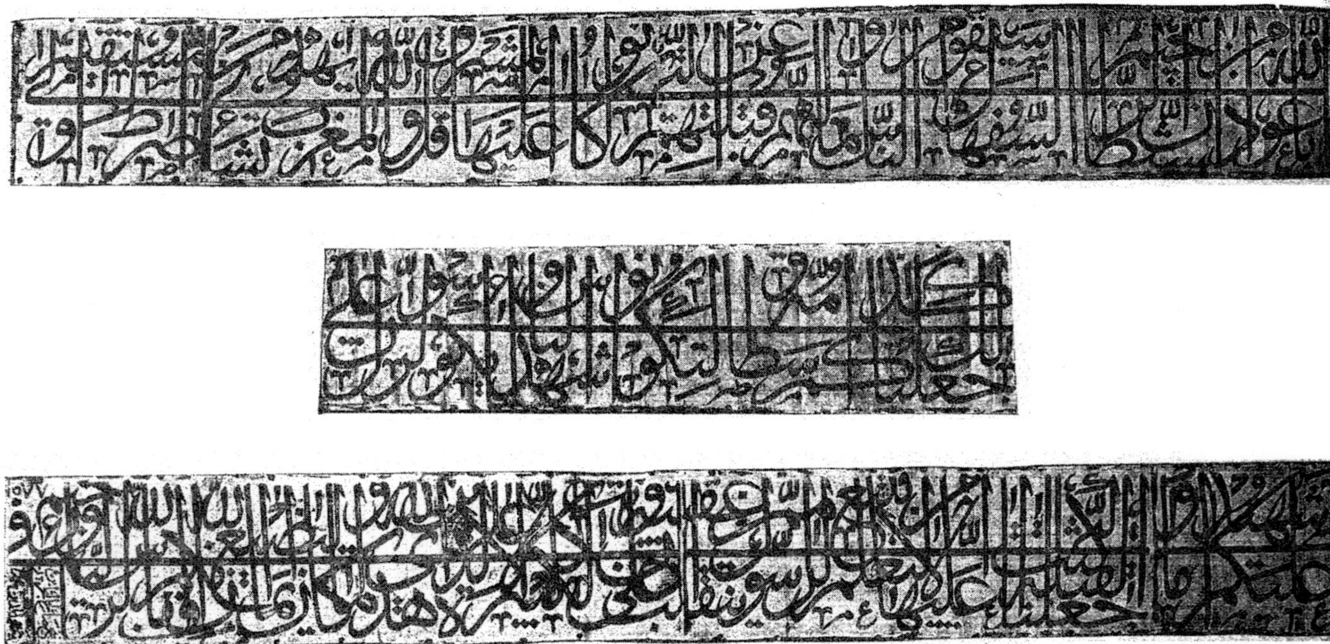

Over the prayer-niche. Great Mosque of Golconda Tombs.

4. Written by Taqiuddin Muhammad, son of Salih of Bahrain." (*vide* plate).

The facade of the mosque is adorned with plastic medallions bearing the following :—

٥- نصر من الله وفتح قريب-وان المساجد لله فلا تدعو امع الله احد ا

٦- الله محمد على فاطمه حسن حسين -عجلوا بالصلوة قبل الفوت -عجلوا بالتوبتة قبل الموت ١٠٧٩(١)

(*Translation*)

5. " The help is from God and the success is at hand verily the places of worship (are set apart) unto God, wherefore invoke not any (other therein) together with God."

6. " Allah, Muhammad, Ali, Fatima, Hasan, Husain. Hasten to say your prayers lest ye miss them, and hasten to repent lest ye perish. 1079 (A.H.)."

(*g*)=Good.

(*h*)=Should be protected.

(*j*)=It has been the peculiarity of the Qutbshahi period that mosques were erected in abundance, and consequently we now have any number of mosques scattered all over the city and suburbs and in the Golconda tombs practically each and every dome is coupled with a mosque. This mosque which is by far the most splendid and the largest mosque of the fort is situated close to the mausoleum of Hayat Bakhsh Begam and as the year of erection of this mosque and the date of death of the Begam is identical, it may therefore be safely asserted that it was built as an adjunct to her tomb. The above mentioned inscription is carved in the prayer-niche in the

(1) Mr. Yazdani has omitted the whole of No. (6) from his reading; although it is important as it records the date of the completion of this mosque. (E.I.M. 1915-16 p. 36).

best Thulth and Tauqi' style, the dimensions of the niche are (76′×50′ 8″). The roof is surmounted by 15 cupolas and the hall is flanked with two lofty minarets on each side. The prayer niche of the Jamay Masjid of the City (No. 7) in addition to the above inscription contains the following verse from the Quran:—

(سبحان ربک رب العزة عما یصفون وسلام علی المرسلین والحمد لله رب العالمین)

Although this mosque was built 71 years after No. 7 still the style of writing is quite identical and this inscription besides exhibiting a masterpiece of calligraphic art shows that these masters whole-heartedly concentrated all their energy in becoming skilful in the art.

No. 68.

(*a*)=The mausoleum of Hayat Bakhsh Begam.

(*b*)=Golconda Tombs.

(*c*)=Sarf-i-Khas.

(*d*)=I-c.

(*e*)=1077 A.H., (1666 A.D.).

(*f*)=The following inscriptions are carved on the sarcophagus in Thulth :—

۱- لا اله الا الله محمد رسول الله علی ولی الله حقا حقا - سورہ ۳ - ایتہ ۱۶ - سنہ ۱۰۷۷

۲- ایتہ الکرسی

۳- سورہ ۲ - آیات ۲۸۵ - ۲۸۶

۴- سورہ ۹۷ - ۱۰۹ - ۱۱۲ - ۱۱۴

۵- ناد علی صغیر - درود شریف

۶- وفات جنت مکانی حیات بخش بیگم بتاریخ بیست وهشتم ماہ شعبان شب سہ شنبہ سنہ ۱۰۷۷

(*Translation*).

1. "Shiite creed. Chap. III, verse 16, the year 1077 A.H."

2. " Throne Verse. "
3. " Quran Chap II, verses 285-86. "
4. " Chap. 97, 109, 112, 114. "
5. " Nade Ali and Shiite Durud. "
6. " The death of (the lady) Hayat Bakhsh Begam whose abode is Paradise, occurred on the 28th of Shaban, the night of Tuesday, in the year 1077. " (A.H.), 1666 A.D.[1] (*Vide* plate).

(*g*)=Fair.

(*h*)=Should be protected.

(*j*)=Hayat Bakhsh Begam, better known as Hayat-Man-Saheba, took a prominent part during the reigns of three Qutbshahi Kings (Sultan Muhammad Quli, Sultan Muhammad Qutbshah Sultan Abdullah Qutbshah), she was the daughter of Muhammad Quli, wife of Muhammad Qutbshah and the mother of Abdullah Qutbshah. Ferishta in describing her marriage ceremony writes that the King gave his exceedingly handsome daughter in marriage to Prince Muhammad the son of Prince Muhammad Amin. This mausoleum is a replica of the tomb of her husband, Muhammad Qutbshah. The Husaini Alam, (No. 35), the Bibi-ka-chashma, the Bi-bi-ka-Alam and Langar, recall the memory of this lady. The village of Hayat Nagar (No. 18), was also a favourite resort of the Begam and the extent of her ambitions may be judged from the incident related in No. 18.

No. 69.

(*a*)=Hira Masjid.

(*b*)=Golconda fort.

---

(1) Mr. Yazdani has given this date as 1670 A.D. (E.I.M. 1915-16 p. 85).

(*c*)=**Sarf-i-Khas.**

(*d*)=**I-c.**

(*e*)=**1079 A.H., (1668 A.D.).**

(*f*)=**The following inscriptions are carved on wooden panels.**

١. شاهنشه دین و قطب شاهان * آن قبلهٔ فیض اهل امید
مانند خلیل کعبه ساخت * کز شمسهٔ اوست ماه و خورشید
از بهر چنین بنای بافیض * سلطان حسین را پسندید
تاریخ بناش گفت هاتف * این کعبهٔ فیض باد جاوید
١٠٧٩
کتبه اسمعیل بن عرب شیرازی

(***Translation***)

1. "The lord of the faith and the Qutb (support) of the **Kings**, the Qibla of bounty for the expectant. Like **Khalil** (Abraham) built a **Kaaba**, from the tassels of which are the Moon and the Sun. For the erection of this bounteous institution, Sultan[1] Husain was singled out by the King. The invisible speaker stated the chronogram of its erection. "**May** this **Kaaba** of bounty remain for ever. 1079, (A.H.), written by Ismail[2] son of Arab of Shiraz."

Below the wooden panels three pairs of medallions consisting of Quranic verses and the names of the Prophet and **his** relatives written in Tughra are carved in the spandrels of the arched openings, as follows :—

٢ عجلوا بالصلوة قبل الفوت
و عجلوا بالتوبة قبل الموت

(***Translation***)

2. "Hasten to say prayers lest ye miss them. "And hasten to repent lest ye perish." (In the spandrels of the right arch).

٣- الله-محمد-علی-فاطمه-حسن-حسین

(1) This appears to be the same Sultan Husain son of Ambiya Quli **Khan** who had built the dome of Shah Shamsuddin Ali Akbar near Ghazi Banda *Vide* No. (27).

(2) **Mr.** Yazdani has given this name as Muhammad Ismail, (*Ibid*).

On the wooden panels of Hira Masjid.

The prayer niche of Hira Masjid.

Sarcophagus of Hayat Baksh Begum No. 68.

(*Translation*)

3. " Allah, Muhammad, Ali, Fatima, Hasan, Husain. (In the spandrels of the left side arch).

۴- ان المساجد لله فلا (۱) تدعوا مع الله احدا

(*Translation*)

4. " Verily the mosques are unto God, therefore invoke not any (other) with God. "

(In the prayer -niche on a panel of black basalt measuring (15′×1′ 4″), in Tughra style the following Quranic Verse 19, Chap. IX. is inscribed) :—

۵- انما يعمر مساجد الله من آمن بالله واليوم الآخر واقام الصلوة
واتى الزكوة ولم يخش الا الله فعسى اولئك ان تكونوا (2)
من المهتدين - كتبه العبد تقي الدين محمد بن صالح البحريني
سنه ۱۰۷۸

(*Translation*)

5. " But he only shall visit the mosques of God, who believeth in God and the resurrection day, and is constant at prayer, and payeth the alms and feareth God alone. These perhaps may become of those who are rightly directed.

Written by the servant (of God) Taqiuddin Muhammad son of Salih of Bahrain. In the year 1078. A.H." (1667 A.D.) (*Vide* plate).

(*g*)=Fair.

(*h*)=Should be protected.

(*j*)=This mosque is situated in an extensive quad rangular enclosure, containing rooms for th residence of travellers and students. In the centre of the platform there is a cistern for ablution. The prayer hall has three arched openings and is flanked with minarets on either side. It is indicated by the date of the inscriptions that it was erected during the reign of Sultan Abdullah Qutbshah.

---

(1) Mr. Yazdani's reading is (بما) (E.I.M. 1913-14 p. 58).

(2) Mr. Yazdani's reading is (يكونوا) (*Ibid* p. 59).

No. 70.

(*a*)=The Mausoleum of Sultan Abdullah Qutbshah.
(*b*)=Outside the enclosure of Golconda Tombs.
(*c*)=Sarf-i-Khas.
(*d*)=I-c.
(*e*)=1083, A.H., (1672 A.D.).
(*f*)=The inscriptions are carved on the sarcophagus of black basalt.

۱- سورۀ ۳ آیت ۱۶ - لا اله الا الله محمد رسول الله علی ولی الله حقا
۲- حقا سنه ۱۰۸۳ ه آیة الکرسی
۳- سورۀ ۲ - آیات ۲۸۵ - ۲۸۶
۴- سورۀ ۹۷ - ۱۰۹ - ۱۱۲ - ۱۱۴
۵- درود شریف - ناد علی صغیر
۶- تاریخ وفات بادشاه جنت بارگاه سلطان عبد الله قطب شاه بن سلطان محمد قطب شاه یوم الاحد سیم ماه محرم سنه ۱۰۸۳ و ولادت با سعادتش بیست و هشتم شهر شوال سنه ۱۰۲۳ جلوس همایونش یوم الاربعا چهار دهم ماه جمادی الاولی سنه ۱۰۳۵ مدت سلطنتش چهل و هشت سال سن شریفش شصت سال

(*Translation.*)

1. "Chap. III, verse 16, Shiite creed. **In the year** 1083 A.H."
2. "Throne verse."
3. "Chap. II., verses 285-86."
4. "Chap. XCVII, CIX, CXII and CXIV."
5. "Shiite Durud and Nade Ali."

6. "The date of the demise of the King of the heavenly abode, Sultan Abdullah Qutbshah, son of Sultan Muhammad Qutbshah, (is) Sunday, the 3rd of the month of Muharram 1083 (A.H.) (April 21, 1672 A.D.), and the date of his felicitious birth (was) 28th Shawal 1023 (A.H.), (November 21, 1614 A.D.) His auspicious accession (took place) on Wednesday, 14th of Jamadil-Awal 1035 (A.H.) (1st February 1626 A.D.). The duration of his reign (was) 48 years and the period of his noble life sixty years."
(*Vide* plate).

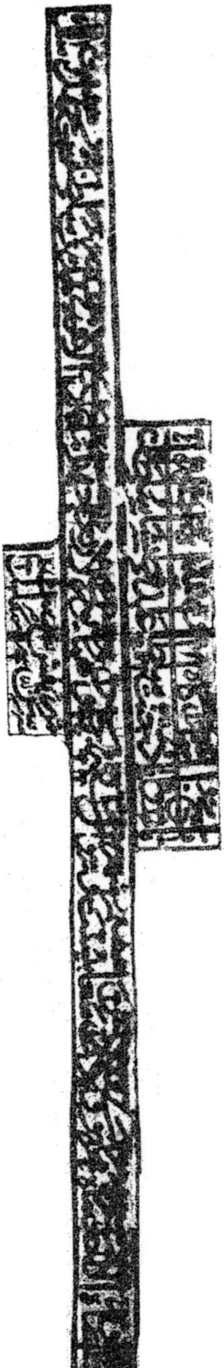

Sarcophagus of Sultan Abdullah. No. 70

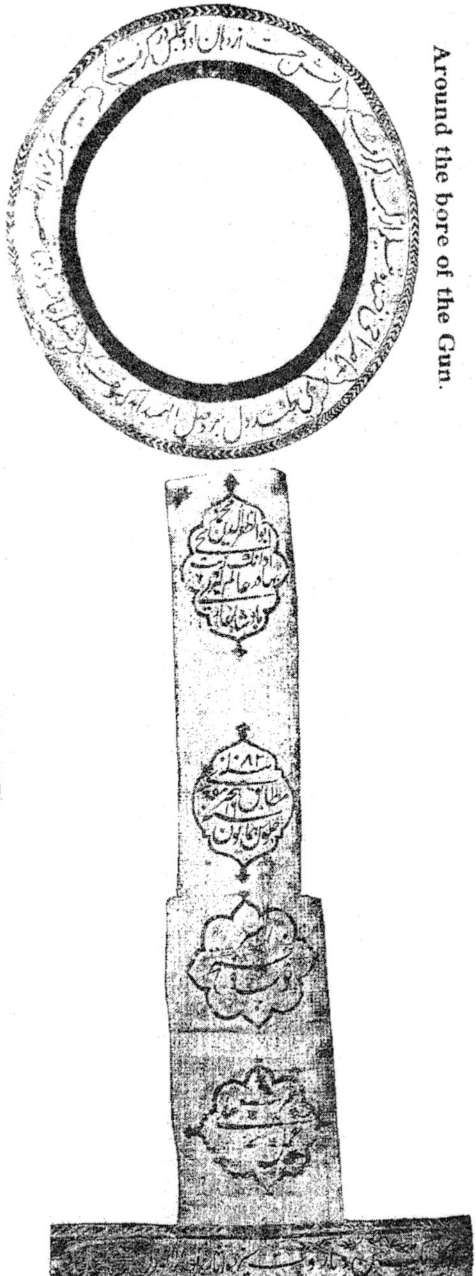

Around the bore of the Gun.

Over Fateh Rahbar Gun. No. 71.

Sultan Abdullah VII.

(*g*) = Good.

(*h*) = Should be protected.

(*j*) = The grand mausoleum of Sultan Abdullah is situated outside the boundary wall of the tombs and is built of the same style of architecture as that of his parents, Muhammad Qutbshah and Hayat Bakhsh Begam. It has platforms of 237 ft., each way and is surrounded by seven arches on each side. The date of his birth is given as 28th Shawal 1023[1] A.H. (1614 A.D.) and the date of his accession 14th Jamadi-I 1035[2] A.H. (1626 A.D.). During the reign of this King, through the good administration of Mir Muhammad Saeed, Mir Jumla, his dominions had reached as far as Carnatic, but the ostentations of Mir Jumla offended the King and he had to seek refuge with Prince Aurangzeb, which brought about the siege of 1066 A.H. and which has been fully described in No. 66. The difference was ultimately settled by giving the King's daughter in marriage to Sultan Muhammad son of Prince Aurangzeb and acknowledging his son-in-law as heir-apparent to the throne of Golconda, but he predeceased Sultan Abdullah and this term of the treaty was fulfilled in the 31st regnal year of the Emperor Aurangzeb, when he became instrumental in exterminating the Qutbshahi dynasty in 1098 A.H. (1672 A.D.).

---

(1) Mir Momin of Astarabad composed this chronogram of his birth (کام بخش جا نها ۱۰۲۳ ھ) and his son Amjaduddin composed the following (خلد ا لله ملکه ؛ بن ا ۱۰۲۳ ھ).

(2) Maulana Raunaqi composed the following chronogram of his accession. (مزین شد جهانی از جلوس شاه عبد ا لله ۱۰۳۵ ھ) (Muhammad Qutbshahi)(MSS).

He was succeeded by his third son-in-law Abul Hasan Tanashah. Abdullah Qutbshah was a just and liberal king, but was not acute in judgment which resulted in political troubles. He was also fond of learning and architecture. The celebrated Persian Lexicon " Burhane—Qaati', " was compiled during his reign and dedicated to him. The accompanying photograph of this king has been copied from the British Museum collection.

No. 71.

(*a*)=Inscription over the **Fateh Rahbar gun**[1].
(*b*)=On the Petla Burj, (Golconda Fort).
(*c*)=Sarf-i-Khas.
(*d*)=II-c.
(*e*)=1083 A.H. (1672 A.D.).
(*f*)=The following inscription is engraved on this gun :—

۱- ابوالمظفر محی الدین محمد (2) اورنگ زیب عالمگیر بهادر بادشاه غازی سنه ۱۶ جلوس همایون سنه ۱۰۸۳ هجری مقدسه

۲- توپ فتح رهبر - عمل محمد علی عرب گله یک من و باروت سیرده آثار پا و بالا بوزن شاهجهانی

۳- تا صراحی خنده تعلیم از لب دلبر گرفت * آتش جست از دهان او و مجلس در گرفت
می طپد دل بهر وصل اما نمی داند که سوخت * شعله جانسوز او تا حضر را در بر گرفت

(*Translation*)

1. " Abul Muzaffar, Mohiuddin Muhammad Aurangzeb, Alamgir Bahadur, Badshahe-Ghazi (the Victorious King). In the 16th regnal year corresponding to 1083 of the holy era of the Flight. "

2. " Fateh Rahbar (Guide to Victory) gun. Foundered by Muhammad Ali Arab. Charge, one maund and gun.

(1) This name is included in the list given in the Maathiri Alamgiri p. 290).

(2) Mr. Yazdani's Decipherment is (محمد محی الدین) E.I.M. 1918- 14 p. 56).

powder, thirteen seers and a quarter, according to the Shahjahani weight."

3. (*Quatrain*).

"Since the (wine) flagon learnt smiling from the lips of the sweetheart, fire has issued forth from its mouth and encircled the assembly.

"The heart is inflamed with passion to obtain union; but it does not know that the flame of her soul-melting beauty has burnt the rival since (she) took him in her embrace."

(*Vide* Plate.)

(*g*)=Fair.

(*h*)=Should be protected.

(*j*)=These verses have been engraved round the bore of the gun, which is 16′ 2″ in length, the diameter of the bore is 2′ 3½″, while the circumference at the other end is 8′ 8″. This gun was one of those which were used during the last siege of Golconda by Aurangzeb. In workmanship and diameter it is similar to its rival on the Musa Burj and was manufactured by the same maker. It is now lying on a bastion called Petla Burj (pot-belly bastion) which is situated on the western wall of the fort.

No. 72.

(*a*)=The tomb of Neknam Khan.

(*b*)=On a platform outside the Mausoleums of Ibrahim Qutbshah and Mirza Muhammad Amin.

(*c*)=Sarf-i-Khas.

(*d*)=I-c.

(*e*)=1084 A.H. (1672 A.D.).

(*f*)=This tomb is situated in an open square enclosure, measuring 26′ 4″ each way. The sarcophagus of the grave is inscribed with the following benedictory verses :—

۱- آیتة الکرسی (سورہ ۲- آیتہ ۲۵۶)
۲- سورہ ۹۷ - درود شریف
۳- هوالباقی
(۱) فرمان جهان مطاع عنایت عنوان وحکم آفتاب شعاع مرحمت بنیان
ازدیوان همیون (1) خلافت
(۲) مشحون چنان شرفصدوریافت‌که مقدمان وکلکرنیان ورعایای موضع
منگلوارم (2) من اعمال
(۳) سمط (3) حنوارہ (4) عرف حسن آباد بالطاف شاهانه امیدوار
بوده بدانند‌که از راه عنایات (5) که شامل حال کافه
(۴) فدویان نسبت از ابتدای شهور سنه اربع وسبعین والف حاصل موضع
مذکوررا وقف لنگروروشنائی وحفاظ
(۵) وخادمان مزار مغفرت پناه جنت مکان نیکنام خان نموده ایم که
تا زمان ظهور حضرت صاحب الزمان
(۶) صلوات الله علیه من الملک المنان مقرروجاری بوده باشد باید که
عهده داران وکارکنان ودیسائیان (6) وتهلکرنیان ومقدمان
(۷) وکلکرنیان سمط (3) مزبورموضع مذکوررا جهت اخراجات لنگر
وروشنائی وخادمان وحفاظ مزار غفران پناه موهی الیه
(۸) مقررومعین دانسته بلاعذر جاری دارند ودرین باب تاکید تمام
وقدغن مالا کلام شناسند واگرکسے ازمضمون فرمان قضا
(۹) جریان تخلف ورزد بلعنت خدا ونفرین رسول الله گرفتار خواهد شد.
فمن بدله بعد ما سمعه فانما اثمه علی
(۱۰) الذین یبدلونه ان الله سمیع علیم - تحریرا ورازدهم شهر
جمیدی الثانی سنه ۱۰۸۴ وفات غفران پناه نیکنام خان دهم ذی‌حجه
سنه ۱۰۸۲ (7)۔ کتبه کلب علی بن محمد صادق (8) عفا عنه (9)

---

(1) It is grammatically incorrect and ought to have been written (همایون).

(2) This name corroborates the version of Maathire-Alamgiri, that the name of Golconda Fort was originally fort of Mankal.

(3) It ought to have been written (سمت)

(4) Mr. Yazdani has read this word as (جنول) (E.I.M. 1915-16 p. 38).

(5) Mr. Yazdani's reading of this word is (عنایت) (*Ibid*).

(6) Mr. Yazdani's reading of this word is (دیسپانیان) (*Ibid*).

(7) Mr. Yazdani has read this date as 1083 (*Ibid*).

(8) Mr. Yazdani has read this as (محمد صادق بن علی کاتب) (*Ibid*).

(9) Mr. Yazdani has omitted to read these words. (*Ibid*).

Headstone of Neknam Khan.

Over Azhdaha Paiker Gun. No. 73.

Neknam Khan.

(*Translation*).

1. " Throne verse. "

2. " Chap. 97 Shiite Durud. "

3. " He [1] is Eternal. The Farman (Royal Mandate) obeyed by the world, prefatory in munificience and the order resplendent like the rays of the sun and orignating in mercy, had the honour of promulgating from the August Court, filled with imperial dignity, to this effect that the Muqaddams (headman), Kulkarnis (accountants) and the royats of the village of Mangalwaram in the division of Janwara, popularly known as Hasanabad, having been expectant of the royal favours, should know, that we, out of our royal bounty, which provides for all of our devoted subjects, have from the beginning of the year one thousand and seventy four, set apart the revenues of the said village as an endowment for the almshouse, the lights, the reciters of the Quran and the servants of the tomb of Neknam Khan, whose sins have been forgiven and whose abode is in Paradise, in order that the revenues be devoted to and spent on these objects until the time of the appearance of his Holiness, the Lord of the Age (Hazrat Mahdi). May the blessings of God be upon him (The 12th Imam) from the bounteous Almighty[2]. It is necessary therefore, that officers, agents, Desayees (accountants of the Pergannahs) Thalkarnis, (divisional accountants), Muqadams (headman) and Kulkarnis (village accountants) of the above mentioned division should regard the said village as assigned and apportioned for the expenses of the almshouse, the lights, the servants and the reciters of the Quran attached to the tomb of the aforesaid person, whose sins have been forgiven, and should not raise any objection to its continuance and perpetuity. And in this

---

(1) I have drawn freely from the English translation of Mr. Yazdani, with slight alterations.

(2) Mr. Yazdani has translated the word (ملک) as King, although it refers to the God Almighty. (E.I.M.1915-16 p. 39).

matter they should observe great care and strict diligence And if anybody disobeys the contents of the irresistable Farman, he shall be overtaken by the curse of God and the imprecation of the Prophet of God. But he who shall change it, after he hath heard it, surely the sin thereof shall be on those who change it, for God heareth and knoweth. Written on the 12th Jamadis-Sani in the year 1084 (A.H.) (25th September 1673 A.D.). The death of Neknam Khan whose sins have been forgiven (occurred) on the 10th of Zil Hijjah in the year 1082 (A.H.) (30th March 1672 A.D.). Written by Kalbe Ali son of Muhammad Sadiq may he be forgiven.[1]" *vide* plate).

(*g*)=Good.

(*h*)=Should be protected.

(*j*)=The above mentioned inscription No. 3 is carved on an arch shaped tablet (3′ 8″ ×2′ 1″) and is fixed at the head of the grave, and is situated on the outer terrace of the Mausoleum of Sultan Ibrahim Qutbshah. Neknam Khan was one of the commanders of Sultan Abdullah and he died on 10th Zil Hij 1082 A.H. *i.e.*, 23 days prior to the demise of Sultan Abdullah (3-1-1083 A.H.). According to the " Madras in the Olden Times," by Mr. Talboys Wheeler, the President of Fort St. George had given the title of Nabob, to Neknam Khan who was the commander-in-Chief of the Carnatic, and it had been from him that they obtained the qowl (contract) for the district of Madrasapatam after the flight of the Rajah of Chandrageri[2]. The year of his demise given by Mr. Wheeler is 1672 A.D[3]., which

(1) Mr. Yazdani has omitted this last portion of the inscription from his English translation (E.I.M. 1915-16 p. 39).

(2) Madras in the Olden Times p. 38. (E.I.M. 1915-16 p. 37.)

(3) Idem p. 42 (*Ibid*).

favourably corresponds to the date (1082 A.H.) given in the headstone inscription of Neknam Khan. Mr. Wheeler has confused Abdullah Qutbshah with Abul Hasan Tanashah when he refers to Neknam Khan on page 18 of his book as being a " Commander-in-Chief of Abul Hasan, King of Golconda or Hyderabad, " as according to this inscription Neknam Khan had expired before the accession of Abul Hasan. This fact is also supported by another history in which Neknam Khan is described as the most accomplished General in the service of Abdullah Qutbshah . The accompanying photograph of Neknam Khan has been copied from the British Museum collection.

No. 73.

(*a*)=Inscription on the Azhdaha Paikar Gun.
(*b*)=On the Musa Burj (Golconda Fort).
(*c*)=Sarf-i-Khas.
(*d*)=II-c.
(*e*)=1085 A.H., (1674 A.D.).
(*f*)=This gun measures 14′ 10″ in length, the diameter near the bore being 2′ 4″, while at the end the circumference is 9′, and contains the following inscription.

۱- ابوالمظفر محی الدین محمد (2) اورنگ زیب بہادر عالمگیر بادشاہ
غازی سنہ ۱۸ جلوس همایون (3) سنہ ۱۰۸۵ هجری مقدسہ (4)

۲- توپ اژدها پیکر عمل محمد علی عرب گلہ یک من بوزن شاهجهانی
وباروت سیئر ده آثار یک نیم پاو بوزن شاهجهانی

---

(1) Basatinus-Salatin, p. 413 (E.I.M. 1915-16 p. 37).

(2) Mr. Yazdani's reading is (محمد محی الدین) (E.I.M. 1913-14 p. 55.)

(3) Mr. Yazdani has read this word as (والا) (E. I.M.1913-14 p.55.)

(4) Mr. Yazdani has written this word before (هجری) and read (مقدسہ هجري) (*Ibid*).

(*Translation*)

1. "Abul Muzaffar Mohiuddin Mahammad Aurangzeb Bahadur Alamgir Badshahe Ghazi (the Victorious King). 18th year of the auspicious reign, in the holy Hijri year of 1085."

2. "The Azhdaha Paikar (Dragon-body) gun. Cast by Muhammad Ali Arab; charge, one maund according to the Shah Jahani weight, gunpowder—thirteen and one eight seer according to the Shah Jahani weight[1].

(*g*)=Good.

(*h*)=Should be protected.

(*j*)=A number of guns are lying on this bastion (Musa Burj) out of which the Azhdaha Paikar is the most important as being one of the four famous guns which were used by the army of the Emperor Aurangzeb during the last siege of Golconda in 1687 A.D[2]. The ball weighing 40 seers was used in charging this gun, it is a replica of Fateh Rahbar (No. 71) and the maker is also identical.

No. 7.

(*a*)=The Mausoleum of Mirza Nizamuddin Ahmad (New) popularly known as the incomplete tomb of Abul Hasan Tana Shah.

(*b*)=Outside Golconda Tombs.

(*c*)=Sarf-i-Khas.

(*d*)=II-c.

(*e*)=1085 A.H., (1674 A.D.).

(*f*)=The following inscriptions are carved over the sarcophagus of Nizamuddin, the other grave contains benedictory verses but bears no name.

---

(1) It weighed 55 lbs. and was defined 40 seers. (E.I.M. 1913-14 p. 56).

(2) Maathiri Alamgiri page 290 (*Ibid*) p. 55.

۱- (۱) الله محمد علی
(۲) شهد الله انه لا اله الا هو والملائکة واولوا العلم قائما بالقسط لا اله الا هو العزیز الحکیم (سوره ۳ آیات ۵-۱۶)
(۳) آیة الکرسی
(۴) سوره ۲ - آیات ۲۸۵-۲۸۶
(۵) سوره ۹۷- ۱۰۹ ۱۱۲-۱۱۴،
(۶) ناد علی - درود شریف
(۷) میرزا نظام الدین احمد نور مرقده رتاریخ ۲۶ شهر صفر روز شنبه سنه ۱۰۸۵ بعد از سه پهر چهار گهری بر حمت پیوستند

۲- الله محمد علی
سوره ۳ آیات ۵-۱۶۔
آیة الکرسی

(*Translation*).

1. (1) " Allah, Muhammad, Ali "
   (2) " Chap. III, verses 5 and 16. "
   (3) " Throne Verse."
   (4) " Chapter II, verses 285, 86,"
   (5) " Chapters XCVII, CIX, CXII, CXIV."
   (6) " Nade Ali, Shiite Durud."
   (7) " Mirza Nizamuddin Ahmed, May his tomb be illuminated, joined the Divine mercy on 26th Safar, Saturday, in the year 1085, 4 o'clock after noon."
2. (1) " Allah, Muhammad, Ali. "
   (2) " Chapter III Verses 5 and 16. "
   (3) " Throne Verse. "

(*g*)=Is in an incomplete condition.

(*h*)=Should be protected.

(*j*)=Sultan Abul Hasan Tanashah [1] who was the third son-in-law of Sultan Abdullah Qutbshah, ascended the throne in 1083 A.H. (1672 A.D.)

(1) The nick-name of Tanashah was given to Abul Hasan because he was very fond of Music, and tunes, besides this in Telugu the word " Tana ", means child and Tanashah was thus nicknamed because he was endowed with several childish fancies.

and reigned for fourteen years. The last siege of Golconda by the Emperor Aurangzeb marked the extinction of the Qutbshahi dynasty and the annexation of the Kingdom of Golconda to the Moghal Empire and Tanashah was confined in the Daultabad fort as a royal captive. It has been a curious coincidence in the History of the Deccan that the Amirs of Sadah (century) after rebelling with the Tughlaq King first declared their independence in Daulatabad by electing Ismail-Mukh, their first King and simultaneously after the dismemberment of the Bahmani Kingdom and the declaration of independence of the Provincial Governors when the last independent King of the Deccan lost his Kingdom he had to pass his last days in the same place (Daulatabad) in confinement, where the first Islamic Kingdom of the Deccan had come into existence. The construction of the present mausoleum according to the practice in vogue at the time was taken in hand by Abul Hasan Tanashah during his lifetime, but owing to the Moghal invasions he could not complete the building and he also could not be buried here, but after his demise in the Chini Mahal of Daulatabad fort in 1111 A.H., (1699 A.D.), he was buried in the graveyard of Hazrat Syed Shah Raju Qattal father of Syed Muhammad Gesudaraz Husaini. The accompanying photograph of Tanashah has been copied from the British Museum collection. The present Mausoleum contains two graves, one belonging to Mirza Nizamuddin Ahmad, *alias* Mir Ahmad, son of Syed Masoom Dashtaki of Shiraz, who was the son-in-law of Sultan

Abul Hasan Tanashah.

Sarcophagus of Fatima Khanum. No. 75.

On the southern wall of Nau Mahal. No. 76.

Abdullah and the other grave next to his tomb bears no name of the deceased. The father of Mir Ahmad having secretly married the sister of Abbas II Safavi, the Shah of Persia had settled in Mecca, and the result of this union was Nizamuddin Ahmad. Mir Muhammad Saeed, Mir Jumla of Abdullah Qutbshah, on hearing the high attainments and the nobility of birth of Mir Ahmad induced him to come to Hyderabad by sending a large sum of money, and offered him the hand of his own daughter. When Mir Ahmad reached Hyderabad Sultan Abdullah was so much pleased with him that he got his own daughter married to him, whereupon Mir Jumla getting extermely annoyed left Hyderabad in despair and joined Prince Aurangzeb[1]. This is another version of the reason for Mir Jumla's proving a traitor to Abdullah Qutbshah; the first version has been already described at length in No. 66.

No. 75.

(*a*)=**The grave of Fatima Khanum.**

(*b*)=**Near No. 74.**

(*c*)=**Sarf-i-Khas.**

(*d*)=**II-c.**

(*e*)=**1087 A.H. (1676 A.D.).**

(*f*)=**The following inscriptions are carved over the sarcophagus :—**

۱- الله محمد علی -سورہ ۳- آیتہ ۱۹ - سنہ۱۰۸۷ھ

۲- آیتہ الکرسی

۳- سورہ ۲- آیات ۲۸۵-۲۸۶

۴- وفات جنت مکانی فاطمہ خانم بنت سلطان عبد الله قطبشاہ بتاریخ بیستم ماہ شوال فی سنہ۱۰۸۷

۵- سورہ ۹۷-۱۰۷-۱۱۲-۱۱۴

۶- درود شریف

---

(1) Maathirul-Kiram by Mir Ghulam Ali Azad Bilgrami.

(*Translation*)

1. " Allah, Muhammad Ali."

" Chapter II, Verse 16, In the year 1087 A.H."

2. " Throne Verse ."

3. " Chapter 2 Verses 285-286."

4. " The death of Fatima Khanum whose abode is Paradise, daughter of Sultan Abdullah Qutbshah, (occurred) on 20th Shawwaal in (the year)1087 (*vide* plate).

5. " Chapters 97, 107, 112 and 114."

6. " Shiite Durud."

(*g*)=Is incomplete.

(*d*)=Should be protected.

(*j*)=Outside the surrounding wall of the Golconda Tombs, this tomb which belongs to the daughter of Sultan Abdullah Qutbshah is situated close to the Mausoleum of Mirza Nizamuddin Ahmad and is not covered by a dome, perhaps owing to the unsettled state of affairs of the times. This lady was most probably the wife of Mir Ahmad.

Inside the Golconda Tombs on the Southern extremity a small dome contains the graves, of two females ; both[1] are inscribed, one belongs to one Fatima and the next grave bears the Tughra of the word " Ali," in eight different styles in best Thulth, it is also inscribed with Throne verse but bears no name.

۱- درود شریف

۱- یا اللہ یا محمد یا علی

۳- وفات فاطمہ بتاریخ ششم شہر رجب فی سنہ ۱۰۳۳

(*Translation*)

1. " Shiite Durud."

2. " O Allah, O Muhammad, O Ali."

3. " The death of Fatima (occurred) on 6th Rajab in the year 1033 (A.H.). "

---

(1) New.

No. 76.

(*a*)=Nau-Mahal.

(*b*)=Outside the fort walls.

(*c*)=Sarf-i-Khas.

(*d*)=I-c.

(*e*)=1170 A.H., (1756 A.D.).

(*f*)=On the Southern outer wall of Nau-Mahal opposite the shrine of Gunday Shah the following inscription in Naskh is fixed, which belongs to the Asaf Jahi period :—

ا و لئک هم خیرا لبریه ۱۱۷۰

(*Translation*).

" These are the best of creatures. In the year 1170 (A.H.)." (*vide* Plate).

(*g*)=Good.

(*h*)=Should be protected.

(*j*)=Nau-Mahal is composed of nine palatial buildings, the material mostly used is teakwood of the best quality. Its present state of preservation is due to the constant conservation measures of the Asafiyah Kings ; each palace invariably contains a small well-kept garden. The other names of these palaces are ' Moti Mahal ' and ' Daulatkhana.'

The shrine of Muhammad Nuruddin, *alias*, Gunday Shah Saheb is situated at the back of Moti Mahal and in the courtyard of the mosque at the head of his grave close to the ' Cheraghdan ' (where the lamp is burnt) a charm is engraved on black basalt, which according to the local tradition cures all ailments, provided it is washed with pure water and the same is given to a sick man for drinking[1].

---

(1) Tawarikhe Farkhunda, Kadir Khani. (MSS).

The following quatrain is given in Tawarikhe Farkhunda, regarding the burial of Gunday Shah here, as it lays down that 30 years after the fall of Golconda (1098 A.H.) one Nimatullah was told in a dream that Muhammad Nuruddin Arab (Gunday Shah) was buried in this place a century before.

ز فتح گولکنڈ بعد سی سال * بشارت نعمت الله یافت ز ابدال
که نورالدین محمد عرب اخیار * درینجا مدفنی دارد ز صد سال
خوشا حالی که مدفن شد لغان خطا بش * ز فقر ایا فتہ بس شغل و اشغال
بعهد قلداری آنجوان بخت * کراماتش ظهور آمد چو فی الحال
بشیخ نعمت الله گفت دیندار * توی صاحب بشارت هم تو ابدال
بنای روضه باید کرد اینجا * کنم تا عرس ز اعمال هر سال
جوار صاحب و فرخنده خوئی * بنای روضه کرد از فضل افضال
ز تاریخ بنایش گفت هاتف * بیا کی روضه با جاه و اجلال
سنه ۱۱۳۰ ھ

Close to the shrine of Gunday Shah on the grave of Nimatullah the following chronogrammatic verse of the Quran is engraved[1] :—

ان تعدو نعمت الله طاب
۱۱۷۰

"If you enumerate God's boons, it is agreeable—1170 (A. H)."

(1) New.

RETROSPECT.

I.

The southern portion of the Indian peninsula lies south of the Narbada, which flows between the Vindhya and Satpura ranges and the plateau of the Deccan lies between the Narbada on the north and the Krishna and Tungbhadra on the south. It is derived from the Sanskrit word Dakshin and is reputed to be a land of evasive mysteries.

The languages of the Deccan are divided into five great divisions :—

The Dravidian (Tamil); the Karnatic (Canarese); the Telingana (Telugu); the Maharashtra (Mahrati) and the Orissa (Uriya). The exact origin of the early inhabitants of the Deccan is quite unknown. So far as the history of this province can be reconstructed, it is evident that the earliest people who visited the N. I. from Northern Russia and the Turanian regions were the Dravidians who spoke Tamil; they were followed by those nations who spoke the Canarese, the Telugu and the Mahrati respectively. These immigrants gradually shifted one after the other from Northern regions and settled into the Deccan.

II.

Little is known in detail of the history of the Deccan before the Brahmanic period. Hindu legends relate that in 500 B. C. three brothers founded three separate kingdoms, all of whom spoke the Tamil language. The Pandya kingdom in the extreme south, the Chola kingdom in the north-east and the Chera kingdom in the north and north-west. Archæological remains and inscriptions bear witness to a series of dynasties of which the most important was the Pandya, who was constantly at war with the Chola.

The conversion of the South to Brahmanism took place about the sixth century B. C. and the earliest historical mention of the Pandya kingdom, whose capital was at Madura, occurs in the Buddhist chronicles of Ceylon. The report of Megasthenes at the end of the 4th and beginning of the 3rd century B. C. mentions the Pandya kingdom as lying at the extreme south of the Indian peninsula. References to the commercial relations existing between the Romans and the Pandya Rajahs are confirmed by the occasional finds of the Roman coins in the Southern portions of India. During 900 A. D. the kingdom of Pandya was at its zenith and its last Rajah reigned in the 11th century.

The next Tamil speaking kingdom of the Deccan was that of the Chola, whose capital was at Conjeevaram (Kanchipuram) and Tanjore. They ruled from 350 B. C. to the end of the 17th century A. D. and ultimately this kingdom was absorbed into the family of Shivaji, the great Maharatta leader of Poona.

The Kingdom of Chera, the third of the Dravidian line, occupied the western coast of Malabar, which ended in the 10 century A. D.

At Kalyani, on the west of Bidar, a Rajput family of Chalukya reigned from 250 A. D. to 1182 A. D. The powerful Chalukyan king Pulakesin II who reigned in the sixth century conquered Chera, Chola and Pandya.

The history of the Deccan during the first Muhammadan era is occupied by struggles between the Rajputs and the Dravidians and by the foundation and disappearance of the Aryan Dravidian kingdoms in the central Deccan, such as the Southern Mahratta kingdom, that of the eastern Chalukya in Kalinga and that of the western Chalukya in the Northern Konkan. On the coast of the Godavery, old Mahrattas reigned at Prathistina (Paitan), and their famous Rajah Shalivahana was the founder of the Saka era, which commences 77 years after the Christian era. Their capital was later on shifted to Deo-Gadh (Daulatabad) and when Sultan Alauddin the Khilji Emperor of Delhi invaded the

Deccan in 1294 A.D., Ram Deo, a member of the same family was reigning there, and it is at this period that the continuous history of the Deccan really commences.

The Andhra Raj at Warangal was ruled by Telugu speaking race. The Ganpati Rajahs reigned there in the 13th century A. D. The territories south of the Godavery, the Golconda, the Madrasapatam and other adjoining towns, where Telugu was chiefly spoken, were under the sway of these Rajahs. The Muhammadans first conquered this Raj in 1323 A. D. and ultimately it formed part of the kingdom of Golconda.

III.

After establishing a Muhammadan kingdom in the north of India in 1193 A. D. (589 A. H.) Prince Alaudidn Khilji, a nephew of Jalaluddin Khilji was the first Muslim who in 1294 A. D. (694 A. H.) invaded the Deccan, and after a siege lasting 25 days, Rajah Ram Deo of Deogadh agreed to become a tributary to Delhi. In the following years when the Prince himself succeeded to the throne of Delhi and Ram Deo having failed to pay his dues, he deputed one of his newly converted generals, Malik Kafoor, to Deogadh in 1306 A. D. (706 A. H.) for the collection of the arrears of tribute and ordered the Governor of Malva and Gujerat to render assistance to Malik Kafoor. When the Malik reached Deogadh, Ram Deo apart from offering any resistance as was expected, willingly went to Delhi accompanied by Malik Kafoor to pay his homage to the king. Alauddin was so much gratified at this that he conferred upon Ram Deo the title of Rajah Rai Rayan and besides bestowing other gifts and favours restored Deogadh to him, whereupon Ram Deo remained a staunch and loyal supporter of Alauddin until his death. In 1309 A. D. (709 A. H.) Malik Kafoor revisited the Deccan and made Rajah Rudra-Deva a tributary of Delhi; he also conquered Madura and built a mosque at Rameshwaram. The third visit of Kafoor in

1312 A. D. (712 A. H.) was marked by the annexation of the whole of Maharashtra and Carnatic and the conquest of the forts of Gulbarga, Raichur and Mudgal. He also imprisoned Sangal Deo the son of Ram Deo (deceased) who had become insurgent at the time, and declared Deogadh the Capital of the Deccan. After the death of Alauddin, his son, Qutbuddin Mubarak Khilji, invaded the Deccan in 1318 A. D. (718 A. H.) and after subjugating other Rajahs he built a mosque at Deogadh which is still extant.

IV.

After the extinction of the Khilji dynasty, Ghazi Khan, Ghyasuddin Tughlaq, son of Ghyasuddin Balban, succeeded to the throne of Delhi in 1321 A. D. (721 A. H.). He deputed his son Fakhruddin, alias Juna Khan to subdue the Rajah of Warangal, but owing to some disagreement among his nobles this expedition proved abortive. A couple of years later Juna Khan returned to the Deccan in 1323 A. D. (723 A. H.) with a large army; he first conquered Bidar (Vidharba of Bhim Sen, whose daughter Damyanti married Nal, so famous in Sanskrit poetry) which was in the province of Warangal and invading other territories of the Rajah of Warangal, captured and sent the Rajah to Delhi as a state prisoner, but the king of Delhi pardoned Rajah Partab Rudra Deva and confirmed him in his government. Later Juna Khan succeeded to the throne of Delhi and assumed the title of Muhammad Tughlaq. He transferred the Capital of India from Delhi to Deogadh and renamed it Daulatabad.

In 1341 A. D. (742 A. H.) when Muhammad Tughlaq left Daulatabad on an expedition to Madura on his way to that place, he lost and interred one of his teeth at Bir with great pomp and ceremony and erected a magnificent mausoleum over it on a square platform measuring 35 feet each way which still survives. The caprices and oppressions of Muhammad Tughlaq produced the natural harvest of insurrections. As a consequence of his monstrous barbarities and idiotic endeavours the state of the kingdom of Delhi became chaotic and the nobles of Sadah[1] rose at this time to avenge the wanton slaughter of 70 of their brother nobles who were mercilessly massacred at Malwa at the bidding of the king. The nobles of the Deccan taking the lead threw off the allegiance of Tughlaq by declaring their severance with the Court of Delhi and selecting Ismail Mukh[2] the brother of Gul Afghan[3] and proclaimed him as their king at Daulatabad, by giving him the title of Nasiruddin Shah. Hasan Gangu Bahmani was given the title of Zafar Khan, who having killed Rai Bhairon, a governor of Tughlaq became sole master of the Mirch and Gulburga. In 1347 A. D. (748 A. H.) owing to the incapabilities of Muhummad Tuglaq all the Muhammadan possessions in the Deccan alienated from the throne of Delhi and continued to remain so until it was finally annexed by the Moghuls in 1687 A. D.

V.

When it was revealed to Ismail Mukh that the popular opinion was entirely in favour of Hasan, he hastened to summon a conference and abdicated the usurped throne of the Deccan in favour of Hasan Gangu Bahmani, who was crowned in the mosque of Qutbuddin Mubarak at Daulatabad on 24th Rabi II 748 A. H. (1347 A. D.). Coins were struck at Daulatabad and the *Khutba* was read in the name of Hasan and he was titled Sultan Alauddin Hasan Gangu Bahmani. He changed the Capital of the Deccan from Daulatabad to Gulbarga, considering the latter place to be auspicious and re-named it Hasanabad. Hasan descended from the family of Bahram Gor and Sassan Bahman, son of Isfandyar hence the *nom-de-plume* of Bahman. But according to another version he is related to have been a slave of Gangu Brahmin, who was a courtier at Delhi.

(1) A Commander of 100 horse.
(2) He was a Commander of 2,000 horse.
(3) He was ranked among the nobles of higher order.

To begin with Hasan undertook the erection of the magnificient Jamay Musjid (Assembly Mosque) of the fort of Gulburga, which is 216 ft. × 176 ft. with an area of 38,016 sq. feet.

In 1362 A. D. (764 A. H.) during the reign of Muhammad Shah, son of Hasan, the fort of Golconda was presented to the king by the Rajah of Telingana, so that it may be reckoned as a frontier of the kingdoms of Bahmani and Telingana ; and in 1424 A. D. (828 A. H.) the Warangal Raj was annexed by Sultan Ahmad Shah Vali Bahmani by the complete annihilation of the dynasty.

VI.

Altogether 18 Bahmani kings ruled at Gulburga and Bidar for about 179 years 1347 (748 A. H.) 1526 (933 A. H.). As a result of the imbecility of Mahmud Shah II, the 14th king of this line, the nobles acquired great ascendancy, with the result that several governors of the Bahmani provinces declared their independence. Sultan Quli, the governor of Telingana, who had remained staunch until 924 A. H. (1518 A. D.) also declared his independence soon after the death of his master in the same year.

Ahmed Nizamul Mulk Bahri was the foremost to establish a separate Nizam Shahi kingdom at Ahmadnagar in 1489 A. D. (895 A. H.). Yousuf Adil Shah and Fat-hullah Imadul Mulk of Elichpur (Berar) followed suite. Owing to the demise of Dilawar Khan Habshi, Malik Qasim Barid came into power and began to rule virtually at the Bahmani capital of Bidar and after his death in 1504 A.D. (910 A. H.) his son Amir Barid wielded much more influence over Mahmud Shah II. In 1520 A. D. (927 A. H.) after the death of Ahmad Shah, son of Mahmud II, his son Alauddin was nominally made a king, who revolted against the aggression of Amir Barid and plotted to kill him, but Amir Barid had him put to death, placing Valiullah, son of Mahmud II on the throne ; three years later he was also done to death and Kalimullah son of Ahmad became king in 1526 A. D. (933 A. H.). Realising his sad plight he approached Babar for help but as he himself was not yet secure, he paid no heed to the request of Kalimulla, who had now no alternative but to quit the country. He therefore fled with his life first to Bijapur where the coldness of Yousuf obliged him to retrace his steps to Ahmadnagar where he remained till his death.

Specimens of Bahmani architecture may yet be seen at Gulburga, Bidar and Firozabad, those of the latter place are now much dilapidated.

Among the five independent kingdoms which were established in the Deccan after the dismemberment of the Bahmani kingdom, the dominion of Imad Shahi at Berar was the first to succumb to the attack of Murtuza Nizam Shah of Ahmadnagar, who annexed this kingdom into his own in 1575 A. D. (983 A. H.) and in 1600 A. D. (1009 A.H.) the Nizam Shahi kingdom of Ahmadnagar was annexed by the Moghals. Amir Barid II, was driven away by one Mirza Ali who usurped the throne of Bidar in 1609 A. D. (1018 A. H.) but later Mirza Ali was imprisoned by Ibrahim Adil Shah in 1619 A. D. (1029 A. H.) who annexed Bidar into his own territories and ultimately in 1686 and 1687 A. D. (1098 A. H.) both Bijapur and Golconda kings were imprisoned by the Emperor Aurangzeb and their dominions annexed to Delhi, thus ended the drama which had in its wake oceans of incidents and experience, of anxiety and suffering and of pleasure and pain, a drama constantly at play in the realm of the Deccan from 1347 A. D. (748 A. H.) to 1687 A. D. (1098 A. H.).

VII.

Sultan Quli a native of Hamadan, belonged to a noble family of Qara Yousuf ; his forefathers being rulers of

Turkestan. He was born of Uwais Quli and when still in his teens Sultan Quli came to Bidar from Persia during the reign of Mahmud Shah II, and was made a courtier of the Bahmani King who was so much pleased with his hunting spirit that the village of Korangal was conferred on him as a freehold and the title of Khawas Khan was also given to him. In 1486 A. D. (892 A. H.) when Africans and the Deccanis plotted to kill the King and entered the fort of Bidar, Sultan Quli saved the life of the King by driving the intruders out of the fort, he consequently became a greater favourite of the king and when Qutbul Mulk Deccani, the Governor of Telingana died in 1493 A. D. (899 A. H.), Sultan Quli was given the title of Qutbul Mulk with the Governorship of Telingana. In 1495 A. D. (901 A. H.) Golconda, Warangal and a few pargannahs were also conferred on him by the King as a freehold. He made Golconda his seat (which was then called Mankal or Mangalwaram), and renamed it Muhammadnagar. After repairing the fort and encircling it with walls and bastions he had several palaces built in the fort and the city of Golconda. He subjugated the rebellious Zemindars of Telingana and adopted a policy of expanding his territory by annexation. At the outset he imprisoned the Zemindar of Rajkonda and invaded the fort of Devarkonda, whereupon Krishna Rai of Vijyanagar, attacked the country of Sultan Quli. The conflicting armies met at Pangal (Nalgunda District) and the fort of Pangal fell to Sultan Quli after a siege of 2 months, an inscription of Qutbshahi period may still be seen over the bund of Pangal tank. After this victory Sultan Quli returned to Golconda and Ghanpura and Koelkonda were annexed.

In 1517 A. D. (923 A. H.) Elgundal and Malangur were also taken by Sultan Quli after a fight with Qawamul Mulk of Rajahmandry. In the beginning of 1518 A. D. (924 A.H.) Sultan Quli erected the famous assembly mosque (Masjid

Safa) at Golconda and inserted several inscriptions over it, in which the name of the reigning sovereign and a prayer for the perpetuity of his reign is inscribed ; which go a long way to prove his fidelity to his master Mahmud Shah II, until his death on 4th Zil-Hij 924 A.H. The inaccurate version of Ferishta that Sultan Quli declared his independence in 918 A. H. has been instrumental in misleading most of the Persian and English historians. After the death of Mahmud Shah II, when Amir Barid had become the sole master of the Bahmani Kingdom, Sultan Quli did not hesitate to declare his own independence, which he did by incorporating his own name in the Khutba and in accordance with the practice of the Kings of Persia he introduced the custom of beating of drums in his capital five times per diem.

During 1519 and 1525 A. D. (926 and 932 A.H.) he was engaged in defeating Shitab Khan, a Zemindar of Warangal, and annexing in his own the forts of Khammammet and Vemalkonda—In 1526 and '27 A.D. he occupied Kondapalli, Rajahmandry and Ellore and the river Godaveri was fixed as his Northern boundary. In 1533 A. D. (940 A.H.) he fought against Ismail Adil Shah at Koelkonda, where one of the soldiers of Ismail, coming out of an ambush inflicted a wound on the face of Sultan Quli, which defaced him for the rest of his life. The sudden illness and death of Ismail on 16th Safar 941 A. H. (1534 A.D.) turned the scales in favour of Sultan Quli, as he got hold of the forts of Koelkonda and Kohir. In 1535 A.D. (944 A. H.) he defeated Rajah Harichand and occupied Nalgundah, afterwards Kondbir also fell to his lot.

Sultan Quli had by this time grown very old and his son Jamshed was yearning for the throne, consequently Sultan Quli was put to death at the instigation of Jamshed by Mir Mahmud Hamadani, on the last Monday of Jamadi I, 950 A.H. (1543 A. D.) while he was engaged in prayers in the assembly mosque of the fort of Golconda.

VIII.

The first endeavour of Jamshed after ascending the throne of his father, had been to blind his younger brother Qutbuddin, who was heir-apparent to the throne. He then diverted his attention towards his sixth brother Ibrahim who lived at Devarkondah, but he soon repaired to Ali Barid at Bidar.

Ali Barid and Ibrahim Adil Shah taking part of Prince Ibrahim Quli attacked Golconda, and in the skirmish which followed one Asad Khan, Commander of Bijapur struck on the face of Jamshed with a sword which permanently disfigured him like his father for the remaining period of his life; in the end Jamshed successfully returned to his capital.

In 1544 A.D. (951 A.H.) he built a fort at Kaolas and occupied Narayan Khed and Ahsanabad, he also took by force the fort of Medak from Ali Barid on which Ali Barid went to Ibrahim Adilshah for help but Ibrahim imprisoned him at Bijapur and ultimately he released Ali Barid on the recommendation of Jamshed, after which Ali Barid and Jamshed remained on very intimate terms. In 1550 A.D. (957 A.H.) Jamshed was laid up with cancer and died in the same year at Golconda.

IX.

After the death of Jamshed his infant son Subhan Quli was placed on the throne and Saif Khan, Ainul-Mulk was sent for from Ahmadnagar for the performance of the duties of the regent during the boy's minority, but Jagdeva Rao, Naikwari, wanted to enthrone Daulat Quli the fifth brother of Jamshed who was a prisoner at the fort of Bhongir owing to his idiocy, and thus to become virtual ruler. Saif Khan soon after establishing himself at Golconda, managed to render Jagdeva Rao submissive, and although Darya Imad Shah of Elichpur had espoused the cause of Jagdeva Rao and Daulat Quli, but Saif Khan succeeded in again keeping

Daulat Quli, a prisoner at Bhongir and Jagdeva Rao was imprisoned at Golconda. This incident made Saif Khan a paramount power in the Deccan which displeased other nobles of the court and hence they made secret overtures to Ibrahim Quli, who after abandoning the fort of Devarkonda for fear of Jamshed and remaining for some times at Bidar, was now passing a peaceful life at the court of Ramraj of Vijyanagar. They sent him an invitation to occupy his paternal throne, on which Ibrahim left Ramraj and on entering the frontier of Golconda, the Naikwaris of Koelkonda helped him in forming an army. When the news of the advent of Ibrahim reached Golconda, the Naikwaris of the fort imprisoned Subhan Quli and on 12th Rajab 957 A.H. (27th July 1550 A.D.) Ibrahim entered the fort of Golconda unmolested and was declared a king. Mustafa Khan Ardastani was appointed Peshwa and Mir Jumla and Ibrahim got his own sister married with Mustafa Khan.

In 1554 A.D. (962 A.H.) Ibrahim Qutbshah in cunjunction with Husain Nizamshah laid siege to Gulburga and Ibrahim Adilshah opposed them with the help of Ramraj. But before the commencement of the operations a sensible letter was sent by Ramraj to Ibrahim Qutbshah which had most salutary effect in the conclusion of peace and the result was that these three Kings met at the Sangam, (the meeting place) of the rivers Bhima and Krishna, and each one of them peacefully returned to their respective countries.

X

As Jagdeva Rao had been instrumental in securing the throne of Golconda for Ibrahim, he soon became overbearing for the King and Jagdeva Rao resorted to his old game of putting Daulat Quli on the throne. Ibrahim becoming aware of the plot put all the perpetrators to death, on which Jagdeva Rao fled to Berar, but in 1556 A.D. (964 A.H.) he managed to attack Elgandal only to be repulsed, whereupon he went to Vijyanagar and settled there with Ramraj.

In 1560 A.D. (968 A.H.) Ali Adilshah, Ramraj and Ibrahim Qutbshah laid siege to Ahmadnagar but Ibrahim apprehending that the fall of Ahmadnagar would overbalance the power of Adilshah left Ahmadnagar abruptly and returned to his capital, after which Ali and Ramraj also returned to their respective countries after concluding a peace treaty with Husain Nizamshah on very severe terms. In 1562 A.D. (970 A.H.) Husain Nizamshah married his daughter Bibi Jamal to Ibrahim, after which Husain and Ibrahim attacked the fort of Kalyan, but Ali Adilshah with the assistance of Ramraj not only drove them out so that they had to beat a hasty retreat to Golconda and Ahmadnagar, but in addition Ramraj and Ali so much harassed Ibrahim that he had to deliver Ghanpura, Koelkonda and Pangal to Ramraj and several villages of Ali were also taken by him before he returned to Vijyanagar.

This growing power of Ramraj gave just alarm to all the Muslim Kings of the Deccan and they resolved to suspend their mutual jealousies and form a general confederacy to extinguish it. Ibrahim stengthened the fortifications of Golconda and subordinated the Naikwaris. In the meantime Ali Adilshah invited a conference of his contemporaries and first of all took Ibrahim into his confidence, who hailed the idea and despatched his minister Khane Azam, Mustafa Khan to Ali Adilshah, thence he went to Husain Nizamshah at Ahmadnagar and succeeded not only in making him a party to the alliance but also successfully persuaded him for a mutual union of his daughter, the famous Chand Bibi with Ali Adilshah and that of the daughter of Ali with Husain. In 1563 A.D. (971 A.H.) after the celebration of these marriages Ali Barid also joined hands and when everything was amicably settled, Ali Adilshah by way of pretext despatched his ambassador to Ramraj with a request that Raichur and Mudgal which originally belonged to Bijapur should be restored to him. Whereupon Ramraj expelled not only the messenger of Ali but similar treatment was meted out to the vakils of other Kings which resided at Vijyanagar. Taking this as an ostensible reason for the declaration of war, Husain, Ali Barid and Ibrahim marched to Bijapur with their respective armies and in company with Ali Adilshah crossed the river Krishna and reached Talicota in 1564 A.D. (972 A.H.), only Burhan Nizamshah remained neutral. On the other hand Ramraj accompanied by his brothers Temraj and Venkatadri took the field with 100,000 horse and 900,000 foot—Husain and Ali Adilshah manifested undaunted courage in opposing the enemy. After a great and decisive battle Ramraj was imprisoned and beheaded, the allied Kings laid waste to Vijyanagar and destroyed the city to such an extent that it gradually sunk to insignificance and is a mass of ruins to the present day.

In 1571 A.D. (979 A.H.) Ibrahim occupied Matiapur and Rajahmundry after defeating Shitab Khan and Vidyadaru Rajah of Cassimcotta, and in 1574 A.D. (982 A.H.) the whole territory of Cassimcotta was annexed to Qutbshahi Kingdom. The Rajah of Kondbir who was not punctual in paying his annuity was brought to book in 1579 A.D. (987 A.H.) with the annexation of Venkonda, Khammam-mett and Kondbir.

After a short indisposition Ibrahim expired on 21st Rabi II, 988 A.H. (1580 A.D.). Besides management of the country he took a keen interest in the population of Golconda. He also repaired and fortified the fort and built a small mosque midway on the steps to Balahisar. The Husain Sagar, Budwell and Kankor tanks, Ibrahim Bagh, Baghe Gulshan and the village of Ibrahimpatan are a few of his productions.

XI.

Ibrahim was succeeded by his 3rd son Muhammad Quli, who founded the city of Bhagnagar in 999 A.H. and erected many buildings besides bazaar, shops, baths, madrasah, and mosques. This city was surrounded by gardens which extended as far as 20 miles in each direction. The Narkhora, Ibrahimpatan, Bhongir and Patancheroo were its four cardinal points.

After conquering the fort of Mussalmurg, Muhammad Quli occupied Nundiyal and Kalabgur in 1594 A.D. (1003 A.H.) Malik Aminul Mulk, his Mir Jumla rendered him distinguished services and subordinated many outlaws.

Shah Abbas son of Shah Tahmasp Safavi's ambassador Aghizlo Sultan first came to the court of Golconda, *via* Goa with many valuable presents during his reign in 1603 A.D. (1012 A.H.) but he had to prolong his stay in the Dilkusha garden of Bhagnagar owing to constant aggressions of the Moghal army and he was allowed to return to Persia in 1609 A.D. (1018 A.H.). On 17th Zil Qadah 1020 A.H. (1611 A.D.) Muhammad Quli expired and was buried in the Langare Faiz asar.

He was very fond of architecture, the following is a list of the famous buildings which were built by Muhammad Quli during his peaceful reign, when the Qutbshahi kingdom was it its zenith of prosperity.

Daulat Khanae Ali (The Royal Palace which was situated near Kali Kaman). The Char Minar, the Char Kaman, the Char-su-ka Hauz, Darush-Shifa, Jamay Masjid (City) Dad Mahal, (where the present High court is situated) Naddi Mahal, the Banat Ghat and Baghe Dilkusha (were situated 4 miles in the northern direction) Khudadad Mahal was composed of seven storeys, *viz.*, —Ilahi Mahal, Muhammadi Mahal, Hydar Mahal, Hasan Mahal, Husain Mahal, Jafari Mahal, and Musavi Mahal. Baghe Muhammad Shahi, Kohe Toor (was situated in the south) Jinan Mahal, (was situated near Amin Bagh) and Badshahi Ashur Khana.

XII

After the demise of Muhammad Quli his nephew Sultan Muhammad, son of Prince Mirza Muhammad Amin, was placed on the throne by Mir Momin of Astrabad, in accordance with the last injuctions of the deceased King. The new king was also the son-in-law of Muhammad Quli, having married his daughter Hayat Buksh Begum in 1607 A.D. (1016 A.H.)

In 1614 A.D. (1023 A.H.) Husain Beg Qibchachi, the Ambassador of Shah Abbas of Persia came to Hyderabad and returned in 1616 A.D. (1025 A.H.) in company with Shaikh Muhummad Ibne Khatoon. In 1617 A.D. (1027 A.H.) two Ambassadors of the Emperor Jahangir, Mir Makki and Jadoo Rao, visited Hyderabad for the first time. Sultan Muhammad received them with due honour and sent a Peshkash of 15 lakhs to the Emperor. On the occasion of Prince Khurram's (Shah Jahan) visit to Burhanpur and Masulipatam in 1622 A.D. (1030 A.H.) when he was forsaken by many of his nobles, Sultan Muhammad treated him favourably and helped him with money.

About 6 miles east of the city of Hyderabad the foundation of a fort and city of Sultan Nagar was laid by Sultan Muhammad in 1624 A.D. (1034 A.H.) but owing to his premature death on 13th Jamadi I, 1035 A.H. (1625 A.D.) the work was abandoned for good. The chief monuments of the reign of Sultan Muhammad was Mecca Musjid and the first Qutbshahi history, the Tarikhe Sultan Muhammad Qutbshahi was compiled in his regime.

XIII.

Sultan Abdullah, the only son of Sultan Muhammad was crowned in the Muhammadi Mahal on 14th Jamadi I, 1035 A.H. (1625 A.D.) after which the Ambassadors of Ibrahim Adil Shah II, the Burhan Nizam Shah III, and the Prince Shah Jahan came to Hyderabad to offer condolence and congratulation on behalf of their masters. In the following year Ibne Khatoon returned to Hyderabad from Persia accompanied by the Persian Ambassador Qasim Beg, the commander of Mazindaran and his son. After a stay of about 2 years Qasim Beg died here and his son Muhammad Quli Beg returned to Persia with Khairat Khan, the Sar-naubat of Sultan Abdullah Qutbshah. The year 1630 A.D. (1040 A.H.) was marked by a severe famine in the Deccan, which however extended all over India. In 1631 A.D. (1041 A.H.) excessive rainfall flooded the city, inasmuch as the water flowed right over the Old Bridge, which played havoc in the demolition of many lofty buildings of the city. In 1632 A.D. (1042 A.H.) the sister of Sultan Abdullah was married to Muhammad Adil Shah of Bijapur and in 1634 A.D. (1044 A.H.) Khairat Khan returned to Hyderabad from Persia. The year 1655 A.D. (1066 A.H.) was earmarked by the surprise visit of Prince Aurangzeb at the instigation of Mir Jumla, Mir Muhammad Saeed of Ardastan, which was only averted after payment of a heavy indemnity, the lowering of the prestige of Qutbshahi king and the marriage of the king's daughter with Sultan Muhammad, son of Aurangzeb. Another daughter of Sultan Abdullah was married to Mirza Nizamuddin, alias Mir Ahmad, who was born of the sister of Shah Abbas of Persia. The marriage of the third daughter of Sultan Abdullah was arranged with Syed Sultan but owing to the opposition of Mir Ahmad she was abruptly given in marriage to Abul Hasan Tana Shah. Abdullah died in 1672 A.D. (1083 A.H.) leaving no male issue and as a result of the favourable disposition of his courtiers, Madannah, Akannah, Syed Muzaffar and Musa Khan Mahaldar, towards Abul Hasan he succeeded to the throne and Mir Ahmad was kept under surveillance in which condition he died in 1674 A.D. (1085 A.H). The famous lexicon Burhane-Qate and a compendium of the Qutb Shahi history (Hadiqatus-Salatin) was compiled during the reign of Sultan Abdullah.

XIV.

After ascending the throne Abul Hasan Tanashah appointed Syed Muzaffar his first Prime Minister, but after a short interval he was dismissed and Madannah succeeded him. The Emperor Aurangzeb who had a long cherished desire to annex the existing dependencies of the Deccan, had now resolved to commence operations. He first conquered Bijapur in 1686, and made Sikandar Adilshah a captive and then after a few months' siege he succeeded in overtaking the impregnable fort of Golconda by the treachery of Qutbshahi nobles and in 1687 A.D. (1098 A.H.) the Qutbshahi kingdom came to an end. The annihilation of the Muhammadan kingdoms of the Deccan gave ampler scope to the rising Mahratta power. After the fall of Golconda the Qutbshahi valuables amounted to 8 lakhs and 51 thousand Huns and 2 crores and 53 lakhs of cash. Abul Hasan was made a prisoner and sent to Daultabad fort in confinement where he died fourteen years later in 1699 A.D. (1111 A.H.) and was buried in the mausoleum of Syed Raju Qattal at Khuldabad. The number 14 had a remarkable influence over the life of Abul Hasan. He spent 14 years in boyhood, for 14 years he remained a devout disciple of Syed Shah Raju Husaini II. He ruled for 14 years and remained in confinement for 14 years. Char Mahal and Gosha Mahal were the two buildings which he could add to the long list of edifices built by his forefathers.

Thirty nine years after the extinction of Qutbshahi dynasty the sun of the house of Asaf Jahi dawned over the horizon of the Deccan in 1724 A.D. (1137 A.H.) when Mubariz Khan, Imadul mulk, the Moghal Subadar of Hyderabad was killed in the battle of Shakar Khera in Berar and since this period a large portion of the territories which once formed part of the five independent kingdoms of the Deccan, is by the grace of God under the sway of Asaf Jahi Kings. The present ruler His Exalted Highness, Asaf Jah VII, is by far the most enlightened and sagacious Monarch and his wise and magnanimous administration is making rapid strides in the moral and material advancement of the country.

FINIS

INDEX

C

D

E

F

I

N

O

P

R

T

U

V

W

Y

Z